Ultimate Judgment

This is a true story.

Only the name of Anthony, along with certain other identifying information, has been changed out of respect for his privacy.

From necessity, depositions have been condensed, although every effort has been made to maintain the integrity, intent and context of each statement.

Ultimate Judgment

A Story of Emotional Corruption, Obsession and Betrayal

Meg Clairmonte and Aurora Mackey

Health Communications, Inc.
Deerfield Beach, Florida

www.hci-online.com

Library of Congress Cataloging-in-Publication Data

Clairmonte, Meg
    Ultimate judgment : a story of emotional corruption, obsession, and
betrayal / Meg Clairmonte and Aurora Mackey.
        p.   cm.
    ISBN 1-55874-831-8 (trade paper : alk. paper)
    1. Clairmonte, Meg.   2. Adult child sexual abuse victims—
Florida—Biography. 3. Sexual child abuse—Guyana—Case studies.
4. Trials (Child sexual abuse)—Florida—Tampa. I. Title: Ultimate
judgment. II. Mackey, Aurora. III. Title

HV6570.3.F6 C53 2001
362.76'4'092—dc21
[B]   00-059661

Publisher: Health Communications, Inc.
                 3201 S.W. 15th Street
                 Deerfield Beach, FL 33442-8190

Cover design by Lisa Camp
Inside book design by Dawn Grove

Contents

Acknowledgments

Of all the people who helped bring this book into being, my deepest gratitude belongs to Meg Clairmonte and the indomitable strength and courage she showed throughout the most painful memories. Meg not only granted me unlimited access to all aspects of her case, but trusted me to write her story without any restrictions.

I am also indebted to Frank Weimann, my agent at Literary Group International, who believed in the power of Meg's story from the start; and to Health Communications for the boldness to publish a story that is so shocking on so many levels. The suggestions from Christine Belleris, Allison Janse and Erica Orloff were greatly appreciated.

Richard Gilbert, a lawyer as brilliant as he is passionate, gave freely of his time to explain the intricacies of Florida law as it pertained to Meg's case. Gilbert's legal assistant, Sondra Fryrear, cheerfully assisted me in obtaining thousands of pages of depositions and court transcripts, as well as photos, videotapes and related documents.

Numerous people also read early drafts and offered invaluable insight: Martin Lasden, senior editor of *California Lawyer* magazine; Steve Simmons, professor of Graduate Writing at the University of San Francisco; and Oakland poet Chris Summers.

Finally, I offer my bottomless thanks to my son, Graham, whose patience and support meant everything to me; and to my husband, John, who has been with me for each word, for each step of the way.

—Aurora Mackey
August 2000

Part I

Digging Up the Bones

If I had not come and spoken unto them, they had not sin: but now they have no cloak for their sin.

—John 15:22

For his eyes are upon the ways of man, and he seeth all his goings. There is no darkness, nor shadow of death, where the workers of iniquity may hide themselves. For he will not lay upon man more than right; that he should enter into judgment with God.

—Job 34:21–23

The worst secret is the one everyone around you knows but never talks about. It's the ghost that lives with you and whispers in your ear, the apparition whose shadow undulates through the air you all breathe, but everyone pretends not to see it. Over time, whatever you think or feel about it doesn't even matter anymore, because there are rules to govern your silence, to keep you from speaking of it:

Nothing is wrong here, and if there is, it is only with you.

This is just the way things are.

You are powerless to change anything, so don't even consider it.

Keep your mouth shut and nothing bad will happen.

Those were the rules in my family, the unspoken ones that permeated every facet of my life, Nick's life, even Mom and Donald's. They are what held our terrible secret firmly in place for three decades, burying the truth so deep that it even went to the grave.

And beyond.

Even after the newspapers wrote all those big stories about what happened, my own lawyers still thought I was in no condition for the whole truth, that I'd collapse or go hysterical or kill myself if they told me everything. There were parts that would have been much too painful, they said, and some things a person was just better off not knowing. That, they told me, was something they'd learned from other trials and cross-examinations: Never ask a question unless you're prepared to hear any answer. And I, in their estimation, was not prepared.

Maybe they were right. Maybe back then I couldn't have handled the knowledge of what my mother made me out to be, or how bad Nick and the priest betrayed me, or what all those doctors thought I could have done in my half-crazed state. Maybe I would have done exactly what those lawyers were afraid of.

But one thing I've learned since then. The truth doesn't stay well buried. The truth wants out of its tomb—even if it has to destroy lives in the process, even if it has to rip a family apart, even if it is forced to leave a path of destruction in its wake.

The truth wants out, and if given a chance it will find a way.

At least, that was what happened to us.

One

You cold?" Ernie asks.

My teeth are chattering and I'm hugging myself, pulling my sweater close to my chest. The lobby feels as if we're sitting under a blasting air conditioner. But maybe it's just me. Even though it's February, and winters here are hardly what anyone could call harsh, Ernie and Nick both look just the opposite of cold. Ernie's spread out in the chair beside me in a cotton shirt and slacks, no tie, and Nick, my brother, is wearing the usual, a T-shirt and jeans. Nick is drumming his fingers on top of a magazine lying on the table beside him—upside down I see it's the *Florida Bar Journal*—and under his armpits are dark patches of sweat.

"I'm freezing. Now tell me again how you know this lawyer?" I say to Ernie, quiet enough so that the receptionist at the long desk across the room won't hear me.

"Meg, don't worry," Ernie says. "I already told you. He's a big estate lawyer, supposed to be one of the best in Tampa. You just go in there and tell him everything, and let him take it from there. Listen to what he has to say. He probably does these kinds of cases all the time."

Nick stops drumming on the magazine. He doesn't believe for a second, any more than I do, that this or any other lawyer in Tampa handles cases like ours all the time.

"But what if he doesn't believe us, Ernie?" Nick asks. "What if he says we're making it all up and throws us out? Wouldn't be the first time we've heard that, would it, Meg?"

Nick gives a snort of disgust, and I know just what he's thinking. He's remembering my mother's face the last time he saw her. And as soon as I recall the image of her standing in the doorway calling out after Ernie and me, my heart thuds in my chest. *You're both a bunch of damn liars! And you and your brother can rot in hell!*

"Nick's right," I say. "Maybe this whole thing isn't such a good idea. Maybe it's just going to mess everything up even more."

Ernie glances at the receptionist and then hunches forward and laces his fingers together. Instinctively, Nick and I both lean toward him as if we're going into a huddle.

"Look," he says quietly. "You want to walk out of here right now, then go ahead. No harm, no foul, okay? I'm sure not going to tell you what to do. But you want to know what I think? You're both scared. Hell, I would be, too. But we've already gone over all of this, all the details. You deserve some compensation for what you've been through. You both go in there with that attitude, and I think everything will be okay. All you need is the right lawyer." Ernie looks at us both to see how we're reacting to his pep talk. "Okay?"

We both nod, but slowly, as if we want him to convince us some more. But there's no time for that. A woman with a neat French bun and dressed in a form-fitting navy suit approaches and says Mr. Arnold will see us now. She leads us down a corridor, her high heels sinking soundlessly into the carpet, to an office at the end. She knocks softly on the door, and then without waiting opens it.

"Ms. Cassedy, Mr. Clairmonte and Mr. Haefele are here to see you," she says to the man sitting at a dark wood desk across the room. She smiles briefly and then leaves us in the doorway.

From where we stand, the office looks as if it hangs out into space. Two walls of solid glass give a full view of downtown Tampa, the Hillsborough River and the harbor, scattered with small boats, just beyond. Heavy clouds scud across the sky from the east. Another storm coming.

The lawyer rises from his leather chair and walks over to greet the three of us, extending his hand first to Ernie, then me and then Nick. Lynwood Arnold is a pleasant-looking man, in his mid-fifties with silver hair and a round, unlined face. He's dressed in a crisp white shirt, red tie and tasteful gray suit, and has the soft spongy look of someone who spends most of his time at a desk. Motioning to a long sofa against one wall, he tells us to make ourselves comfortable, and then sits in an armchair opposite us. But no sofa on Earth can make me comfortable. Sandwiched between Nick and Ernie, I'm shaking so badly I'm certain I'm visibly vibrating the whole sofa.

"Well," he says, looking first at Nick and then me.

There can be no doubt that Nick and I are brother and sister. We both have the same wiry black hair and coffee-colored skin that came from having a black father and white mother. Ernie, on the other hand, looks like Robert De Niro in *Raging Bull,* that movie where he's all beefed up and street tough as a boxer.

"I understand from Mr. Haefele's phone call that your step-father recently died," Mr. Arnold says. "And that you recently received a document concerning his estate?" I nod and then, when he doesn't say anything more, hand him the folded piece of paper I've been holding. He scans it, nods, and then lays it on the coffee table. "This is a notice of administration," he says. "Are you aware of what that is?"

"We're kind of aware," Ernie answers. "Something about a time limit to challenge the will? But that's why Meg and Nick are here. They got the notice in the mail three weeks ago. They wanted to know their legal rights. And that's why I called you."

If Lynwood Arnold thinks it's strange that Ernie's doing the talking for Nick and me, he doesn't show it. He just nods thoughtfully and crosses one leg over the other. "And Nick, you received a copy of this document as well?"

"Uh, not really," Nick says. "I don't exactly have a permanent address right now. I'm kind of staying with friends. Meg called me and told me about it. She and Ernie live together, so that's where it got sent. And then we all talked it over, and then we decided to. . . ." His voice trails. "We want to know what it means, just like Ernie said."

"I see," Lynwood Arnold says. "Well, what the document means is pretty much what Mr. Haefele—"

"Ernie is fine," Ernie says.

"All right. It's pretty much what Ernie said. The notice gives you thirty days to challenge your stepfather's estate, or else you forfeit any future right to do so. After that time, you would have no legal right to contest the will or challenge the estate—it's essentially 'forever hold your peace.' Since the document was dated three weeks ago, that only gives you seven more days to respond."

"She sent it after she threw us out," Nick says.

"Pardon?"

"After our mother threw Meg and me out," he says. "She did it right after that."

He picks up a yellow legal pad. "Before we get to issues related to the estate, I need to ask you a few questions. Now, your stepfather's name was . . . ?"

"Donald Sahlman," Nick says, and then spells it.

He writes it down. "Your mother was married to him when?"

"In 1983. So for about nine years," Nick says. "But she'd known him for years before that. Since she met him in Guyana. Meg and I were kids."

The lawyer writes something on the legal pad. "Any idea why your mother hired a lawyer? Why she's asking for a formal response from the two of you about your stepfather's will?"

"Sure," Nick says. "She thinks Meg and I are a bunch of liars. Greedy liars is what she called us, didn't she, Meg? Anyway, she thinks we're just mad because we were left out of the will."

Lynwood Arnold studies Nick a moment. "And are you?"

"Mad?" he asks. "Nah."

He nods, jots something else down. "Have you met your mother's lawyer yet or had any conversation with him—Charlie Luckie?"

Nick shakes his head.

"And do you know for a fact that you haven't been provided for in your stepfather's will? That you've been excluded?"

"Absolutely," Nick says. "Meg and I have known that for years, haven't we, Meg? You see, the way it always was, Donald was going to leave half of everything to our mother—she used to be Patricia Clairmonte but she's Patricia Sahlman now—and half to his son from his first marriage, Don Jr. Meg and I always knew we'd be left out of it. We never expected him to do anything different."

"And can you by chance estimate the value of the estate? If you know, of course."

Nick grins. "Oh we know, all right. At least seventeen million. Maybe more."

Lynwood Arnold's pen stops over the notepad, but his

expression doesn't change a bit. If he's as big a lawyer as Ernie said, I suppose he's used to talking about big money.

"I see," he says. "And what did your stepfather do?"

"You mean his work? For a living?" Nick asks. "Donald used to be the owner with his brother Jack of Sahlman Seafoods, right here in Tampa. It's the biggest seafood company in the entire world. Donald and Jack owned a huge fleet of shrimp trawlers, and they even had a seafood plant down in Guyana. That's where my mother first met him back in the 1960s, working as a secretary. Anyway, Donald sold his share of the company in . . . I don't know, about 1979, wasn't it, Meg? Yeah, twelve or thirteen years ago. For seventeen million. He always boasted about that. Then he retired and lived the good life. Didn't he, Meg?"

The whole time Nick's been talking, my heart has been thudding in my ears. My hands won't stop shaking either, even though I've been pressing them tightly between my knees. Even to me Nick's voice sounds arrogant and cocky, as if Donald's money, and the fact that he's dead, explains or justifies our entire reason for sitting here. As if the mention of seventeen million dollars should be enough in itself, and the rest of it should be the lawyer's problem to work out.

When Nick stops talking, Lynwood Arnold turns his eyes on me. It's obvious by the way he's waiting for me to say something that he's wondering, *So is this how you see things, too? Are you like your brother?* I want to open my mouth and tell him there's so much more to it than any will, any inheritance, that Nick isn't necessarily speaking for me, but I'm paralyzed. It feels just like one of my recurrent bad dreams—the one where I'm running through a swamp and something horrible is chasing me, deep under the water, but I can't scream. Nothing comes out but a high-pitched squeak, like air escaping from the stretched end of a balloon.

"Margaret?"

I jerk my head. Lynwood Arnold is looking at me, waiting.

"Excuse me?"

"I asked whether you had given thought to challenging the will," he says. "Whether that is your intent."

My intent. Three or four months ago, while Donald was still alive, I could have said perfectly what my intent was. When I knew he'd be dead very soon, there was only one thing I wanted. But ever since that day two months ago in Father Venard's office, my intent, my entire focus, had been completely blurred. It was just like the priest said: *But now that he's dead, Margaret, it must be obvious to you that your goal is gone now, that your goal is no longer possible. You must realize that, don't you?*

Ernie reaches over and takes my hand. "It's okay, Meg," he says softly. "Just tell him. You have to tell Mr. Arnold or he can't help you. He's got to know what he's dealing with, okay? Tell him about what Donald did to you so he'll know. It's okay."

I grip Ernie's hand.

The script has already been written for me; and this is what Ernie expects me to do.

I always do what's expected of me.

If it gets bad I can cut myself off from what's happening to me.

I'm good at this: I can separate myself from the shame and not feel a thing.

"Just tell him, Meg," Ernie says again.

And then, when I do open my mouth, the words pour out like a waterfall. They stream out without punctuation, almost without breathing. It is a torrent of words, propelled by the force of every day I have remained silent. I'm telling this perfect stranger, this Southern gentleman with silvery hair and an expensive suit, the most horrible and shameful things any person could tell another human being. Things that, until just two months ago, only one other person in the world has ever heard me say.

"I know you don't believe me," I say to the lawyer. "I know you won't believe any of this but it's the truth, and I don't care if you believe me or not, because I'm sick of everyone saying what a good man Donald Sahlman was, because he wasn't. And you want to know why I'm here? Because no one has *any idea* who he really was or *what* he really was or how he tortured me my entire life. Abused me my entire life! And if one more person tells me what a saint he was I'll *scream!*"

I sink back against the sofa. I've stopped trembling. All that's left is the anger, the fury, the thought that I don't even care now what he thinks of me, whether he believes me or not. The hell with him and anyone else. It's out now. I've taken it as far as I can go. I did what Ernie said to do.

No one says anything right away. Then Ernie breaks the silence. "So you can see what I meant on the phone, Mr. Arnold. These kids have been through a lot. A hell of a lot. And Nick has, too, haven't you, Nick?"

Lynwood Arnold looks at Nick. "Your stepfather did this to you as well?"

Nick nods, but his expression has changed. All of his previous arrogance and cockiness is gone. Suddenly he looks nervous, like a rabbit staring down a rifle barrel. "It was pretty much the same thing as Meg, Mr. Arnold. I just wasn't around it as long as she was. I kind of ran away."

Lynwood Arnold writes again on his legal pad. "And you are how old now?"

"Thirty-two. Meg is thirty. She lived at home a lot longer than I did. Until she was twenty-five. That's when she married Tom Cassedy. They're divorced now." Nick swivels to look at me. "You know, Meg, maybe you should tell Mr. Arnold what Mom and Donald did when they found out you were getting married. Or when they found out you were pregnant."

All at once I feel as if I've just taken my clothes off in front of a window without realizing that binoculars were trained on me. I don't know why I hadn't fully realized it before, but it hits me then that Nick and I might have to talk about everything, expose every tiny piece of our lives. But it's too late to cover up now. The lawyer has already heard enough to know it's all about filth and horridness. Part of me feels as though it would almost be a relief if he threw us all out right here and now.

"Well," he says, "first of all, I'm not going to tell you I've ever handled a case like this before. This isn't within my area of expertise. Primarily I deal with wills and trusts."

Nick and I glance at each other. Both of us have been following Ernie's advice, to see what the lawyer said and then take it from there. But the way Lynwood Arnold is talking, it sounds as if he's about to send us packing. And suddenly I feel an odd sense of desperation. When I first walked into his office I had no idea what I wanted. *What is your intent?* But now that we're about to be dismissed, the idea of just walking away from this seems as if it would be the worst thing of all—as if Donald would be winning again, controlling me even from his grave. I picture Donald in his marble casket, his eyes closed, smiling and then whispering, *I told you no one would believe you, Margaret. Who'd you think they'd believe—a rich white man like me or a little nigger girl like you? You think anyone would ever believe a word you say?*

"You think we should forget it, don't you?" I say. My voice is quavering with anger. "That's what you're thinking. Who's going to believe someone like me saying things about a rich man like him? You think I'm lying, don't you?"

Lynwood Arnold tilts his head. "I didn't say that," he says slowly. "But from what you and your brother have said, it sounds to me as if neither of you is talking about challenging the will. Neither of you has said you think you have a right to be included in the will. Am I right about that?"

Nick and I glance at each other and then, even though we've never discussed this, we both nod.

"What you're talking about," Lynwood Arnold goes on, "actually sounds more like a personal injury claim."

A personal injury claim. I always thought that's what people sued for after they were in an automobile accident or if they slipped and fell in a supermarket. It never occurred to me we could do something like that against Donald. But then the reality of what he's suggesting strikes me. "But how do you sue a man who's dead?" I ask. "How are you supposed to get anyone to believe what he did now that he's gone?"

Lynwood Arnold folds his hands in his lap. "Well, that's a good question," he says slowly. "And the short answer is, not easily."

He's going to throw us out right now, I think. He'll do it politely, but here's where he buzzes his receptionist so she can show us the way out.

"I think there's someone you should meet," he says. "A personal injury attorney here in this building. I don't know what he'll say, but would you be willing to talk with him, answer some questions?"

I can't answer for Nick, but to me it's a reprieve I didn't expect. At least Lynwood Arnold hasn't slammed the door in our faces.

"I'll talk to anyone you want," I say.

The second I set eyes on the lawyer Lynwood Arnold introduces us to the next day, a lead ball drops in my stomach. Richard Gilbert is take-your-breath-away gorgeous: six foot three, with dark blond hair and lapis-blue eyes set into a strong, kind face. He's probably not much older than I am. Talking to Lynwood Arnold was like forcing yourself to tell intimate things to a doctor, someone you imagine only could be interested in the facts, but this other lawyer is a whole different story. *No way,* I think, *can I tell this man what happened.*

But I'm wrong about that. Richard Gilbert is soft-spoken

and has a gentle refinement about him, almost as if he'd stepped off the elevator out of a different century. It doesn't take long before I sense I can trust him. I feel it even though I get the distinct sense he's sizing me up, that while he's asking me questions he's also trying to determine how easily I could lie to him.

Richard Gilbert is particularly interested in my mother's part in everything. He asks me several times what she knew, what she saw, what she did. It would be impossible to go into everything right now because it would take ages, so I tell him just the basics: what happened growing up in Guyana, after we moved to Florida, before I got married to Tom Cassedy, after my son Cameron was born, after my divorce, what my mother did after Donald died. I rattle it all off so quickly, almost without taking a breath, that I wonder how much of it he's hearing.

Richard Gilbert is sitting in an armchair beside Lynwood Arnold. He's watching me the entire time, not writing anything down. I can tell by his face that I've shocked him, although I don't know by which part. "And in all those years, you never told anyone?" he asks. "Not one person?"

I shake my head. "Just Ernie."

"And your mother, she denies everything? She says none of it ever happened?"

When I nod he puts his elbows on his knees and places his fingertips together, prayerlike, to his lips. "I realize you came here expecting me to give you an answer about what I think about all this, from a legal standpoint, that is," he says. "And unfortunately, I'm afraid I can't do that."

I open my mouth to protest, but he raises one hand, signaling me to let him finish. "But right from the start I need to tell you and Nick what a lawsuit would mean. From what I understand your stepfather was an extremely wealthy man with an apparently good reputation. He's also dead and can't defend himself. Right now I'm not going to go into all the legal difficulties of bringing charges against a dead person— and there are lots of them.

"But I will tell you this: Bringing *any* kind of claim against your stepfather, just by the nature of his wealth and status alone, would be bound to get all kinds of publicity," he goes on. "Horrendous publicity. I'm talking about the newspapers, television, everything. Every aspect of your life would be opened up to that. And believe me, I've seen what that can do to people. You open up the newspaper, and there you are on the front page. The most intimate details of your life, right there for everyone to read about."

Lynwood Arnold, who until now has been sitting quietly in a leather executive chair, clears his throat. "There's also the problem of the timing," he says. "Perceptually, that is. Since neither of you talked about this abuse to anyone until after your stepfather died, the question that would be bound to come up is: Why did you wait until now, until your stepfather is dead and can't defend himself, to say anything?"

Nick is rocking slightly on the sofa. His eyes are moving from side to side as if he's already picturing an imaginary headline: *Sex Abuse Shocker! Unemployed Cocaine Addict Sues Dead Millionaire Stepfather.* It's obvious, at least to me, that Nick is weighing the risks, that he's trying to figure out if the publicity would be worth the possible payoff. But not me. I don't know exactly what's happened since the day before, but I don't need any time to weigh anything. My trembling is over; my fear seems to have disappeared.

Now I want to fight. Now I want to tell what happened. If nothing else, I want just one person to believe me. *And if I can tell it to someone like Richard Gilbert, I think, I can tell it to anyone.*

Nick stops rocking. He sits upright and looks at both the lawyers and then me. "All right," he says. His voice is suddenly determined, as if he's just figured it all out. "I don't care anymore. Let's go for it. Let's nail the son of a bitch."

Richard Gilbert leans forward and laces his hands together. His brows furrow, and already he seems to understand that Nick is unpredictable, that his mood swings could be a problem.

"Meg," he says, turning to me, "how clearly do you remember things that happened? How well do you think you could tell us everything?"

I don't know why he's asking me that. "I already told you what Donald did, what my mother did. Ask me whatever you want. I'll tell you whatever you want to know."

"No," he says, "that's not what I mean." He shifts in his chair and crosses one leg over the other. "Lynwood and I would need you to tell us exactly the way things happened. Not just *basically* what happened, but all the details, everything you can remember. And let me tell you why. Most people, especially if they're important or respected, go to great lengths to conceal their bad deeds. That may sound like an obvious fact of human nature, but it's worth remembering. On the outside, they may appear to the world to be one thing, and then—as you and your brother are suggesting—in reality be something completely different. And those people are usually highly invested in maintaining that illusion, in covering their tracks. That's what makes it so difficult in cases that boil down to one person's word against another, where there are no witnesses.

"But there's always something," he goes on. "If you dig deep enough there are always signs, always clues the person leaves behind: People who might have seen something or suspected something, medical records. It could be a lot of things. And that's what we'd be looking for now, Meg. Those signs, those clues Donald Sahlman left behind. Anything that would help us prove what really happened." He's staring at me intently, gauging how I'm reacting. "Do you think you could do that? Help us find proof of what Donald Sahlman did to you?"

I'm nodding my head, but I can't bring myself to tell him what I'm really thinking.

I remember everything, but no one else was ever there. No one except my mother ever saw or knew a thing, and now she's lying through her teeth. For thirty years, I never told a soul. Nick didn't know about me, and I didn't know about him. Donald is dead now, and we'll never find any proof. We won't find it, because there isn't any.

Not even that I am the one who killed him.

I look at Ernie and then the lawyers. After a long moment, I nod. "I'll try," I say.

Two

CLIENT FILE: Margaret "Meg" Cassedy
INTERVIEW: First Session; February 1993
SUBJECT: Full Text of Client's Background Statement
ATTORNEYS PRESENT: Richard Gilbert, Lynwood Arnold

Sometimes I try to think of this another way, but what it always comes down to is this: Donald Sahlman was there, deciding what my life was going to be like, from the very start. Even before I remember him, before I ever set eyes on him. With only a blurry mental picture of a light-skinned baby girl, he must have wanted me near him.

Even then.

In 1962, I was just a few weeks old when my mother left me behind in Barbados with my father and took Nick and Granny to live with her in Guyana. More than once, I asked her why she'd done that, hoping, I'm sure, that she would change the answer she always gave, that she would alter the story so that it was a painful separation she was forced to make, a gut-wrenching decision made for my own benefit. But that answer never came. This one story always remained the same.

"Because your father was a drunk and an abuser, and he hated Nick the worst," she'd say. It never made sense, never explained a thing. If he was such an abuser, then why didn't she take me with her to Guyana, too?

I don't remember my father, Ronald Clairmonte, and what little I do know about him comes from my mother. But since her telling about him has changed over the years, it's hard to know what the truth is. One thing I know for certain, no matter what she says, is that he was an incredibly handsome black man, with the same light skin, high forehead and chalk-white smile of a young Harry Belafonte. Nick actually looks a lot like my father. But I'm also going by just one picture, which I rescued the day my mother tore up all the photos from that part of her life.

The picture was taken in a room in Barbados with my father's friends and relatives gathered in a semicircle. My mother, the only white person in the room, is standing in a sleeveless dress near the corner of the picture. She's looking across at him suspiciously, her brows furrowed, as if he's just done something awful. But my father is just smiling away, completely oblivious to whatever she's thinking.

When I was little, my mother told me he'd been an underwater welder. She said he had no education but could charm the skin off a snake, which was the closest she ever came to saying she ever loved or cared about him. Later on in America, though, my father got a whole new background. In her new version, he wasn't black anymore: He was a French islander, a highly trained engineer who died in a tragic accident.

Still, I don't know how she expected anyone to believe that part about his not being black. Even though Nick and I are light-skinned and conceivably could have a lot of possible backgrounds, it doesn't take a genius to look at us and figure out we're sure not French. But maybe she said it because of the way Donald felt about black people. For as long as I can remember, he talked about how he had nothing against "niggers" and thought everyone should own one, how black people shouldn't be allowed to vote because they're just jungle bunnies, how the reason they're such good football players is because they learned it running from the police, how America would be a lot better off if the South had won the Civil War. Even though he'd talk like that when Nick and I were right there in the room, my mother never said a word. She'd just keep cooking or looking in the refrigerator or whatever she was doing, and pretend as if she didn't hear him. As if the entire topic was no concern of hers.

Right after she moved to Georgetown, Guyana, my mother

got a job as a secretary at a seafood company. It was at least partially owned by Donald's company here in Tampa, which is why Donald or his brother Jack took turns flying down there on business five or six times a year. Donald would stay for weeks or months at a time at the home he and Jack owned in Bel Air, which was a beautiful neighborhood across town from us where all the rich people lived. I guess you could call Bel Air Georgetown's version of Beverly Hills.

Not long after she started dating him, Donald offered to go to Barbados and fetch me. He'd never even set eyes on me, but my mother said he told her it wasn't right to leave me there. A mother, he said, shouldn't be without her daughter.

"If it hadn't been for him, I would have left you there," she said to me once. "And then I was going to let him go get you, but I didn't want him running into your father."

There was a time when I imagined that was because my father wouldn't have given me to Donald in a million years. Drunk or not, he wouldn't have just handed me over. But later on I learned what my mother must have meant. She wouldn't let Donald go because she was afraid he would see the man she was once married to. And she couldn't risk having Donald see my father's obvious blackness. The way I figure it, hiding our background was a game they must have played from the start, with her pretending Nick and I were French kids and Donald pretending to believe it, and all the time him talking about how much he hated niggers and her ignoring it and taking his money and jewelry and clothes. The most charitable explanation I can give for her is that, back then, maybe she thought she had to. Maybe she thought that latching onto a rich man and putting up with everything was the only way she could survive.

When I was very young, my mother told me she'd been forced to drop out of school when Granny had her first nervous breakdown and couldn't work anymore. She said she'd worked as a secretary ever since she was sixteen, and from then on the responsibility for Granny, who only got worse over the years, had fallen squarely on her shoulders. After she divorced my father and ran away to Guyana, she said, the burden got even worse. Now she had four mouths to feed and a job that barely got us by. But that story also changed. In her later telling, my mother didn't have to drop out of school at all. Somewhere along the way she'd learned to play the violin and the piano quite well, and in Guyana I heard her tell people she'd earned a Ph.D. in music back in the islands. Many years later in Florida, she told it still a different way: She said she'd gotten a master's degree in music through a correspondence course with a university in England. So I guess you'd have to ask her what the real truth is. But good luck getting it.

Even now, people tell me they think my mother's attractive. It's hard for me to think of her that way, but I can see why they might say it. She's an inch shorter than I, five feet exactly, and has dark glossy hair, dark eyes, and a perfect cream complexion that reminds me of movie stars from the 1940s. Ernie once said she reminded him of that bitchy television actress Joan Collins, especially with her accent: It's a blend of the British from Guyana and the language of the West Indies, lilting and clipped, which makes everything she says sound haughty or disapproving. Maybe it was that exotic accent that attracted Donald when he first met her. That, or the fact she had Nick and me.

What my mother saw in Donald is a different question. Never in his life could anyone have called that man attractive. He had a ring of sparse hair around a pointed bald head, and a large nose and acne-scarred skin that reminded me of volcanic rock. If it hadn't been for his thick black Buddy Holly glasses, which magnified eyes the color of shark skin, he was the kind of man who'd be perfectly safe at a police lineup. Utterly plain, utterly forgettable.

Still, Donald seemed to have no awareness at all of his plainness, of what bordered on ugliness. At times, it even seemed as though he thought just the opposite of himself. He walked in long forceful strides, laughed loudly, and whenever he talked it was in a deep authoritative Southern drawl, as if he clearly expected to be listened to, as if he automatically assumed he'd be admired. He was arrogant and opinionated, and on top of it had a temper with a flash point somewhere at curb level. But if all that weren't enough to discourage my mother, there was another small detail. He was already married and had a grown son. He told us his wife, Bette Louise, was a total invalid confined to bed in Florida.

But there was, of course, his money. The scent of it hung on him like some overpowering cologne. It was there in the way he dressed, his clothes starched and pressed to perfection; in the way he loved to talk about all the things he owned—his forty-two-foot yacht, his home overlooking a canal in the best part of Tampa, the new luxury car he bought each year; in the lavish gifts he bought my family. To my mother, being so close to all that money must have been intoxicating. And listening to him talk about everything he owned in Florida must have been like hearing about another world—one that was beautiful and graceful and filled with lovely things, one as far away from the slum we lived in that you could get.

In Guyana we lived in a little white house on stilts, which is how most of the houses in South America were built. But that one house had been divided into three flats for three families, so it felt as though we all were on top of each other. In many ways, it was like a mini-population sample: Upstairs was an Indo-Guyanese family descended from India, and downstairs an Amerindian family who shared their space with an Afro-Guyanese couple. Our apartment, on the second floor, had two bedrooms about the size of large closets: one for my mother and me, and one for Granny. Nick slept out on the sofa under the one small window overlooking the street. It was cramped and dark, and even though my mother kept it as clean as she could, cockroaches bigger than my thumb crawled the walls and scattered whenever the lights went on.

Up and down the street were other houses just like ours. All of them were run-down and paint-chipped and jammed close together, with just a small strip of dirt separating the front doors from the street. A few had dilapidated porches, and most didn't have phones. Some families, like the Ethiopians with twelve kids across the street or the Indian family next door, didn't even have electricity. There wasn't a single flower anywhere, just a few coconut and papaya trees, but even then there was no smell: It was as if we all were living in the middle of a picture taken in black and white. Amid the rusty cars that stood in driveways, some propped on blocks and never moved from one spot, my mother's car was the only one on that street that looked good. It was new and shiny and green, a gift from Donald.

I remember the first day I found out I was getting to go over to Donald's house in Bel Air. I was four years old, and he had called my mother to tell her he wanted to pick me up for lunch. Even though we saw him several times a week at our apartment, I was so excited, because this was the first time he was taking me instead of Nick. Whenever my mother came back from visiting Donald in Bel Air, she always talked about all the huge homes and big gardens and how beautiful it was, so that just thinking about it made me ache to see it, and just waiting for him to arrive seemed like an eternity.

I was wearing my church clothes, a light-blue dress with little buttons down the front and black patent-leather shoes, when Donald drove up in his white car. My mother didn't walk outside with me, but she reminded me to be good and do whatever Uncle Donald said. I got into the front seat with him, and I could barely contain my excitement. He was wearing shorts, and as he drove away from our house he took my hand and rubbed it up and down his leg. "Aren't I hairy?" he said. I laughed and said, *"Yeah!"*

We drove to the other side of town, where the landscape changed completely. Wide boulevards with tall arching trees formed a green tunnel as we drove under them, and huge houses with expansive gardens flew by like something out of a dream. With the windows down, my hair, which stretched down my back, blew gently against my face in the warm breeze. I don't think I'd ever been so happy or felt so special in my life. Pretty soon we drove up to a big, black iron gate. Donald stopped the car and got out to open it. As he did, I looked up the long driveway and saw a huge garden that had orchids and roses everywhere: yellow roses, red roses, pink roses, with the smell so sweet I could have swum in it. The white three-story house was beyond the garden, and I wanted to jump out of the car right then and put my nose into all the flowers.

Donald drove up and parked the car, and we walked up the stairs to the front door. Once inside, my eyes must have been like soup bowls as I looked at everything. The living room had high ceilings and beautiful dark wood furniture, and French doors opened out onto a balcony that stretched the length of the house. There was even a sofa on the balcony where you could sit and listen to the birds or smell the flowers, and then you could come back inside into the cool lovely air conditioning, which we sure didn't have at home. He led me into the dining room, where there was a round dark table and four chairs with black-and-white checkered seats. Against one wall was a long narrow table where Lucille, the cook, came in and put the food. Lucille was a big black woman and very kind to me.

"Hello, how are you?" she said, smiling down at me. "I hope you like what I'm cooking for lunch." She went back into the kitchen, and Donald and I sat down at the table. I could see my reflection in a big gilded mirror on the wall, and I grinned at myself just to make sure I wasn't dreaming. Lucille came back with two plates for the rice and beef stew and poured me a big glass of milk. Everything tasted so delicious, and I remember thinking, *This is how it must feel to be a princess.*

After we were done eating, Donald told me I had to take a nap. I'd never taken a nap before—my mother worked during the day and Granny never paid any attention to what Nick or I did—but he told me that's what civilized people did after lunch. *Civilized,* I thought, *must mean sleepy.* We got up and walked into the kitchen, where Lucille was putting things away in a big cupboard. I stared at all the food there—we sure didn't have that kind of food at home—and then I spotted a big bowl of vanilla pudding. I loved vanilla pudding. "Would you like something else?" Lucille asked me. I looked up at Donald, hoping he would nod so I could have some, but when he didn't I said, "No, thank you." And then Donald took me down the hall.

There was one bedroom to my left, a bathroom on the right, and then a second bedroom with a double bed and white bedspread. Above it hung a mosquito net, a veil, that was draped in a circle all around it. There were two big pillows on the bed, and then I saw one cute, tiny pillow in the middle. I ran over to it, thinking he'd put it there just for me. "Oh look! A little pillow!" I said, picking it up.

"That's my pillow," he said. "I put it between my knees when I sleep. I'll let you use it now, Margaret, but at night it is mine."

There was a dresser by the door where Donald put his wallet and the change out of his pockets. "After your nap," he said, "I'll give you a quarter."

A quarter! That was a lot of money—enough to buy candy for Nick and me both. And just for sleeping! But right away I worried about what would happen if I was too excited to sleep. Would he still give it to me? Maybe I'd have to pretend.

Donald reached over and shut the door and locked it real slow, real gentle-like.

"Why are you locking the door?"

"I told you, we have to take a nap. Lucille is in the kitchen, and I don't want to be disturbed." He started to take off his clothes. He took off his shirt and put it on the dresser, took off his shoes, his belt and then his pants. In his white underwear, he went over to the bed and lay down. I stood in the middle of the room looking around, and finally he patted the side of the bed for me to come over. He told me to take off my clothes and shoes. I had trouble undoing the little buttons of my dress, so he did that for me. He pulled my dress over my head so that I had just my panties on.

He told me to sit next to him on the bed, Indian-style. I wasn't thinking anything was strange, because I looked up to him. I knew he was Mom's special friend, so I just did what he told me. He was lying down. And then he pulled off his underwear.

Suddenly I was very scared. Donald sometimes took Nick into our bathroom to wash him, so I'd seen my brother naked a few times before. But Donald looked like a horse I'd once seen by the side of the road. And right then I started to wonder what was going on. I didn't understand, because I thought I was supposed to be sleeping. He reached over and took my hand. "Let me show you how this is done," he said.

He wrapped his hand around my hand and put it on him and started going up and down, up and down. I tried to pull my hand away, but he said, "No, you've got to peel the skin back, like this." I was very, very scared. I kept thinking, *I wonder where Mommy is?* I knew something was wrong and looked at the door. "But we're not sleeping," I said. "Aren't we supposed to sleep?"

"We're going to sleep when we get through," he said. "After that, if you still don't want to sleep, you can go out and play with Lucille in the kitchen while I sleep." He tightened his hand on mine and did the movement. I wasn't even doing it. My hand just went numb and limp. He said, "You have to go all the way down to the base." He kept on going and going and going. I moved my hand away real quick. "Don't move your hand!" he said. "Don't move until I'm through!" And then all of a sudden he started to shake. To jerk. And then all this white stuff came out.

I was terrified. I thought I was killing him. That he was dying. I didn't know what was happening. I said, "Oh my gosh! Are you okay? Are you all right?"

"Don't worry, Margaret. It just feels oh-so-good."

I took my hand away, but he grabbed it back again. He glared at me as if he was going to hit me. I was so scared I started to get very hot. I felt my heart beating very hard. "Don't you move your hand," he said. "You're not allowed to move until I tell you." There was all this white stuff on my hand, and it was so sticky and nasty I wanted to cry. And then he rubbed it all over the top of my hand. "Don't worry," he said. "We'll wash it up in a little bit." Then he just lay there. He took his hand off mine. And I thought, *Oh good, he didn't die.* I was so relieved he hadn't died.

He got up and took a white towel and washed everything off of him and then me. Then he walked over to his closet where his suits were hanging. He reached down and took out a camera, a Polaroid, and showed it to me. He said, "Now we're going to take some pictures." Donald told me to take off my panties and stand on top of the bed. I didn't know what to do. He stood at the foot of the bed and took a picture, and it popped out of the camera. "Now turn to the side," he said. He took another. He told me to put my hands on my hips, to give him a back view, to grab my ankles. He took more pictures.

"Are you going to show these to Mommy?"

"Oh no, this is our secret," he said. "Only daddies and daughters do this. You're not allowed to tell anybody. This is our secret."

"Why?"

"Because," he said. "I already told you. Daddies and daughters are the only ones who do this. All daddies and daughters do this. Mommies and daughters don't do this. And it's our little secret. You're not even allowed to tell Debra." Debra was my best friend who lived downstairs from us.

He looked at the pictures for a few minutes, and then took a pair of silver scissors from the dresser and cut them into little pieces. I asked him why he was doing that. "Because we don't want them around. Other people come to the house, too. Important people from my company. We don't want anybody to see them because it's our secret." Then he told me to put my clothes on and go over to the dresser. "There's some money there like I told you. You can have a quarter or two if you like. Now, you can either stay and take a nap with me, or else you can go outside and play."

The minute he said "nap" again, I wanted to get out of there. He'd already used the word before, and it hadn't been a nap at all. So when he said it again, I was afraid it might happen again. I got dressed very quickly—I didn't want him to change his mind—and as I was leaving I took a quarter off his dresser. Then I quickly took another. I unlocked the door and went out to the kitchen. Lucille was washing the lunch dishes.

"Oh, are you up from your nap already?" she asked.

"Yeah," I said, "but I didn't sleep."

"You didn't sleep?"

"No."

She looked at me and dried her hands on her apron. "Well then, did you maybe want something else to eat?"

I thought for a moment, and then nodded. "I'd like some pudding now, please."

Three

By the time I was six, Donald's bimonthly visits to Guyana had a regular, predictable quality to them. In many ways, we could have set our clocks by what happened to us when he was in Georgetown.

On his first day back from Florida, he arrived at our flat carrying a big bag of gifts, which he perched on his knees on the sofa and then theatrically asked Nick and me if we knew what he'd brought us. Only after we'd called out the proper response—"Show us, Uncle Donald!"—did he slowly reach into the bag and retrieve the items, holding each one up for us to see. There were huge flat lollipops with whorls of colors, packets of Dentyne gum, oversized bars of chocolate with almonds, brightly colored sourballs wrapped in cellophane, and then came the clothes: little dresses with bows and lace for me, shirts and shorts for Nick. Even though Donald had only been gone at most a few months, he treated every one of his returns like Christmas.

My mother, too, was showered with Donald's presents. He brought her perfume and clothes and jewelry—gold and diamond necklaces and bracelets and rings she oohed and aahed over. Sometimes, after she opened every gift, he handed her a thick envelope, which she'd slip into her purse with her eyes cast down. One day, Nick and I came home to a baby grand piano in the middle of the living room, its shiny black lid propped open so we would see the tiny white hammers and metal strings inside. It took up so much room you had to turn sideways to get to the sofa. My mother, who'd been forced to do her practicing on a small organ at the Sacred Heart Catholic Church near our flat, was speechless by what he'd done. For weeks afterward, every time she walked past it she let her fingers run lightly over the ivory keys without making a sound, as if touching it was the only way she could believe it was really there.

I was always happy that first day Donald arrived from Florida. Part of me, I admit, even looked forward to it. I'd carry his candy into the bedroom I shared with my mother and spread the chocolate and sourballs out on our bed, and then I'd stand in front of my mother's mirror and try on the little dresses he'd gotten me. For a few hours, that would be all I would think about: the candy I'd share with my best friend Debra; how pretty I'd look going to church in my new clothes.

But then the dread would set in. It swooped down on me, a cold chill deep in my stomach that felt like snow. The candy and clothes were only part of Donald's ritual, only the beginning; what lay ahead of me made me shudder. As often as I tried to believe that *maybe this time he won't do it anymore,* deep down I knew it wasn't true.

My mother no longer told me in advance that Donald was coming by the flat at lunchtime. She didn't have to, since he came every day. The only question was whether he'd take Nick or me, which we didn't know until the last moment. While she was away at the seafood plant, Donald drove up in his white car and honked the horn, the engine idling as he waited for us both to come outside. Granny, as always, sat in her frayed armchair in the corner of our living room staring blankly into space, oblivious to whether we came or went or were even there.

"Come on, Margaret," he said when it was my turn. Or, "In you go, Nicholas," when he wanted to take my brother.

The drive over to Bel Air was no longer beautiful, no longer exciting or special. I felt like a lamb going to slaughter. I wished it had been Nick going instead of me. As Donald crossed town and passed under the tunnel of trees, I'd stare out the window watching the rose gardens and huge homes fly by, saying silent prayers that something would make him take a different route or turn the car around or get a flat tire on the way. But nothing like that ever happened. It always ended the same.

He'd take me inside the dining room for the lunch Lucille had prepared. After we finished eating he'd announce it was time for our nap, and then came the long walk down the hallway to the back bedroom, with each step the knot in my stomach tightening so that sometimes I was afraid I would vomit. But it was that sensation, actually, that gave me an idea.

One day it occurred to me that if I simply kept on eating—if I used up all of Donald's nap time at the table—I wouldn't have to go with him into the bedroom. So the next time at the table with him, I began chewing each bite very slowly, taking the tiniest of sips of milk. I stared at my plate so I wouldn't have to watch him as he leaned back in his chair, his hands folded in his lap, staring at me.

"Hurry up, Margaret," he said. "You're dawdling with that food."

I chewed a bit faster, drank more milk. The important thing was to keep eating so he wouldn't think I was done. But my stomach was getting full. That's when I asked to go to the bathroom. I went inside and locked the door, leaned over the toilet and put my fingers down my throat. When I was finished, I came back to the table and asked for another plate of food.

He was immediately suspicious. "You've already had your lunch, Margaret. What's wrong with you?"

"I'm hungry, Uncle Donald. My stomach is still growling. If you put your ear right here," I pointed, "you can even hear it."

His eyes narrowed, and then he reluctantly asked Lucille to bring me a second helping. Lucille came in and put the plate down in front of me, and nodded gravely. "Hope she don't have the worm, Mr. Sahlman, sir," she said.

Donald watched me take each bite. He drummed his fingers on the table and breathed in little snorts through his nose. Finally, he pushed his chair back brusquely and took my plate away. "You've had enough now. I need my nap." He walked into the kitchen and gave the plate to Lucille. Even though it hadn't worked as I'd planned, going to the bathroom had delayed it. By the time I was seven, I vomited practically every day he took me for lunch. The only time I didn't was when one of Donald's business associates happened to be at the house, too. Sam Fazio, a dark-haired man who used to smile at me from across the table, sometimes ate with us before heading back to work. But even if Sam was there in the house, that didn't stop Donald.

Donald was no longer satisfied with having me sit Indian-style on the bed and moving my hand up and down on him. He made me lie naked with my legs apart while he put his mouth on me, and then forced me to put my mouth on him while he gripped the sides of my jaw. I choked and gagged and tried to cry out because of the pain in my face, but that only made him clench my jaw tighter. He never released me until he was through. It made him angry if I ever complained or moved, and it always frightened me to hear his voice drop down real low, real threatening, whenever he said, "Very bad things will happen if you don't do this, Margaret. All daughters must do this."

Afterward he took Polaroids of me, which he always cut into tiny pieces before putting them into the wastebasket. Then he'd point to the dresser. "Take your two quarters now, Margaret. And don't forget." I always shook my head, letting him know that I wouldn't. "This is our little secret," he always said. "Only daddies and daughters do this. It's how they show their special love. No one else must ever know. No one."

Later, I sat in the kitchen with Lucille, watching her pull baking ingredients out of the cupboard and listening as she told me stories about her childhood. Sometimes she handed me a big wooden spoon and helped me stir a bowl full of thick batter. Afterwards I'd follow her out into the garden as she snipped roses and brought them inside to put in vases. With the smell of cake or cookies or muffins filling the kitchen, Donald slept. Donald forgot about me then. And when he got up again, he stopped in the kitchen only long enough to have a bite or two of whatever Lucille and I had made.

"Good-bye, then, Miss Margaret," Lucille would say to me, pressing a warm cookie or muffin into my hand. And then Donald drove me back to our flat, dropping me off outside, before heading back to his office.

In the evenings, after my mother returned from the seafood plant, Donald came back to our flat. He no longer wanted to eat meals at our apartment; his house, he said, was so much nicer. All of us would pile into his car for the drive back to Bel Air to have dinner. Nick and I and Granny usually sat at the table and said nothing, while Donald asked my mother the same questions he always asked: So how was your day? Anything interesting happen at the plant? Do you need anything? How's that car been doing?

Back then, my mother wasn't at all supercilious or arrogant the way she got after we moved to America. If anything, especially whenever she got around Donald, you would have called her mousy or timid. Sometimes it seemed as though she was afraid of him, of displeasing him, as if the two of them had some unspoken agreement about how they were supposed to behave together, except that sometimes she wasn't always perfectly clear about all the rules. And maybe, if you think about it, it's not hard to understand why. Donald was married, and she was a practicing Catholic who went to Mass every Sunday. There weren't a lot of rules for a situation like that. Maybe that was why, in all the years we were in Guyana, I can't remember a single time I ever saw any kind of open affection between the two of them, with the sole exception of occasional hand-holding. It might explain why there wasn't a single instance that ever made me think she loved him or that he felt that way about her. The two of them always seemed like actors.

At the dinner table in Bel Air, my mother never once had anything interesting to say to him. Probably, looking back, it was because nothing new or different ever happened to her, but she still always responded to his inquiries the same way. She'd give a shake of her head and a small smile, and then she'd turn the conversation to him: Nothing much, but how was your day? What have you been up to? Then we'd all sit there and listen while he went on about all the lazy workers at the plant and how he shouldn't expect anything more from those people anyway, how sometimes he wondered why he even bothered trying to get an honest day's work out of niggers because they were all the same.

There was never a word about having brought Nick or me over for lunch. Not from him, and not from Lucille, who silently came in from the kitchen and cleared our dinner dishes from the table.

After dessert, we'd all go into the living room, where Donald would pull out a box of slides and put it into his projector on top of a small table. He loved his slides. With Granny, Nick and me on the sofa and my mother in an armchair in the corner, he'd flip off the lights and then focus the blurry beam of light filled with dancing dust motes onto the wall. Image after image clicked above our heads as he narrated what we were seeing: an orange sunset with huge silvery clouds above Tampa Bay; his yacht moored behind his home on the canal; his family's land up the east coast of Florida at Fernandina Beach, where his ancestors used to have a plantation full of slaves. Donald brought boxes of pictures on each trip to Guyana. Each night we watched them with the same resignation and silence that would mark, in many ways, our entire relationship with him.

From the time I was two years old, Donald had given Nick and me baths at our flat. But now that he brought us all over to Bel Air at night, he gave us our baths there. After his slide shows, while my mother stood in the doorway looking on, he had me stand naked in front of the tub for inspection before I was allowed to step into the water. Crouched on his knees, he spread my lips and peered closely between my legs. Sometimes he said I had pimples that required a special cream he'd bought, but usually he just talked about an unpleasant odor.

"I talk about this all the time, Patricia, but she really smells bad down there," he'd say. "She stinks. I think she's been getting too much sugar. You need to watch that."

My mother would just nod her head. "I've noticed that, too," she'd say. She furrowed her brows as if I was something despicable, something loathsome. "You are a very dirty girl, Margaret," she'd say, and then disappear to play her violin while Donald washed me.

Afterward, when I was in my pajamas, it was Nick's turn. My mother, Granny and I sat in the living room until Donald was through and Nick was in his pajamas, too. Then Donald helped Granny out to the car, and by the time he came back to the house we'd all be ready to leave. We got into his car and he drove us home, Nick and me sleeping with our heads on Granny's lap in the backseat.

The same thing, I knew, would happen the next day.

From the deposition of Salvatore "Sammy" Fazio, conducted by Richard Gilbert

"I saw Margaret Clairmonte when she was a young girl . . . in Georgetown, South America. I do remember seeing her where I lived occasionally. And I've seen her with her mother many times as a young girl, but I don't remember specifically where."

"Were you working for Sahlman Seafoods at the time?"

"I worked with them, yes."

"Did you stay in the Bel Air house?"

"I stayed in two houses. One was the house that the Fazios rented [in Georgetown], and one was the house that belonged to the Sahlman brothers [Jack and Donald]. The Sahlmans lived alone and I lived alone at times. So from time to time I would move into their [Bel Air] house so that we would have somebody to eat and talk with. As I recall, the Sahlmans didn't stay down in Guyana very long. They might have stayed down there a week or two. I never stayed more than seventeen days. I would be coming back to Florida at that time."

"And how many times did you do this?"

"Almost two years off and on . . . I'm speaking of the years, probably 1972 to 1973."

"Is that the only time you spent with either Jack or Don Sahlman?"

"We socialized often, but I lived [at Bel Air] from the time in question. If I hadn't been living with the Sahlmans, I never would have seen the young girl. I would see the mother at work because she worked down where I worked. I probably met Pat Clairmonte the first year she came to Georgetown. . . . As I recall, Pat had fled from Barbados for whatever reason and had come to Guyana and had no friends or family."

"Would you socialize with Don and Pat?"

"Don was the type of guy that was early to bed and early to rise. He didn't go out very often at night as I recall."

"You say you saw Margaret where you lived. In which house did you see her?"

"I saw her at the Sahlman house. As I remember it, she would pop in in the middle of the afternoon and be there half an hour or so, drink a Pepsi-Cola and have cookies and leave. And I remember it because I always had to put my clothes on when she came. The maid and the cook were always there. She would stay, have a Coca-Cola and then they would leave."

"You say, 'They would leave.' Who is they?"

"The little girl. Margaret. And Donald Sahlman."

"Where was Pat?"

"I don't know."

"Did Pat Sahlman spend the night there?"

"I don't remember them ever staying for dinner, let alone staying for the night. And I lived there."

"What were you doing during the day?"

"We were working. Some days I would go home at 3:00, some days at 4:00, some days at 5:00. I had no particular schedule to get to the house. But I always came home for lunch at noon."

"When would you see Meg, or Margaret?"

"I don't remember ever seeing her in the morning or at lunch time. I recall it being in the late afternoon. I remember the little girl loved Pepsi."

"How old was Meg when you saw her down in South America?"

"Maybe seven years old, maybe ten."

"And when you saw Don and Meg together without Pat in South America, what were they doing?"

"I'll repeat. She was a child. They would come to Donald's house. I would be there. I would strip down sometimes and have my shorts on even though the maid was there. The little girl would come in and zoom straight to the kitchen. And I would go in my room and put a pair of pants on. I would come out. [Donald] would say, 'How about some cookies?' Now this is in the living room. 'Okay, Meg, let's go.' And they would leave. It's half an hour at most they would be there."

Four

When Donald finished his month-long business trip in Georgetown and finally went back to Florida, it felt the way it did when the torrential Guyana rains suddenly stopped and the sun came out, when the air was crisp and clear and clean. I felt a lightness inside me, something I didn't recognize at the time as relief. My time was my own again, and until my mother got home from work, Nick and I could do as we pleased. If it seemed like Christmas the day Donald arrived, it felt like the start of summer when he finally left for America.

In the afternoons, my friend Debra and I would walk around the neighborhood wearing sunglasses and pretending we were teenagers, or sit on our paint-peeled front steps sipping lemonade in the hot sun. Later, all the neighborhood kids gathered to play cricket out in the street, the ball thonking against the wooden bat as we yelled and ran and cheered. As dusk approached we played hide and seek, our whoops and screams echoing into the pink and orange sky. Only when we were so drenched in sweat and exhausted that we couldn't bear it anymore would we slowly disperse, all of us disappearing back in our houses to cool off in our bathtubs.

I forgot about Donald then. As soon as he was gone, it was as if he didn't exist. My mind somehow pushed him out of my thoughts as if I had shoved him over a cliff. Sometimes it seemed as if the world stopped moving while he was in Guyana and only started up again after he left.

It's difficult to know, of course, what my mother felt when Donald went home again to his bedridden wife and son in Tampa, when he returned to his million-dollar home on the canal and his yacht and all the things he always talked about. Sometimes, though, I think it must have been like Cinderella at the stroke of midnight, when all the beauty and elegance and lovely things suddenly go *poof!* and what's left was the stark reality of her life, a cockroach-filled tenement and a boring job at a seafood company and three people depending on her to keep it all going.

She couldn't even go anymore to the Pegasus, the new luxury hotel and country club Donald had joined. On hot evenings, and practically every weekend, he'd take us all swimming in its huge pool, letting Nick and me gorge ourselves on the magnificent buffets with curried rice and salads and cakes and cookies and trifles. While Donald aimed his new movie camera at Nick or me and said, "Show me a dive," or "Walk to the end and then come back at me with a big smile," my mother sat by the pool in her big sunglasses, talking with friends or reading romance novels.

But there was no Pegasus when Donald left for Florida. There was no fine food or envelopes stuffed with money or bags of groceries when she needed them, either. The moment Donald stepped onto that plane, that's what she must have been left with: *Poof!* The dull, heavy reality of her life.

When Donald was in America, my mother did go out in the evenings with friends to a restaurant or movie, about the only two things you could do in Georgetown. She started going over to Sacred Heart Catholic Church, too, where she once had practiced the organ. A new priest had come to the parish, Father Andrew Morrison, and my mother said he was looking for an organist who could help the congregation grow. She thought it would be a nice change for her, and so once or twice a week she tucked a stack of music under her arm and drove over to the church.

"I'll be back late. You do whatever Granny says," she'd say to Nick and me as she headed out the door.

What Granny said to us, of course, was nothing. To Nick and me, Granny was as much a fixture as the sofa or the lamp or the piano. For as long as I can remember she was like someone living inside a fish tank: the way she stared at you with that blank look, the way her mouth opened and closed but she didn't say anything, the way she rarely moved from her chair near the window except to shuffle to the bathroom and back. From the time I was little, Granny had the same expression I once saw when one of the neighborhood boys accidentally got hit in the head with a cricket bat: wide-eyed and bewildered, as if every thought had just been knocked clear out of her head. Nick could be pounding on me or chasing me from room to room—his favorite thing to do as soon as my mother walked out the door—and Granny wouldn't even blink.

According to my mother, Granny hadn't been able to handle the change of life. I didn't know what that was, but I made up my mind it would never happen to me. It wasn't until many years later, in America, that I found out what Granny's real condition was. When my mother was a teenager, Granny was diagnosed with schizophrenia. For nearly forty years, up until her death, she lived in a heavily medicated world that consisted of one armchair or another, staring blankly into a space none of us ever entered.

Sometime when I was about seven or eight—I know this because I had already started school—Father Morrison began making regular visits to our flat whenever Donald was in America. He was an extremely tall man with pale blue eyes and the white hair you only see on people who have been very blond all their lives, and he walked with a noticeable limp. The only thing I knew about him was that he'd come from England and that his heavy accent, very proper and formal, wasn't at all like what we normally heard in Guyana. I was used to seeing him each Sunday at Mass and later in the youth group he started, but now we saw him during the week as well.

Father Morrison would arrive shortly before dinner with a small oblong box in his hands. He sat on the sofa with Nick and me and did magic tricks while my mother cooked in the kitchen. He was good at the magic, too: He made playing cards float to the top of a deck, thick metal rings pass through each other like butter, pennies fall out of our mouths. "Oh no, what is this?" he said one time, and then reached behind my head and produced a bouquet of flowers. "You have been hiding those flowers from me, Margaret Clairmonte, and they were right there inside your head all along!"

Nick and I always burst out in amazed laughter. We adored him, and thought it was especially wonderful that sometimes, in the mornings, he even came to the flat to take us to school. Our mother, too, seemed particularly affected by him; after he left the flat, she sometimes leaned against the door and said, "Oh, isn't he *nice!* Such a *nice* man!" She seemed happy in a way I'd never seen her with Donald.

A few times, my mother took us with her when she drove over to the church for a practice session. Nick and I brought along books or homework and sat in a back pew while Father Morrison sat on the organ bench beside my mother, their backs turned to us. While my mother played "Firmly and Truly I Do Believe," he rested one hand on her shoulder or rubbed her back, occasionally reaching out with his free hand to turn the pages of her music.

The only thing we didn't understand was why he changed so dramatically on Sundays, when suddenly he acted stiff and formal around my mother and as if Nick and I were nothing special to him. As the children walked into the building for the youth group after Mass, he greeted us all the same way. "Hello, Margaret; hello, Nicholas; hello, Andrea; hello, John . . ."

Nick and I knew better than to call him what we now did in private. He had already explained that whenever we saw him at church, we never should call him what we did at the flat: Uncle Andy.

"Hello, Father Morrison," we said to him quietly, and went inside with the other children.

Donald's returns to Georgetown put an end to Father Morrison's visits, along with my mother's weeknight practice sessions at the church and her dinners with friends. The four of us, including Granny, still attended Mass each Sunday— my mother said the reason Donald never came with us was that he was a Methodist—but other than that, Father Morrison went the way of my walks around the neighborhood with Debra or our neighborhood cricket games in the street. Whenever Donald was in town, whatever life we had established in his absence simply stopped. Our lives now revolved around him.

I have no idea what my mother said to the priest to explain his sudden banishment, which lasted anywhere from a few weeks to a couple of months depending on Donald's business schedule. But whatever it was, Father Morrison seemed to respect it. He was cordial as ever to her at church services, and even inquired how my confirmation studies were coming along. I didn't have the courage to tell him how difficult it was for me to think about catechism when Donald was there, how hard it was for me to concentrate on the Ten Commandments or original sin when I knew he was always waiting for me. In fact, I didn't have the courage to tell anyone at all.

At school, there were a few times I considered talking about what was happening to me. I attended the Winfred Gardens School, a large white two-story building that was about fifteen minutes from our flat. Even though Winfred Gardens was private and co-ed—and, presumably, paid for by Donald—Nick went to St. John's, a private school for boys, which meant we never saw each other until late in the day. It never occurred to me then that there was a reason we were separated like that.

By the time I was nine, and going to Bel Air at lunchtime was no longer possible, Donald had begun to pick me up in front of the school at the end of the day. I never knew when it would happen. In contrast to when I was younger, when he came every day like clockwork to our flat, there now was no pattern to when he'd show up. All day long I'd sit in the classroom and wonder what was going to happen to me later, getting more and more nervous as the day wore on. My book would be opened to a page and the teacher would be talking to the class, but sometimes I heard only phrases of what was being said:

As a British colony, Guyana's political, economic and social life during the 1800s was dominated by a European planter class, and what was this called? That's right, children, the plantocracy . . . (Maybe he won't come for me today.) *And members of the plantocracy, who controlled the working conditions for the majority of the population, had links to British commercial interests in London, and often they had close ties to the governor, who was appointed by what? Yes, that's right, the monarch* . . . (But he wasn't there yesterday, so he'll probably be there today. He usually never misses two days in a row.) *The next social stratum consisted of freed slaves, many of them light-skinned, from mixed African and European heritage* . . . (What if he gets a flat tire like last month? Then I could hurry before he got here and I could make up a story. . . .) *And who was at the lowest level of society? That's right, class, it was the majority, the African slaves. . . .*

My grades were barely average, and I'm sure the teachers all thought I was slow.

At the end of the day, as the children lined up for dismissal in front of the main doors, I'd have a pit in my stomach, not knowing what I'd see when the doors opened to the driveway filled with cars and awaiting parents. My eyes would sweep across the front lawn, preparing to see his white car and Donald walking toward me saying, "Let's go, honey." But some days he wouldn't be there. I'd run down the driveway toward the street clutching my books to my chest, glancing at the other girls getting into their fathers' cars. Always I looked for a sign—a kiss, a protective glance, a hand placed just so—that would indicate it was happening to them, too. But I never could tell.

Winfred Gardens' headmistress was a large, light-skinned woman the kids all liked, and she seemed to like me as well. Often I brought her roses from Donald's garden, which she placed in a vase on her desk. More than once I thought about going to Mrs. Fernandez in private and asking her what had become a burning, unanswered question: Did all the girls at the school really have to do what Donald made me do? Mrs. Fernandez had a gentleness and kindness about her, and if there was anyone I could trust it would be her. But in the end I always rejected the idea. If Donald ever found out I'd told her, I'd be better off dead. I can't tell you exactly what I thought would happen, because it wasn't my physical safety that worried me; it was more the look Donald got when he glared at me and said, "If you ever tell anyone, very bad things will happen. You'll burn in hell, Margaret." And somehow I knew Mrs. Fernandez would tell him.

Sometimes, too, I considered asking one of my girlfriends. In our school, several grades were combined into one large classroom, and so there were many girls both older and younger than I who might have been able to tell me what I longed to know. I thought of asking three girls in particular: Allison, a blond-haired girl who lived with her father and mother; Kuwali, a thin, black girl whose mother had remarried; and Senata, a beautiful girl who was part Indian, and who seemed sophisticated and knowledgeable about practically everything.

But how would I bring it up with them? I thought of offhanded things like, "So, what kind of stuff does your dad do?" Or, "So, do you like being with your dad?" But I never could bring myself to say it. Always there was the fear: What if they had kept the secret and were shocked I would reveal it? Donald said all daddies and daughters did what we did, that all daughters had to keep the secret. And if that was true, what if I was the only one who broke that promise?

And so I said nothing. I didn't ask Mrs. Fernandez, I didn't ask any of the girls at school, and I didn't even ask Debra, who years earlier had stopped asking me why we never spent time together whenever my Uncle Donald was in town. I never confided in Nick, either, since we'd never really been close—and especially because he now took every opportunity to roam the neighborhood or go over to friends' houses. And I certainly said nothing to my mother. She knew full well that Donald still gave me baths and peered between my legs to make sure I was clean.

At the end of the school day I lined up with the other girls, my heart pounding, the fear gnawing at my insides. I stood beside Allison and Kuwali and Senata as they laughed and talked cheerfully, and wondered if they really could feel that way if they were facing the same thing I was. *But maybe,* I thought, *it was an act.* The same one Donald had instructed me about. Whenever I wasn't with him, he had said, "You always need to put on the happy face, Margaret. I don't want to hear from anyone about you having one of your sad faces."

Even that seemed like a threat: If he heard from anyone that I didn't look cheerful, bad things would happen then, too.

✝ ✝ ✝

From the deposition of Patricia Sahlman, conducted by Richard Gilbert

"I was born in British Guyana, South America. December 26th, 1938. My mother's name is Mary and my father's name was Joseph."

"Where did you go to school?"

"I don't understand, I can't hear you. Speak louder. I have a hearing problem."

"Where did you go to school?"

"I went to school in Guyana."

"And you went through what grade?"

"I went through twelfth grade."

"And were you as a child ever the victim of any sexual abuse?"

"Never."

"Were you married before you were married to Donald Sahlman?"

"Yes. To Ronald Clairmonte. 1959. In Barbados, West Indies."

"And what was Ronald Clairmonte's race?"

"He was half white and half islander, which is a kind of mixture."

"When you say islander, you mean a black person?"

"No, not black. He was not black."

"What is an islander?"

"It's sort of a mixture between French, Spanish, English, Portuguese. . . . There's a lot of races in the Caribbean similar to America, and everybody intermarries."

"Do you know what portions or races made up Mr. Clairmonte?"

"English, French. I would say a small portion of Negro, Portuguese."

"You say a small portion of Negro. What color was he in terms of complexion?"

"He was her color."

"By her, you are referring to Meg Cassedy?"

"Margaret."

"And then did there come a time when you got divorced from Mr. Clairmonte?"

"Yes. Sometime in the sixties. In Guyana."

"So you moved without him while you were still married?"

"That's right."

"Did you meet Don Sahlman before your divorce or after your divorce?"

"Before. I was working for a shrimp company in Guyana, and I met him there."

"When you first began dating Don Sahlman, did you know that he was married?"

"Yes."

"What did he tell you about his relationship with his wife?"

"He was very unhappy."

"Do you know when Mr. Sahlman got divorced from his wife?"

"I don't recall a year."

"Were you intimate with Mr. Sahlman prior to the divorce?"

"Do I have to answer that?"

"Yes, ma'am."

"Yes."

"And when you were dating Mr. Sahlman in Guyana, did he provide any financial support for you?"

"No."

"Did Don Sahlman have a concern for the hygiene of your children?"

"Yes."

"What did he do to demonstrate that concern? Did he show them how to bathe themselves?"

"Yes."

"He showed Nick how to clean himself?"

"Yes."

"Did he show Meg how to clean herself?"

"Yes."

"Were you present during these?"

"Yes."

"What did he tell Nick? Do you recall?"

"Well, a boy should take care of his private parts."

"What did he tell Meg?"

"Same thing."

"Why didn't you tell Meg how to take care of her private parts?"

"I was kind of shy and embarrassed to do it."

"How old was Nick when he showed Nick how to clean himself?"

"Probably eight, nine."

"How old was Meg when he showed Meg how to clean herself?"

"About the same."

"Did he periodically check them to see if they were cleaning themselves?"

"Yes."

"How would he check Nick?"

"He would just tell him to go take a bath."

"But would he check his genitals?"

"No."

"How would he check Meg?"

"She would just tell him to come and see if she bathed clean."

"She would ask him to come in and look at her?"

"Yes."

"How old was she when she did this?"

"Twelve, thirteen."

"Up to what age?"

"Around eighteen."

"So she would be in the bathroom, and she would ask Don Sahlman to come in and examine her to see if she had bathed clean?"

"Yes."

"Were you present during these occasions?"

"Yes, always."

"You were always present. What would he do, Don Sahlman?"

"She would open her legs and ask him to see if she was clean, and we would both say 'Yes, you're clean,' or 'No, you're not. Take another shower.'"

"So, he would simply look at her?"

"Simply look at her."

"And you two, the two of you together, would examine her?"

"Yes."

"How many times were you and Don Sahlman checking her?"

"I don't remember how many times, but, you know, whenever she smelled."

Five

I'm not sure why we left Guyana, but two things happened the last full year we were in Georgetown, in 1973, that stick out in my memory. The first stands out because it was the first time I ever truly wished that Donald was dead.

In the past, Donald had always flown from Tampa. For some reason, though, that year he and a business friend decided to sail to Guyana on Donald's yacht. My eleven-year-old mind envisioned it as a huge clipper ship with hundreds of tiny masts, like something out of the 1800s, that had a long pointed bow that sliced through the waves. I can't tell you why, but something about Donald being on that yacht, coming slowly through the sea toward Guyana, gave me a sense of impending doom. At night I lay in bed next to my mother and pictured Donald on the deck as a storm began brewing on the horizon, and then I envisioned huge gusts of wind blowing the ship up and down like a bobbing cork. Then came the final gust, provided by the power of my mind: It shoved the yacht on its side, lifting it practically all the way out of the water, so that Donald was catapulted into a black churning sea that swallowed him up like the whale closing its mouth down on Jonah.

Gone. Drowned at sea. Lost forever.

And then I looked over at my mother's face on the pillow beside me and got a horrible feeling of guilt. Those were sinful thoughts, wishing anyone dead, and God would punish me for having them. I whispered ten Hail Marys.

Donald wasn't all bad, really. If it hadn't been for him, we wouldn't have had a thing. My mother wouldn't have her piano or her beautiful clothes, and Nick and I sure wouldn't be studying French at our private schools. Without him, all of us would have been dirt poor just like all the other families around us. Besides, my mother and Donald had already been together at least nine years—and surely, I thought, she must care about him after all that time? Surely she had to feel something for him even if she didn't show it?

But there still was Father Morrison from church, our "Uncle Andy" at home, which made me wonder. As soon as Donald left for America, it was as if we'd all been listening to a record from which someone had lifted the needle, and then suddenly it was dropped back down again in the same spot, with the same music playing as before. Father Morrison picked up coming over to the flat during the week as if no time at all had passed. He joined us for dinner in the evenings or took us on picnics on weekends, and frequently he drove Nick and me to school.

But something else made me wonder about my mother's real feelings for Donald. There also was that strange thing Father Morrison said to me in the car one day when I was about eleven. "From now on, Margaret," he said, "I'm going to call you M. M. Is that all right with you? Would you mind if I called you that?"

"M. M.? What does that mean? Like the candy?"

He glanced over at me. "Oh no," he said, smiling strangely. "M. M., for Margaret Morrison. Would you like it if that were your name?"

I didn't know how to answer him. He was a priest, and I knew priests couldn't get married. But he was still smiling and waiting for me to say something. "I guess you can call me that if you want," I said.

"But would you like it if that really were your name?" he persisted.

"Sure," I said slowly. "I guess it sounds all right." The rest of the way he tapped his thumbs against the steering wheel, smiling the same strange smile.

One night not long after that, I woke up from a nightmare. Something had been chasing me through the jungle and when I opened my mouth to scream, no sound came out. When I bolted upright, my mother's side of the bed was empty. It was pitch black in the bedroom and the flat was completely silent, the families above and below us asleep. I got out of bed quietly and walked toward the kitchen. That's when I saw them.

My mother's back was to me, and her head rested on the priest's shoulder as they hugged each other. Quickly I stepped back into the shadow and tiptoed back to the bedroom, praying they hadn't heard me. Neither of them had seen me—I was sure of it. But my heart still pounded, and I trembled under the covers.

Not long after that, Donald and his business friend arrived on the yacht from Tampa. Father Morrison did the usual, turning stiff and formal whenever we saw him at Mass and staying away from us at home. In the evenings our family went over to Bel Air, and everything was the same as it always had been, with Donald picking me up sporadically at Winfred Gardens and doing everything he'd always done to me. There was only one time I ever thought Donald might have some inkling about Father Morrison. It was one night in Bel Air, out of earshot of my mother, when he said, "That priest loves your mother, you know. He's been talking about taking a sabbatical." But that was the extent of it. It wasn't until much later, when the priest reappeared in our lives in America, that I found out just how much Donald had truly disliked him, how jealous he'd been and the lengths he'd go to get rid of him. But I guess I'm getting ahead of myself.

In any event, Donald finally went home again. He and his friend set sail for Tampa and Father Morrison, once again, returned for dinners and breakfasts and picnics. It's possible we all would have gone on like that for years, if my mother hadn't gotten a phone call one morning that changed every-thing. Nick and I didn't know who she was talking to, but we knew she was hearing something bad. Her hand was pressed to the side of her face, and she looked as if she'd just wit-nessed her own death. After she hung up, she turned and saw Nick and me standing there.

"Donald's yacht sank," she said, in a tone that almost sounded if she thought it was our fault. "Off the coast of the Dominican Republic. One man drowned, and the other man was rescued. No one knows yet which man it was."

She maneuvered her way around the piano and sat down on the sofa, and stared out the little window to the street. For a long time she didn't move. Finally, she whispered toward the glass, "Donald might be dead. *Dead!*"

None of us talked about what would happen if it were true. Maybe we each had our own idea of things, all of us torn about how we'd feel if he were really gone. I didn't cry and I didn't feel any happiness, and to tell you the truth, I have no idea what I was feeling—except for a tinge of fear. I re-membered how I'd lain in bed and imagined his yacht capsiz-ing and Donald sinking to the bottom of the ocean, and I prayed to God it wouldn't be my fault if he were dead, that my sinful thoughts hadn't caused it. While we waited for some word of what happened, it was as if all of us were in limbo, frozen in time. Donald's fate had become linked to our own.

Donald, of course, didn't die. It was his friend who drowned after the yacht ran into bad weather and capsized.

Donald told us later that he and his friend were both catapulted from the deck, and he dove under the water repeatedly to find his sailing partner. "Finally, I just had to give it
up," he said. "He was gone, the boat was gone. It was dark,
and I had to save myself." Exhausted, he climbed inside the
one life raft and waited for help. He never explained why his
rescuers weren't certain which man had died, and none of us
asked.

After that, things were different. I can't put my finger on it,
but something changed. My mother became much more
solicitous whenever Donald was around, fawning over him in
a way I'd never seen before. But she also became much
colder in the way she talked to me. "You're a very stupid
girl," she said when I didn't understand my homework.
"You'll never amount to a thing." Donald, in turn, became
much nicer to her, asking her, for example, where she preferred to have dinner instead of automatically taking us over
to Bel Air. But just like my mother, he also got more aggressive with me. After school in the back bedroom, he lay on top
of me and rubbed himself violently even though he knew his
full weight hurt my back terribly. I'm only 100 pounds now,
so when I was eleven I was even smaller. But he didn't care.
Several times he tried to penetrate me, ordering me to lie still
and be quiet so Lucille wouldn't hear. It was only by constantly squirming under him—which made him even
angrier—that I managed to avoid it. But each time I moved
like that, my back felt as though a knife had gone through it.

Things with Father Morrison, too, had changed. He still
came to our flat whenever Donald went home to Florida, but

there was a sadness about my mother I'd never seen before. It was as if she'd been wrestling with something for a long time that she hadn't wanted to be true, and then finally had accepted it. To this day I believe she truly loved that priest. But after Donald's brush with death, some inner curtain must have fallen. Perhaps when she held that phone and heard about Donald's disappearance, she truly had seen her own death: the death of everything she had and the nice life she'd come to know.

Perhaps that was why, near the summer of 1974, I wasn't completely surprised by Mom and Donald's announcement. Nick, Granny and I had all gathered in the living room at Bel Air to hear, as my mother had put it, "an important question." It was Donald who posed it.

"How would you all"—in his Southern drawl it came out like "jawl"—"like to come to America?" he asked. "How would you all like to live in Florida instead of here?"

America. What incredible pictures sprang instantly into my head! For years, we'd been watching Donald's slides of Tampa and St. Petersburg and Jacksonville; we'd seen the pale green water and white sand at Longboat Key, the lights of Sarasota at night, the big houses overlooking lakes and canals. And to live there!

Nick and I looked at each other, wide-eyed, and then at Donald. Of course we wanted to live there. Who wouldn't want to? When did we get to go? Would we have to buy special things before we went? How long would the airplane trip be? What was the weather like there? Where would we go to school? Where would we live?

"Don't you all worry about all that," he said. "I'll be takin' care of everything."

✝ ✝ ✝

From the deposition of Charles "Jack" Sahlman, conducted by Lynwood Arnold

"What do you understand to be the issues in this case?"

"A bunch of plaintiff lawyers got together and got somebody to make certain allegations and a case was filed against my brother. Pretty much the same as the trash you released to the news media."

"Did you ever have occasion to travel to Guyana in connection with your job duties?"

"Yes. About six times or twelve times a year, depending on what the circumstances were."

"Did you ever travel to Guyana, South America, with your brother, Donald?"

"No."

"So you were never down there at any time when he was there. Is that correct?"

"That's correct."

"When did you first meet Margaret? We'll call her Margaret."

"It was subsequent to the time my brother married Pat Clairmonte. After that."

"When your brother would travel to Guyana, how long would he typically stay down there?"

"About the same length of time I did. And that varied anywhere from one month to one week."

"Would you describe your relationship with your brother as being close?"

"It was a close relationship, but it was not a social relationship."

"Did you ever talk about personal things?"

"Rarely."

"Was it unusual for your brother to have an extramarital relationship with someone?"

"I don't know."

"Are you aware of the boat that was owned by Donald Sahlman?"

"Of course I was. It was a forty-one-foot Hatteras."

"Do you recall a cruise that your brother took with Jack Walburg on the boat?"

"Yes. He was an architect. All I know is that they were cruising along at night, and Donald was sleeping down below, and the boat ran into a rock or something off Haiti or the Dominican Republic. I went over to the house [in Tampa] and tried to do what I could to console Bette Louise and subsequently picked Donald up at the airport. And of course, we discussed that. I think the boat sank, and I think it was declared a total loss."

"Did you talk to the Coast Guard about the accident?"

"No."

"You don't recall a telephone call from the Coast Guard to Bette Louise regarding the accident?"

"No."

"You're not aware that there were two women on the boat at the time of the accident?"

"I don't believe there were any women on the boat at the time of the accident."

"You don't recall a conversation that you had with Bette Louise Sahlman regarding her notification by the Coast Guard that there was one woman rescued and one woman died?"

"No. I would say if that word got out to you, it's a fabrication of some kind."

"Have you ever seen any racist behavior in your brother?"

"No."

"Did you ever hear him refer to black people as 'niggers'?"

"No."

"Is that a word that would have been unusual to have been used in your household growing up in Fernandina Beach?"

"In Fernandina Beach, my parents taught us that it was an entirely inappropriate word to use."

Six

True to his word, Donald had taken care of everything. By the time we stepped off the plane in Tampa in mid-September of 1974, just a few weeks after my twelfth birthday, he already had rented us our own apartment, enrolled Nick and me in school and looked into getting my mother a secretarial job. The paperwork for bringing us to America had been put into motion by him in Guyana, and soon he even was going to help us become U.S. citizens. "You all are in the land of the free now," he said. "The home of the brave." I had no way of knowing how brief our new sense of security was going to be.

My mother's friends in Guyana had all predicted we'd get culture shock in America, with its tall buildings and Kentucky Fried Chickens and six-lane freeways, with everything so strange and brightly lit and fast-paced. But the truth is, right from the start it felt as though this was where we'd been destined to be all along. Florida seemed like one of my recurrent dreams—one that had seeped into my pores during Donald's years of slide shows—and now was both familiar and odd at the same time.

Mostly, though, everything struck us as wonderful and luxurious. The first time we walked into our three-bedroom apartment at the Aegean Towers, a brown stucco building that was right next door to St. Patrick's Catholic Church on Manhattan Boulevard, my mother actually danced. She twirled around the living room with her arms outstretched like a child's helicopter game and cried out, "Oh Donald, I can't *believe* we're here! It's gorgeous! Absolutely gorgeous!" And it was. There was a big bright kitchen with a new invention called a microwave oven, air conditioning, high white ceilings that looked as if they'd been sprayed with sparkly cottage cheese, and Donald even had made sure it was fully furnished right down to the linen closet filled with towels and sheets. All we did was unpack our suitcases, the only things we'd brought with us. My mother and I shared a double bed in one bedroom, but Nick even had his own room at the end of the hallway. Granny took the third bedroom, which was the size of two rooms back in Guyana.

Within a week of our arrival, Nick and I began attending the public junior high school just ten minutes away. Immediately

I was taunted for the strange way I talked. "What are you, anyway?" one boy asked me as I walked down the hall. It was obvious he was asking me about my race; there were only about five black kids in the entire school, but all of them were darker than me. "I'm from the islands," I replied, repeating what Donald had instructed Nick and me to say if anyone ever asked. Never, he said, were we to reveal to anyone that we were black. "From Barbados," I added. The boy seemed to accept that, but I suspected it was because asking me anything more would have revealed his ignorance of what people from the islands are supposed to look like. As it turned out, though, it was the same reaction I got from everyone.

From the first Sunday on, we all began attending Mass next door at St. Patrick's. It was easy to feel comfortable in the small brick church, with its forest green carpeting and bright modern stained-glass windows; the people were all friendly, even if some did occasionally look at my mother and then quizzically at Nick and me, and my mother immediately liked it. She offered to play the organ and joined the choir, and began going to practice on Thursday evenings. On Sundays, without Donald, we always sat in the same back pew, all of us dressed in our finest clothes.

If Donald was concerned about being spotted around town with us, or about news of our existence ever getting back to his son and invalid wife, he gave no sign of it. At least four evenings a week he picked us up at the Aegean Towers in his brown Cadillac convertible, driving us down Kennedy Boulevard to a restaurant or winding through Hyde Park to the harbor with the top down. On the nights he stayed over

I slept with Granny, who turned out to be a much quieter sleeper than my mother. Once, Donald even dared to take us past his home with Bette Louise at Culbreath Isles on the other side of town. It was a two-story mansion with columns out front that looked like a miniature version of the White House. Behind it, on the canal that ran beyond the pool and back lawn, was his new Hatteras cruiser, the *Bette Louise*. He'd bought it to replace the one that sank. Soon, he said, he'd take us all out on Tampa Bay.

For the first month or so, I really thought it had ended. Donald hadn't touched me once, except to examine me in our bathroom in front of my mother. I truly believed that coming to America somehow meant that part of my life was over, that he was done with me that way. What I didn't realize was that he simply hadn't had an opportunity.

Not long after that—I can't remember when this was, exactly—Donald moved his boat from behind his house to the Imperial Yacht Basin, which was just ten minutes from our apartment in the opposite direction from my school. The boat yard was in a run-down area off Gandy Boulevard, and it seemed strangely seedy for Donald's tastes: Railings were rusted and the docks weathered, and men with tattoos and big bellies lay on the decks of their small boats drinking beer. But the rented boat slip, Donald told my mother, would make it more convenient for all of us to go out with him. If he moved the boat from behind his house, his wife wouldn't have to know each time he was gone. Pretty soon all of us were heading on the boat across the bay to St. Petersburg for lunch on weekends.

Have you ever had a dream you've never had before, but you still know exactly what's going to happen in it? That's what it was like the first time I saw Donald's brown Cadillac parked in front of my new school one day. My heart skipped a beat, my hands got sweaty and I felt suddenly nauseous. As I walked down the steps with the other kids, he leaned over, flung open the passenger door and grinned. "I thought we'd go over to the boat and do a few things to clean it up," he said. "I really could use your help."

Suddenly it was as if there was a full choir inside of me that yelled out at the same time: "No!" I did not want to get into the car with him, I did not want to be alone with him. But I couldn't tell him that. "I have a lot of homework to do, Uncle Donald," I said. "I really need to get started on it."

"You can do that later, Margaret. I really need your help on the boat. You don't want to make your dad mad, do you?" He lowered his voice. "Because you know what can happen if your dad gets mad."

Silently I slid into the front seat with him. At the boat yard, we climbed up the cruiser's small metal ladder. For a few moments, I stood alone on the deck while Donald went down below. It was sweltering, the air so hot and humid I could barely breathe, but I was still trembling. There were a few other boats nearby, and in the distance a woman called out something about an ice chest and a man yelled back, "What, honey?" I was listening to the couple, to the water lapping against the boat, to the sounds coming from below deck. My brain felt like a moth in a jar.

Maybe I'm wrong. I'm not wrong. But he hasn't bothered me

*since Guyana. But now he's got the boat here. Maybe he really
just wants help with the boat. He doesn't want help. Do something, quick. What am I supposed to do?*

It felt as though I stood there forever. Finally he came back
up, held out his arms and waited for me. "Why don't you
come and give your old dad a hug?"

Oh God, I wish I didn't have to tell you this. I wish I didn't
have to think about this ever again. Every time I picture the
mustard-yellow sheets on the boat's bunk bed, the yellow
towel, the yellow Dial soap, I feel as though my insides have
been stained that color, as if there isn't enough water in the
world to get me clean. So I'm going to tell you this part quick
and then I won't say it again. After this first time on the boat,
it was always the same, so you won't have to hear this again.

He took me down below, laid me on the bottom bunk, took
off my panties and turned on the light above him so he could
examine me. He had a phobia about germs, and I knew what
he was going to tell me. It was the same thing he'd said ever
since I was four years old. "You smell very bad, Margaret.
Let's wash, why don't we?"

He lifted me up and placed me on the edge of the tiny sink.
The metal faucets dug into my back. He turned on the water
and washed me, and then dried me with the towel. Then he
put me back on the bed and opened me up. "There," he said.
"It smells and looks so much better. Just like it should."

As he knelt down and put his mouth between my legs, I
looked at the friendship ring Debra had given me right before
we left Guyana. And right then I went away, just as I'd learned
how to do. It was nighttime in Georgetown; Debra was probably

getting ready for bed. I could picture her unfastening the bands from her long braids, untwining her dark hair and shaking it loose. The little light in the corner of her bedroom cast her face into soft half-shadow, and in her pretty flowered nightgown she was taking the broom she always left by the door and lifting the handle high above her head. Right at that moment I pictured her giving three taps on the ceiling: Good. Night. Meg. Too late, she would remember I was not upstairs anymore. I was in America. And she would think of me, too: She was picturing my face, just as I was doing with her, and it would be daytime in Florida.

I imagined Debra's thoughts: *Meg is at the ocean. Her hands are outstretched, her long hair rippling in the breeze. It isn't at all like the shoreline of Guyana with only marshes and swamps and long stretches of mud flats as you approach the ocean, where the water is shallow and brown. No. It's just like Meg's postcard. She's running along a white sand beach with scattered palm trees bowing over the turquoise water, "Wish you were here" across the bottom.*

Donald reached for a condom, moved on top of me and began rubbing against me. I was not to worry if I got pregnant, he said into my ear; he would take care of it if it happened. "I will not penetrate you," he said, "but I will try just a little."

I pictured Debra in her bed with just a sheet covering her. It was too hot and humid for a blanket, just like in Florida, and her bedroom window was open enough to gently flutter her curtains. She could hear the steady hum of insects outside. It was soothing, that rhythmic bizz-bizz-bizz and tucka-tucka-tucka coming out of the darkness beyond the screen; Debra was closing her eyes and thinking about me again. *Meg has water on her feet now. She's standing still, looking out at the ocean, white foam between her toes. As she dives into the water, brightly colored fish dart around her fingertips. . . .*

Donald angrily pulled off the condom. He had the same expression he got when I had lingered too long at the lunch table at Bel Air. I was too small for him, he said, and I wouldn't stop wriggling away from him. "Sit next to me, then, down there." I moved off the bunk and sat on the floor as he rolled onto his side and put it into my mouth. He pushed his thumbs under my chin and gripped my head so I couldn't move.

Meg is swimming straight out toward the horizon, a blue and green sea with pale blue sky above. No one is watching her as she flops her arms up and down toward a gray fin in the distance. She's not afraid of it! Meg swims closer and closer toward the triangle sticking out of the water, but it's not a shark. How did she know? It's a dolphin that will carry her on his back, carry her to shore because she's gone too far out now. . . .

"Do not move, Margaret. It feels so good. I'm going to. . . ." He gripped my jaw tighter with both hands, and I began choking. Debra's face disappeared.

He got up and stepped over me. In a cabinet was a bottle of pale yellow Listerine, which he swished and spat into the sink. Then he did something odd. He placed his hands on both sides of his face and began pushing his thumbs down his cheeks, as if he were drawing imaginary lines.

After a moment I asked, "What are you doing?"

"I need to milk my saliva glands. Get the germs out. I don't want to catch anything from you." He kept drawing the lines down his cheeks.

I hadn't moved from where I was sitting. "Well come on, then," he said, picking my clothes off the floor. "Stop gawking at me and let's get dressed now. We've got to get home. You've got homework, and then you've got to cook." I reached for my panties, but Donald took them out of my hands. He put them up to his nose. "I think I'll keep these," he said. He placed them in a brown supermarket bag and tucked it in a hidden hatch under the mattress. "I'll give them back to you the next time you visit." He winked. "I'll let you exchange them."

As we drove back toward the apartment, Donald looked over at me. "No sad face, Margaret." It was as familiar a warning as to never tell anyone. "When we walk in that door," he said, "I want you cheerful."

✝ ✝ ✝

From the deposition of Nicholas Clairmonte, conducted by Charlie Luckie

"Where are you employed?"

"Right now I'm not employed."

"How old are you now?"

"I'm thirty-two."

"Have you read the complaint that has been filed in this action on your behalf?"

"Yes, I have."

"When did this claimed abuse of you by Mr. Sahlman start?"

"The first time was probably when I was about five years old. It happened at his house in Guyana. He told my mom he was going to teach me how to clean myself. I'm not circumcised. We went into the bathroom and he started holding me and pulling the skin back and telling me that's how you do it, and would you do it to me? I don't exactly know what I said, but I did it. He told me I had to practice. After that was over, he took me into the back bedroom, his bedroom, and started fondling me some more. That was the beginning of everything."

"Where was your mother at that time?"

"She was in the front room, the living room."

"Did you say anything to her?"

"No, sir. Because he had already told her that he was going to do it."

"To show you how to clean yourself?"

"Yes, sir."

"What is the next incident that you recall where Mr. Sahlman, as you say, abused you?"

"It was sometime within the same time period. He started licking me down there and making me lick him in the same place."

"Where did this take place?"

"In the same house. At Donald Sahlman's home."

"Where was your mother when this happened?"

"I don't recall."

"How did you happen to be at his home?"

"He would take me and Meg over there for lunch and, you know, talk to us, take us for rides and whatever else people do with kids."

"Was Meg there on the occasion when you say that there was this licking going on?"

"No, sir."

"Where was she?"

"I don't recall."

"When is the next incident that you recall of Mr. Sahlman supposedly having abused you?"

"There's a lot of incidents, and I can't put a specific time period or date. It continued from that point on until I was twenty-one."

"Was it always the type of abuse that you've described previously? Was it always the same?"

"No. It progressed from there to penetration."

"Penetration?"

"That's right."

"Anal penetration?"

"Yes. Mr. Sahlman penetrated me, yes."

"When did this start?"

"I would guess at about seven or eight years old."

"Did any of them [your mother, grandmother or Margaret] know that what you say was happening was going on?"

"Not that I know of."

"All right. Tell me what happened between you and Mr. Sahlman after you moved to Tampa in as much detail as you can."

"We became closer as far as, you know, seeing each other on a more regular basis because he was, you know, he lived here. We moved to the Aegean Towers Apartments, and at that point in time, to sum most of it up, it got worse. It got to be two to three times a week."

"And two to three times a week he was doing what to you?"

"Anything he'd like. Anal sex, oral, fondling."

"Where did it happen?"

"Mostly down on the boat. . . . It was at the Aegean Towers, too."

"And the acts of abuse which you have mentioned, that is physical abuse, stopped when you were twenty-one?"

"It might have been twenty-three. I don't remember."

"At the latest you were twenty-three?"

"When it actually stopped. I was propositioned later on when I was twenty-eight, twenty-seven, twenty-six."

"Okay. But nothing happened?"

"I didn't do anything, no."

"Okay. And how did it take place that it stopped?"

"I ran away from home."

"How long were you gone away from home?"

"Approximately three to four and a half years."

"And where did you live in that three or three and a half years?"

"Pensacola, Florida. . . . The first couple of months I looked for a cooking job but there was none available. I eventually got a job on the offshore oil rigs."

"Do you know what year you came back from Pensacola?"

"I don't recall."

"And you say that Mr. Sahlman propositioned you, but from that time on nothing happened?"

"That's right."

Seven

When you've got a secret someone else knows, you're always in danger. They could reveal it when you're not there. They could betray you, and you might never even know how or when it happened. Everything your secret-holder does or says is a threat: You've got to watch them, listen to what they tell people, make sure no one says something that could open up a door. You've got to control their environment. That's what it must have been like for Donald. For years I'd held his secret, but until I got to Tampa I didn't know about his lie, too. He had to know that one day I'd find out the truth—that most fathers and stepfathers and mothers' boyfriends only kiss little girls goodnight on their foreheads—but he still had to make sure that whenever I did learn it, no one else would. He was so afraid of discovery, in fact, that even a hand gesture sent him into a panic.

It was November, two months since we'd left South America. Just as he'd done when I was at Winfred Gardens, Donald already had begun arriving in front of my new school with no set pattern. On the rare days his car wasn't there, I'd run all the way from the Winn-Dixie market on the corner to our apartment, my stomach lurching every time I spotted a brown car. Looking back, I suppose I should have put it together that Nick was never home on the afternoons I was granted a reprieve, but I didn't. It never even occurred to me.

One day, I arrived home and saw Donald and my mother sitting on the sofa. That was a rare thing to see after school: Donald, in a suit and tie, reading a magazine, and my mother, who hadn't found a job yet, with a romance novel in her lap. Donald nonchalantly flipped a page, and without looking up said, "Where's Nick?"

I didn't know. I told him Nick usually went out the back door of the school because his last class was close to it, so I rarely saw him at the end of the day. "Well, the boy shouldn't be running around the city, Patricia," Donald said. "Not with no one knowing where he is."

"I'll talk with him about it, believe me," she said. Then she looked up at me. "There's a list on the counter of things we need from the market, Margaret. As soon as you wash up, we need to go get them."

I set my books down on the dining room table. I was used to helping her with the shopping—I now went to the market several times a week and also cooked our dinner. My mother didn't want her hands ruined for the violin with soaps and chemicals, either, so usually I did most of the cleaning. I picked up the list off the counter, and then remembered something. "Uncle Donald?" I asked, holding up my middle finger in the gesture I'd seen two angry boys make to each other. "What does this mean?"

Donald leaped off the sofa, grabbed my arm and twisted it behind my back. "Don't you *ever* do that again, Margaret," he bellowed. "Do you hear me? Never, ever again!" Then he turned to my mother. "Did you see that? I don't want her going there anymore, Pat. I should have known she'd learn filth at the public school. I'm yanking them both out of there. You're never going back to that school again, Margaret, do you hear me? It's filth, that's what it is, and I won't have it!"

"But I just—"

My mother slapped the sofa with her palm. "Quiet!" she yelled. "If Uncle Donald says you're not going to that school anymore, you're not going there anymore! Now get over to that market, and get the things we need for dinner!"

I would have gone right away, but Donald stopped me. "You know, Patricia, I do notice a bad smell from her. Maybe she should wash before she goes. We don't want anyone at the market getting a whiff of her."

My mother wrinkled her nose. "I know, it's very bad, isn't it? You stink, Margaret. Go in and let Uncle Donald make sure you wash correctly." Donald followed me into the bathroom.

After I finished, he called to my mother, spread my lips with his fingers and asked her if I passed inspection. "You still smell," she said. "Do it again. Or Donald, *you* do it for her." And then she walked away.

The next day, Donald enrolled Nick and me in Tampa Catholic, a practically all-white high school about an hour away by bus. For reasons I still don't understand, I was placed in the ninth grade—two grades higher than the previous school I'd attended for only two months. Nick, who was fourteen, was put into the tenth grade. Most of our classmates were at least two years older. Nick and I still told everyone we were "from the islands," which seemed to satisfy our schoolmates about our racial background. And we both were working on getting rid of our British accents. Whenever I was alone, I practiced saying the American "a" that felt as though I was talking through my nose. "Can't, can't, can't," I repeated, and then in my normal speech, "cahnt, cahnt, cahnt."

I understand now why Donald did what he did. He must have thought the subject of sex would never come up in that Catholic environment. But he was wrong. Because it was there, in a sex education class, that I found out his big lie. There wasn't a single moment I realized it, no one, great flash of awareness that what he'd been telling me all those years wasn't true. If anything, the word "incest" came to me as if upon cat's paws.

He's not Catholic, so maybe he didn't know. But he said it was how all daddies and daughters show their special love. He knew that was a lie! He had to know!

That means he tricked me into sin!
But he's not really my father; he's not really my stepfather.
Maybe it doesn't count. Oh my God, I'm so dirty, so filthy inside.
I've sinned too long to ever be forgiven. I could never, ever con-
fess to Father Obert, to anyone what I've done. Oh God, please
don't hate me. . . . You must hate me. . . .

I never told him I knew. Not in so many words.

But somehow, whether it was the way I looked at him, or turned my head away from him on the boat, or the tone in my voice when I pleaded with him and said "Please don't . . . ," Donald knew I'd learned the truth. He knew it as certain as if he'd been sitting in that classroom right beside me.

Sitting on the edge of the boat's lower bunk one day, he looked at me sideways like a hawk eyeballing a rodent. "What's this *please don't?*" He mimicked my voice. "You want to go back to Guyana? Is that it?" He got a small smile. "Because I can arrange that if you'd like."

I didn't say anything. "You want me to tell you somethin', Margaret? Your mother didn't have two pairs of panties to her name when I met her. You probably don't remember that, because I've been takin' care of you all so long it just seems normal to have nice things, doesn't it? And all the nice things you and Nick and your mother and Granny have, that's because of me. Isn't that right, Margaret? You think you'd live in a nice apartment if it wasn't for me? Think your mother would have nice clothes? Or her jewelry? Or a kitchen full of food? Think you'd get the chance to be an American citizen? Let me ask you somethin'—" He jabbed his finger in the air at me. "What kind of life do you think a little nigger girl like you would have without me? Ever thought about that?"

I was trembling so badly I couldn't speak.

"I tell you what kind of life you'd have, Margaret. You'd be right back where I found you. And where I can send you back—" He snapped his fingers, "—like that. So here's the way it's going to be now, all right? I can send you all back to the slum I found you in, and your mother can go right back to her cockroaches. But you can be damn sure she won't have a job at my company anymore when she gets there, so don't forget about that. Or, you can do what I want and shut up about it. Do what we've always done. It's your choice. You can show me how nice you can be to me, or you and your whole family can get deported. You know I can do it, too. Now, which one's it going to be?"

After that day, Donald never talked again about how all daddies and daughters did what we did. From then on, whenever he took me to the boat or came to the apartment while my mother was at choir practice, he threatened me. My choices, as far as I could tell, were clear. Either I did what he wanted and never told anyone, or all of us would get sent back to Guyana, where my mother would be jobless and we'd live in worse poverty than ever before.

There was no doubt in my mind that Donald was rich and powerful enough to do it. And if I crossed him—as my mother did just one time, when Father Morrison soon reappeared in our lives—I was just as certain that he would.

6757058862

READER/CUSTOMER CARE SURVEY

BA1

We care about your opinions. Please take a moment to fill out this Reader Survey card and mail it back to us.
As a special **"thank you"** we'll send you exciting news about interesting books and a valuable **Gift Certificate**

Please PRINT using ALL CAPITALS

First Name [ ] MI. [ ]
Last Name [ ]

Address [ ]

City [ ] ST [ ] Zip [ ]

Phone # ([ ]) [ ] - [ ] Fax # ([ ]) [ ] - [ ]

Email [ ]

(1) Gender:
○ Female
○ Male

(2) Age:
○ 13-19   ○ 40-49
○ 20-29   ○ 50-59
○ 30-39   ○ 60+

(3) Your children's age(s):
Please fill in all that apply.
○ 6 or Under   ○ 15-18
○ 7-10   ○ 19+
○ 11-14

(8) Marital Status:
○ Married
○ Single
○ Divorced / Widowed

(9) Was this book:
○ Purchased For Yourself?
○ Received As a Gift?

(10) How many HCI books have you bought or read?
○ 1   ○ 3
○ 2   ○ 4+

(11) Did this book meet your expectations?
○ Yes
○ No

(12) How did you find out about this book? *Please fill in ONE.*
○ Personal Recommendation
○ Store Display
○ TV/Radio Program
○ Bestseller List
○ Website
○ Advertisement/Article or Book
○ Catalog or Mailing
○ Other _____

(13) What FIVE subject areas do you enjoy reading about most? *Choose 1 for your favorite, 2 for second favorite, etc.*

	1	2	3	4	5
Self Development	○	○	○	○	○
Parenting	○	○	○	○	○
Spirituality/Inspiration	○	○	○	○	○
Family and Relationships	○	○	○	○	○
Health and Nutrition	○	○	○	○	○
Recovery	○	○	○	○	○
Business/Professional	○	○	○	○	○
Entertainment	○	○	○	○	○
Sports	○	○	○	○	○
Teen Issues	○	○	○	○	○
Pets	○	○	○	○	○

Rank only FIVE.

BA1

9396058864

(25) Are you:
○ A Parent?
○ A Grandparent

(18) Where do you purchase most of your books?
Please fill in your top TWO choices only.
○ General Bookstore
○ Religious Bookstore
○ Warehouse / Price Club
○ Discount or Other Retail Store
○ Website
○ Book Club / Mail Order

(20) What type(s) of magazines do you SUBSCRIBE to?
Fill in up to FIVE categories.
○ Parenting
○ Sports
○ Fashion
○ Business / Professional
○ World News / Current Events
○ General Entertainment
○ Homemaking, Cooking, Crafts
○ Women's Issues
○ Other (please specify) _____

It was 1975, a year since we'd left Guyana, when Father Morrison called our apartment. "Is that you, M. M.?" he asked.

"Uncle Andy!" I said excitedly. "Where are you? Are you in Guyana?"

He was, but he was coming to America. He had some church business in Tampa, he said, and wanted to come visit us. "Would you like that, if I came to see you?" he asked. After I told him how much I missed him, he asked to speak with my mother.

We met him, about a week later, in the parking lot of a variety store on the Dale Mabry Highway. At the time it didn't occur to me that there was a reason for the odd meeting place. As soon as we spotted Father Morrison leaning against a parked car, my mother got out of the new Ford Maverick Donald had bought for her, and Nick and I scrambled out of the backseat. Just like any other shopper, he was wearing slacks and a cotton shirt with no clerical collar. All three of us hugged him at the same time.

"Ohhh," said my mother, who seemed overcome with emotion. "Oh Andrew, it's so good to see you. So good." In the bright sunlight his blue eyes seemed even paler, and he was grinning from ear to ear.

"Well, look at you all, then," he said. "You've grown, M. M. You too, Nick. And such smart clothes. You look like proper little Americans!"

I thought she was about to cry. After a moment, we all walked inside the store, with Uncle Andy limping beside my mother as she absently picked items off the shelves and then put them down again. They talked about ordinary things:

how we liked Tampa, all the people back in Guyana my mother missed. He told her he was going to be in town several more days and would love to see us again. She looked at her gold watch with little diamonds around its face.

"Let me call you," she said. "I'm afraid we have to get back now before. . . ."

"Oh, that's fine," he said, grinning. "I understand, you have things to do. But you'll call me later and let me know, then, won't you?"

"I will, Andrew. It's just that we have to get back now and—"

"It's fine. I understand. Just call me."

When you're raised on secrets, you get an instinct for keeping them. That's why I have no idea, to this day, how he found out. Nick and I never said a word to Donald about Father Morrison's visit, that's for sure, and my mother never would have told him, either. But the next day, Donald arrived at our apartment looking mad as hell.

"I know that priest was up here visiting you, wasn't he?" he asked my mother. She looked at him with wide-eyed innocence. I thought she might downplay it—*So what if a priest visited me?*—or even point out that Donald was still married and didn't exactly have the right to control her life.

"I don't know what you're talking about," she said, and then turned and walked toward the bedroom she and I shared. Donald followed her.

"He was here, wasn't he?"

I peered at them from the doorway. Donald was standing

about two inches away from her, his jaw muscles flexing. "No," she said. "No, he wasn't."

Donald shoved her hard onto the bed. She fell back with a startled expression that quickly turned to fear. I thought he was going to hit her.

"I don't know what—"

"Tell me the truth!" he yelled. "I know he was here, so tell me the truth or you'll regret it!"

"All right," she said, jerking her head up and down. "All right, yes, he was here. But he just—"

"But nothing, Pat." His voice had dropped an octave, menacing and threatening. He leaned over her and put his face close to hers on the mattress. "He is not going to visit us anymore, Patricia," he said. "That priest is not visiting any of us anymore. Do you understand that? Your meeting yesterday was the end of it."

She was breathing rapidly, still jerking her head up and down. Maybe she was trying to figure out the same thing I was: How did he know? Had he got someone to follow us? We met Father Morrison in the late afternoon, when Donald should have been at his company. And even if Donald had been at the store, we would have seen his brown convertible. So someone else had to have told him. But who?

"All right, yes, all right," she said.

"Say it. Say that you won't see him ever again. Say it so I hear it."

"I won't see him," she said. "I promise I won't see him again."

Donald stared at her a moment longer and then stood

upright and nodded. Not only had he just eliminated another threat to him, but he also had made it abundantly clear that he now controlled us. Somehow, Donald knew what we did, where we went, to whom we talked. And when he shoved her onto that bed, in one swift motion he had conveyed a message to us all. If we ever betrayed him, he would know.

✛ ✛ ✛

From the deposition of Olivia Brooks, conducted by Richard Gilbert

"Did you ever work for Bette Louise and Donald Sahlman Sr.?"

"I was a housekeeper, shopped, did something of everything. While they were married, for about fifteen years. Until 1979."

"Do you know anything about the relationship between Don Sr. and Margaret? Do you know who Margaret is?"

"I've seen her. I don't know her. I guess the first time I realized he was having an affair is when she was small. Mrs. Sahlman had just had a back operation."

"Was Bette Louise Sahlman bedridden?"

"Yes. More or less. It was very bad. One day I was going to deliver some things back to the mall for Mrs. Sahlman. And at Columbus Drive and Dale Mabry I saw Mr. Sahlman and Pat in the yellow convertible. And the little girl was in the middle jumping up and down. They didn't see me, I don't think. I thought it was awkward, because his wife was home sick. You wouldn't be riding around with a child jumping all

over you in a car unless you're having an affair. . . .
But I couldn't tell her that, a sick lady. I wouldn't
want nobody to tell me anything to hurt me."

"Did you find out anything else about Don's relationship with Pat?"

"Well, on occasion I would see them. I was taking
Mrs. Sahlman one time to the beauty shop. She usually called him every time she would go. But this particular day I told her, 'You don't have to call every
time you go somewhere because, hey, you go sometimes, then you see things that you should see.' By
the time I picked her up, she was standing outside
waiting and got in the car. And then he pulled up, too.
Donald. I guess he was taking them, Pat and the children, home. And he was shocked to see us out at that
time of day. He was home by the time we got there.
He wanted to know why she didn't call him and let
him know that she was going to get her hair done."

"Had Bette Louise seen Don?"

"No, but I told her. And she already knew by then.
She suspected something all along. She had hired an
investigator. She told me she found out what she
wanted to know."

"Did you have occasion to see Don and Pat out
before the divorce, other than what you've described
so far for me?"

"Once in a while she had us go down there to watch
and see what was going on. We was investigators."

"You were the investigators? You and Bette Louise
went out?"

"I went. She told me to go and I went. And I waited.
And I saw where they went and when they came. I
went in the mornings, and I saw them in the

evenings. And I would come back in the afternoon and saw them come home. I'd park the car and sit there and watch them when they came and picked up the kids, wherever they took the kids."

"And what would you do with this information?"

"She sent me. So I would tell her. Who else would I report it to?"

"Mrs. Brooks, would you take a look at this? It is supposed to be a copy of a diary of sorts. Would you take a look at it and see if you can recognize it?"

"I think this is Mrs. Sahlman's writing."

"Is that your signature on the last page, ma'am? It says, 'All information in tablet agreed to and witnessed by.' Then it lists Ms. Mary Harber and yourself. And then you signed that?"

"Yes."

"When you were serving as an investigator, did you ever go down to the boat and watch at the boat?"

"We went to the boat, but nobody was there."

"Did Bette Louise go with you?"

"She went with me and rode in the car."

"How often did you go down to the boat?"

"About six or seven times, something like that. But a good many years before they got a divorce, the boat was parked at the house. We only went there after he moved the boat, after he had to move out. Because the boat was at the house."

"So when he moved out, he moved the boat to the marina? The Imperial Marina?"

"Yes, because he wasn't living at the house anymore. Before that, the boat would have been docked in front of the house. They had it right at the house. I looked at it every morning when I went there."

"When did that boat get moved to the dock? When did he move the boat? Do you know when he moved out?"

"Whenever they filed for divorce and the lawyer told him he had to move out. That's when he moved the boat."

✝ ✝ ✝

From the alleged diary of Bette Louise Sahlman, with factual data as supplied by Olivia Brooks

November 19th, 1975. Olivia (maid) spent night with me. Donald at woman's apartment.

Nov. 28th. Friday. Donald left home before 7 A.M., before I was awake. Did not tell me where he would be or where he was going. Did tell me a few days before he would be away for a few days. At 10 P.M. Donald's red Mercedes parked at woman's apartment. Was there all night.

Nov. 29th. Saturday. Donald, woman and two children (boy and girl) were seen at Gandy and Westshore, heading for Imperial marina for Donald's boat. Parked car at boat and got in boat.

Dec 7th. Sunday. Donald left house at 7:30 A.M. His car at woman's apartment all day and night. Was supposed to be going to Sarasota to have boat fixed.

Dec. 9th. Boat gone. Donald phoned from office. Told me he had been shopping for boy's toy train and steam engine.

Dec. 11th. Found pictures in Donald's Mercedes. Pictures of a dark skin boy and light girl.

Dec 22nd. Donald left house at 6:30 A.M. Went to Fernandina Beach, spent that day and night there. Came back to Tampa to woman's apartment and spent night. Jan. 23rd, 1976. Donald's car parked at woman's apartment overnight. When he left home, told me he was going fishing on his boat until Monday the 26th. Jan. 26th. Donald's car at woman's apartment. Seen leaving at 7:35 A.M. with boy.

Feb. 8th. We both drove to store to get milk. I mentioned my car seat was still uncomfortable. Donald blew up. Had tantrum in kitchen when we returned, threw garage door opener on floor, broke it into pieces. Told me he never would go any place with me again. I was frightened because of past experiences with his temper. I went to bed immediately and stayed in my room until he left next A.M.

Feb. 9th. Donald continually asks Peg and me what a young girl should wear and how she should fix her hair and where they should go for different things.

Feb. 19th. Donald offered to get some medication for my back from drugstore. Medicine he returned with was purchased a week ago on my prescription without my knowledge. A strong pain pill that I had stopped using almost completely. Says he is now taking strong sleeping pills all the time because he can't sleep. Says he is in a turmoil.

May 14th. Nancy, a salesperson at the Cadillac agency, called me looking for Donald. She sold us two cars and has been very friendly. She said Donald had been down to Cadillac agency with a young girl about thirteen, and said she looked Puerto Rican. He introduced the girl as his daughter and called her Margaret. He went around and introduced her to other employees as his daughter. Nancy wanted to know who she was because she knew we had one child, a son.

July 6th. I ask him to move out.

July 14th. Donald living on boat. Mary Harber saw Donald coming from boat at 7:00 A.M. with boy. Boy evidently spent the night. Donald took boy home and stayed thirty minutes and then left alone.

Eight

For my three closest friends, Valerie Eyring, Terry McCullough and Carol Llosa, being a senior at Tampa Catholic High School meant going to football games, proms, beach week and after-school clubs. Friday and Saturday nights meant dates with Mike or Steve or Robert, dinners at restaurants on Dale Mabry followed by a movie. My own experience in no way resembled theirs. Sometimes I felt as though I lived in a different universe, one I viewed as if through the wrong end of binoculars.

"Boy, your parents sure are strict," I heard more than once

when I explained for the hundredth time that I wasn't allowed to date or attend any after-school functions. Donald's standard answer to me was that girls who did that sort of thing always ended up pregnant. "They treat you like a nun or something," my friends said.

Once, a few months before graduation, Valerie Eyring pressed me about it. Valerie was a straight-A student, slim with long blond hair, and always had a date for the weekend. I had leaned against the locker next to hers and said I wished I didn't have to wait until I was eighteen to go out on a date, when Valerie put her books inside and turned to look at me. "Why can't you, Meg? You're *sixteen*," she said. "Okay, so you're a bit younger than us, but you're still a *senior*. You're going to *college* in September, right? So how come you can't do *anything?* Not even a *movie* with a boy? Not even *shopping* with us?"

The words slipped out before I could take them back. "If I went out with a boy, my parents would check me."

She furrowed her brows. "What do you mean, 'check' you?"

"Never mind, Val, just forget it." I'd already said too much. "How'd you do on the history test?"

Even if Valerie had asked what I'd meant, I wouldn't have told her. I couldn't have told anyone. The year before, while I was in the eleventh grade, Donald had showed me how to douche in front of my mother. His examinations had also changed. He still inspected me every time he took me to his boat, but now he did it at home as well. We had just moved from the Aegean Towers apartment into our own three-bedroom house on Juno Street, a ranch-style home with a neat little garden and palm trees out front. Whenever Donald came over in the evenings, he made me lie on the bed I shared with my mother while she stood at the foot of the bed and watched. He pulled off my panties and made me spread my legs, and then shined a flashlight to see if I was clean or not.

"I wish this weren't necessary," he'd say over his shoulder. "I wish there was an easier way. I sure don't enjoy this, you know."

"I know," my mother would answer, and let out a long sigh.

Sometimes he said I had pimples or a "foul-smelling" discharge, and rubbed a white cream on me while my mother looked on. After I was permitted to put my panties back on, this was followed by a breast exam. For several years I had suffered with painful lumps in my breast, along with back pain and throbbing in my jaw whenever I chewed. Donald attributed the breast lumps to all kinds of things—too-tight bras, too much sugar, too much dairy. After he finished inspecting me, he told my mother to take off her shirt so he could check her as well. The two of us would sit there on the edge of the bed, naked from the waist up, while Donald fondled our breasts. More than once he left the room and came back with a camera, snapping pictures of the two of us sitting there together and smiling on command. He did that a lot over the years, and in different locations. In one picture, my mother and I are standing naked in a hotel room, both of us smiling into the camera as if we were in bathing suits at the beach.

Eventually, Donald did take me to a doctor for the breast

lumps. Even though Donald introduced me as his daughter, the doctor didn't seem to think it at all strange that Donald insisted on being present in the exam room. As I sat shirtless on the tissue-covered table he explained, as if I wasn't even there, that surgery was probably my best option. "I'm pretty sure that what she has are benign cysts," the doctor said to Donald. "Of course, you never know for certain until you get in there." In all, three benign cysts were surgically removed.

When the pain in my jaw got so bad I could barely open my mouth, he took me to another doctor, who put both hands on either side of my face and asked me to open and close my mouth. Beneath his fingers I could feel a click and pop, and then I saw a perplexed look cross his face. I had a condition, he told Donald, called temporomandibular joint syndrome or TMJ. It affects the jawbone where it moves up and down in the socket. He said he didn't understand it, because I was very young to have that kind of problem. I thought: *Why don't you tell him how I got it? Explain to the nice doctor what caused it.* But Donald just shook his head as if he was just as baffled as the doctor.

Right around that time I did actively try, for the first time, to avoid going to the boat with Donald. Stupidly, I thought my mother might help me. One night when the two of us were alone, I told her I really didn't want to go there anymore, that Nick should be helping Donald on the boat after school instead of me. That's a terrible thing to have said, I know that now, but at the time I had no idea of anything that was happening to my brother. I just thought it would get me off the hook.

But the second I said it, my mother looked at me as if she was about to slap me. "Donald has been very good to us, Margaret. He's given us *everything* we have. And you can't do this one small thing for him after all he's done for you? You'll go to that boat when he asks you, and I don't want to hear any more about it. Not one more word of ingratitude out of your mouth. You disgust me."

She walked out of the room, and a few minutes later I heard her playing her violin. *You know what happens to me there, but you don't care at all,* I thought. She was ordering me to go. She had her house, her car and her jewelry, and I felt like the exchange. I went to bed that night feeling like a burnt offering.

Nick, I'm pretty sure, had no awareness of anything that was happening to me back then. During my senior year he was practically never home, since he'd gotten a job right after graduation at the Winn-Dixie market as a bag boy and later at a restaurant as a short-order cook. Around that time, according to my mother and Donald, he'd also begun using drugs, his clothes frequently permeated with a heavy sweet smell they said was marijuana.

"You're going down the wrong path, Nick, hanging around with the wrong people," Donald told him on the rare evenings he was home. "Good boys don't do drugs, Nick. You have to change your ways. You'll end up dead in the gutter."

While Donald told him about the evils of drugs, Nick just listened. He didn't deny it, didn't even offer up any excuses. "Okay," he'd say, after Donald was through. "I'll try to do better." And then we wouldn't see him for at least a week.

When he did come back it was only to retrieve clothes or do laundry, and then he'd stay away even longer. He did that, back and forth, for a long time.

By that time Nick was a foot taller than I, six feet and skinny. His face looked as if it had been chiseled from hard toffee. He always seemed angry, eager to get out of the house as soon as he could, and sometimes I wondered why he didn't just move out with his new girlfriend and be done with it. Secretly, I hoped he would. For sixteen years I had shared a bed with my mother, and if Nick left I knew I could claim his room. All I wanted was my own bed, my own door to close.

But I also was angry with my brother. Angry in a way I never could have put into words. All those years Donald had been going after me, and Nick was always gone. Gone roaming the neighborhood in Guyana, gone with friends when Donald came to get me at school, gone when he could have been there on the boat and protected me. It was almost as if he knew he was abandoning me to something, as if he intentionally was leaving me behind to bear the brunt of everything. I felt a wordless fury at him for leaving me alone.

In the meantime, I tried my best to have some kind of a life, to occupy myself while I was alone with Granny and my mother was at her new secretarial job at the University of Tampa. On the days Donald didn't pick me up and take me to the boat, I threw myself into cooking. While my friends shopped for new outfits to wear on dates (Donald always accompanied me to clothing stores and selected outfits for me), I pored over recipes, each day looking for something new or different or exotic to prepare for that evening. Once a chore and obligation, cooking now was the only thing I was permitted to do with no restrictions. And so it also became my salvation. After school I made fresh breads and appetizers and salads; I whipped up creamy soups or vichyssoise and potato lyonnaise; I found unalloyed joy in watching the blade of my knife slice through skin and bone as I prepared chicken menuire or chicken cordon bleu. I made crepes suzette and cherries jubilee, baked cookies and tarts and Black Forest layer cakes from scratch, until the entire house smelled like the finest restaurant and bakery in town. When Donald and my mother sat down to the table each night they got five-course meals, the whole nine yards, and if there's one thing in my life I'm proud of, it's that. If you told me three hundred people were coming for dinner tomorrow night, I wouldn't even blink. I'm a great cook, and you can ask anyone you want about that.

There were, too, brief respites from Donald's abuse. Sometimes, in fact, he even used his boat for its intended purpose. On weekends, just as he'd done over the years, he occasionally took my mother and me out on Tampa Bay, across the glistening water to St. Petersburg. Sometimes he invited some of his friends or relatives along, or told me I could invite one of my friends. On rare occasions, Nick joined us. We'd shut off the engine and anchor under the clear sky, munching on sandwiches and listening to the shriek of gulls, the four of us probably resembling any other normal family out for the afternoon. But we never went out very far on any of those trips. My mother, who couldn't swim, had a terror of the open sea. In all the times she ever went out on his boat, that was her unchanging condition: only if we go where we can still see land.

I have no idea where Donald's wife thought he was whenever he was with us, or even if she cared. My mother had told me at one point that Donald had been living briefly on his boat during a trial separation, but I have no idea when that was, or even how long he was there. To me, Donald was always on his boat. That, or at our house. But it did occur to me that maybe Bette Louise was quite happy having him gone all the time, and where he was wasn't important as long as she had his huge house and all his money. And maybe, she wasn't really an invalid. *Maybe,* I thought, *that was just another one of his lies.*

Nine

Right after my high school graduation in June 1979, Donald proposed a boat trip down to the Florida Keys. It was, he said, to be a graduation gift to me, along with a vacation for my mother. "You can even bring a couple of your little girlfriends," he said to me one evening in our living room. "And Pat, it'll give you a nice rest. It'll be fun."

The instant he said it, I knew it was all show. He knew full well my mother had never gone further out to sea than the other side of the Gandy Bridge, and that even if the sea didn't terrify her she'd never in a million years leave Granny and her precious dog all alone in the house. Amazingly, though, she actually hesitated. And for a second, I saw a worried look cross Donald's face. Then she shook her head and said, "I don't think so, no," and Donald breathed again. But he had to keep on with it.

"Aw, come on, Pat. You need to get away. It'll be fun."

"I wouldn't enjoy it. I really wouldn't. Plus I have to work, and there's Granny. But you go on without me. You go have your fun."

There's an adage about safety in numbers, and that's what I clung to. As we motored away from the Imperial Yacht Basin about a week later, I assured myself that Donald wouldn't dare do anything to me in the presence of Valerie Eyring and Terry McCullough, both of whom had been thrilled at the idea of finally getting to see the Keys. Terry and Val would act as my shields; as long as I stayed close to them I'd be fine. The boat had two bedrooms, a master and a second one with two bunks and a foldout sofa, and I figured the three of us could keep to ourselves, especially at night.

Right away, Val and Terry put their small suitcases in the closet of the second bedroom, and I put mine beside the sofa. As we cruised south past Sarasota and Venice, past Charlotte Harbor and Sanibel Island and Fort Myers, the three of us smeared ourselves with oil and lay on deck in our bathing suits while Donald steered from the flying bridge not far above our heads. Even though he could see us, the wind made it impossible for him to hear us as we swapped stories about teachers we had loathed or loved, students we thought would make it or bomb in college, our favorite all-time moment over our four years at school. None of us realized it at the time, but what we were doing was saying good-bye to a part of our lives that was gone forever. Lying there in the hot sun, each of us was trying to ease into the future. Terry was thinking about attending Hillsborough Community College and becoming a physical therapist, and Val was talking about moving out and getting a job somewhere so she could take her time figuring out what she really wanted to do. As I listened to them, it occurred to me that I'd never once envisioned a future for myself, that I'd never once pictured myself at any point in time other than the present. "Maybe I'll go to the community college, too," I said, although it was the first time I had considered it.

Throughout the trip, Donald snapped pictures of us. With the boat on autopilot, he took them when we dozed, when we put on sunscreen, when we stood up to go below deck. For each one I smiled; I pushed out of my thoughts what my friends might think whenever Donald put the lens too close, and calmed myself by Val and Terry's demeanor toward him. Several times they mentioned how nice he was, how rich he must be to have such a great boat. *Maybe,* I thought, *everything's going to be all right after all.*

It was dusk when we reached Naples that first day. Donald steered the boat into the marina and docked. There was a warm breeze, and the lights of the city in the distance gave a soft blurry glow. The sky and water were both a pinkish silvery blue, and close by were small harbor shops and restaurants. The walkway was crowded with people leisurely eating ice cream cones, pushing strollers or peering into store windows. After we hosed down the boat and got more gas, he took us to dinner at one of the nearby seafood restaurants. He didn't say very much. Even though he seemed to enjoy listening to Val and Terry, and laughed when they said they wanted to take a bucket of seawater back home because it was so blue no one would believe them if they didn't, I still felt jumpy. I guess I sensed that something bad was going to happen.

On our way back to the boat, we picked up a few groceries at a small market. As we approached the dock, I could tell Val and Terry weren't happy about the thought of going to sleep so early, but neither seemed to have the courage to say anything. It wasn't until we got back on deck that Val turned to Donald and stammered through her request.

"Do you, uh, think we could maybe walk around for a while, you know, maybe just do some window shopping?" she asked, nervously twirling a strand of her long blond hair around one finger. "You know, uh, just look around and stuff?"

"Why sure," he said. "I don't see why not, as long as you don't make it too late. We need to get an early start tomorrow."

"Oh we won't be late, we promise," Val said over her shoulder and scampered below deck. Terry and I followed her. We all changed into sleeveless dresses and sandals. I watched as Terry pulled her dark hair back with rhinestone combs and put on lipstick, which Donald forbade me to wear, and then as Val groaned at her reflection in the small mirror and said, "Well, that's about as good as it's going to get." I told her I thought she looked great. "Not next to you I don't," she said. "Do you see the way men drool over you? Standing next to you makes me feel like a bag lady." I told her she was crazy. But it still made me happy that she complimented me like that.

Back on deck, Donald looked at the two of them approvingly. "You girls go on and have yourselves a good time," he said. "But you know what? My back's really been acting up. Something fierce, actually. Sittin' in that chair drivin' the boat all day really does it to you. Margaret, you wouldn't mind stayin' back with me and givin' me a back rub, would you? I'd really 'preciate it."

Val threw me a strange glance. "You're not coming with us?"

My heart instantly began beating wildly. They absolutely could not know. If they ever found out—if anyone ever found out, even suspected it—I'd kill myself. One time, Terry had come over to our house and Donald had said, in front of her, that he needed to examine my breasts for lumps. He'd done it right there, in front of her, but I'd acted as if it had been nothing, that all fathers did that kind of thing all the time. Later on she told me she'd thought it was "kinda weird," but I had just shrugged and changed the subject.

But this would be a subject I wouldn't be able to change. And the thought of them knowing what Donald had in mind terrified me. "You know, I'd better not, I really shouldn't," I said rapidly, the way I get sometimes. "His back gets really bad sometimes, really bad, and he really needs me to massage it, it's the only thing when it gets really bad, but I'll go with you next time, you just go on without me, don't worry about me."

"You sure, Meg?" Terry asked. "We can wait around until

you're done if you want. We don't mind waiting while he gets his massage, do we, Val?"

Donald waved them off. "No, no, you girls just go on now and have yourselves a good time. We could be a while. And don't you worry about us. We'll be fine."

You already know what happened after they left, so let me just pass over that part. I said before that it was always the same on the boat, and somehow I'd learned to think about other things while it was happening. I was so used to what he did to me that the second it started, my insides instantly went dead. It was as if I became a life-size doll with no heart, no mind, no feelings. I became a robot. He owned me and had programmed me; he could do whatever he wanted with me. It wasn't until Val and Terry returned and I heard them walking around on deck that I suddenly felt as if I might vomit. I was so afraid, and at the same time I was filled with horrible shame. Donald pushed me toward the edge of the bunk. "Go on, then," he said. "You know what you have to do."

Quickly I put on my clothes and went out to explain to Val and Terry that I couldn't sleep in the same room with them because Donald needed more back rubs. I knew he was listening. My heart pounded. And somehow, I made it sound plausible. They both rolled their eyes and groaned as if they couldn't believe I'd been saddled with an invalid, but at least I didn't see any suspicion in their eyes. I picked up my suitcase as if it was the most normal thing in the world to do, and carried it into the master bedroom.

The rest of the trip, when we docked in Marathon or St. Marcos and finally Key West, it was the same. During the day we'd go sightseeing, to Ernest Hemingway's house, to the top of a lighthouse, to the little tourist shops near the ocean, and after dinner we'd all go back to the boat. Terry and Val would shower, get dressed up and then go back on shore, into the warm night without me. When they got back, the door to the master suite would be closed. Donald got up just long enough to poke his head out and say hi to them, to make sure they'd gotten back all right, and then close the door again.

As far as they knew—and what I prayed they believed—I was already sound asleep.

From the deposition of Theodore H. Blau, Ph.D., a psychologist hired by the defense, conducted by Richard Gilbert

"The plaintiff presents very detailed memories from early in her life. And one of the characteristics of the recovered memory syndrome is remembering in great detail, when in actuality general recollection is pretty vague for the early years. Even in the middle years, from six to thirteen, memory tends to be spotty. And the great specificity of her description is concordant with the research on recovered memory."

"Would you agree with the proposition, Doctor, that if an event is repeated over and over again in a similar pattern, that that event reinforces its memory and your ability to recall it? You would agree with me, would you not, that where a victim of child abuse, for instance, is the victim of a repeated course of conduct by the same person, she tends to have an ability to recall that conduct in a fair amount of detail because of the nature of the repetition?"

"Well, I've seen it both ways. I have seen it as great detail which later proves not to have occurred, (or) which later proves to have occurred in a different setting and had been transferred in the memory. Which is what the research on memory tells us: that there is an exchangeability of time and place and persons and events. The idea that memory is very specific and very exact is a myth that we all rather fondly ascribe to. And actually, we remember bits and pieces and fill in as best we can. A person with so-called excellent memory fills in in an excellent way. And the research on several people witnessing the same event and then reporting what they remember is distressing to a lot of people because different people perceive and remember in different ways."

"You have an article in your file entitled, 'Woman Recants Incest Tale That Sent Father to Prison.' What utilization did you make of this article?"

"Well, that's just one of a large number of pieces of research that happens to be left in the file. . . . About 300 cases of sexual abuse accusations against parents have been recanted over the last couple of decades. So it's not an unusual situation. This does happen."

"Do you know, Doctor, are you familiar with the statistics on the amount of child abuse that goes on?"

"Oh, there's all kinds of statistics. And they're all questionable. . . . We have no scientific instrument that can measure with any degree of reliability or validity whether a person has been sexually abused."

"But there have been studies of child abuse victims, and those studies indicate that there are certain symptoms suffered by most child abuse victims. Is that not true, sir?"

"No sir, it's not. Symptoms are extremely variable. . . . You could make a list of these symptoms, and you will find people who have had clearly defined, documented, corroborated child sexual abuse and have none of them."

"You indicate in your report that there are signs of symptom exaggeration which may represent deception. Tell me what are those signs."

"First of all, we made a variety of measures of her intellectual response. And the variation is such to suggest . . . that she was manipulating her responses, ranging from very poor to very good on the intelligence tests. Her performance on the memory scales are such that one would expect her to have very poor immediate, intermediate and long-term memory—and yet she demonstrated good memory on one of the intelligence tests. The inconsistency is . . . one of the many measurements of a propensity to symptom exaggeration, faking bad, deceit or malingering."

"You would agree that she is submissive?"

"At times, and at other times, very angry."

"You would agree that a person that we have described such as Meg would have a need to be believed?"

"Yeah, I would assume so."

"And would you not also agree that when a person such as Meg who has a need to be believed is tested, that she may exaggerate her responses out of a plea for help?"

"Well, there is such a concept as an exaggerated profile, as a cry for help. But not of the style that I saw on her test results. I don't see it as a plea for help."

"But you would agree that it can be—"

"More likely a need to manipulate her environment. If you call that a need to be believed, it's akin to the need for the murderer to be believed by saying he wasn't there at the time of the crime. Sure, they have a very strong need to be believed. But they are distorting the facts."

Ten

Donald never talked about private things. Not to me, and as far as I could tell, not to anyone else. He never talked about Bette Louise or his grown son, except maybe to mention that Don Jr. had been doing some work for him at his seafood company. And the only thing he ever said about his relationship with my mother was that she was a cold fish. He told me that a lot—that he wouldn't be forced to get his satisfaction from me if my mother would react to him. But I sure didn't react to him either, so that was just one more of his lies. Just one more justification for going after me all the time.

I'll give an example of how he could keep things to himself. None of us, for instance, ever expected him to get a divorce. By 1979 he was almost sixty, and it wasn't as if he was dying to finally marry my mother. Several times a week he slept over at our house—I'd sleep with Granny those nights—and the arrangement seemed to suit my mother just fine. So it wasn't as if she was pushing for it. But that year, a few months after we came back from the Keys, he surprised us all by announcing he'd finally filed the papers. He said he was planning to buy a home on Occident Street, in an upscale neighborhood overlooking a canal, with a pool.

One night after that, he came over and said he'd figured it out. He had more money than he'd ever need in ten lifetimes, so what was the point of killing himself? He said he could sell his half of the company to his brother Jack and enjoy life, travel and do all the things he'd never had time for. He was ready, he told my mother and me, to finally get out of the rat race and relax. We could go to Europe. Or maybe Hawaii. So what did we think?

It was hard to tell if my mother, who kept nodding her head in little jerks, was truly happy at the news. Maybe she was remembering stories she'd heard about men who retired and then followed you around the house telling you what to do, or listening on an extension phone while you talked with friends. She was still working as a secretary, and quitting her job to travel would mean she'd be completely dependent on him. I'm guessing, but I still think she was reluctant to give up that part of her life without some kind of guarantee. And if she'd had any idea how many times Donald had threatened behind her back to deport her to Guyana, she probably would have demanded one.

My own reaction was more immediate. As soon as I understood what he was really saying, my throat felt as if I'd swallowed a fishhook. If he didn't go to the office anymore, he'd have time on his hands. And Donald's free time, I knew, was my enemy. Just the way he looked at me when he said *I think it's high time I savor the fruits of my labor,* I knew exactly what he had in mind. Right then and there I decided to join Terry at the community college, that I'd ask her to show me how to enroll. She'd been trying to talk me into it for weeks, and suddenly it seemed like a partial solution. At least it would get me away from the house in the afternoons. Within the week I signed up for a few general education classes. I felt small and ghostlike as I walked across the campus each day into the plain stucco buildings. Down the crowded hallways past students several years older than me, all of them in clusters of noisy enthusiasm, I moved with a sensation that reminded me of times I had accidentally cast my shadow onto one of Donald's slide shows. I was present, and not present. What defined me was not where I was, but where I was not.

I also enrolled in a ballet class off campus, where the women were all about my age and doing it as an alternative to aerobics. There was something pleasantly distracting about feeling pain in my feet as I went up on my toes, something soothing about disciplining my body to twirl and jump and bend. It was there that I also met Darley Davies, who quickly became one of my closest friends. Darley was thirteen years older than I and already had been married and divorced. She's tiny like me but even thinner, and had short-cropped brown hair that made me think of a bird the way she danced. Darley's the type of woman who says whatever is on her mind, no holds barred, so you never have to wonder what she's really thinking. But probably what attracted me most was her happiness, her huge enthusiasm for life. I wanted to know how she got that way. Pretty soon we started going to lunch or shopping together, and afterwards she'd sometimes come over to the house and talk to me while I cooked. Donald never liked her, although he and my mother never said anything in her presence. "If you ask me," he'd say after she left, "that girl comes from the wrong side of the tracks."

Nick, by that time, had already made his full escape. One day he'd come over to the house, packed up a few more clothes and told us he was going to Pensacola to visit his girl-friend for the weekend. "Don't forget you promised to cut the grass on Monday," my mother said as he walked out the door. Over his shoulder Nick said he wouldn't. And then he just never came back. He didn't call, didn't tell us where he was, and it wasn't until several months later that he told us he'd gotten a cooking job at a Pensacola steakhouse. He said he was living with his girlfriend and was happy and doing well, that he had no intention of ever coming home. It was obvious it really hurt my mother, who'd always been much closer to Nick than me. She'd always been so different with him, hugging him all the time, and now she walked through the house with a stunned look on her face. "How could he do it to us?" she said over and over again. "What have we ever done to be treated like this?" Personally, I was glad for him. I'd been angry with him for abandoning me, but I'd never wished anything bad upon him.

Immediately, I took his room. Whatever things he'd left behind I put into a closet, and then I set about making it my own. I bought a pretty bedspread, hung a few pictures and then draped my rosary—the light blue one Father Morrison had given me for my Confirmation—over my bedpost. For the first time in sixteen years I didn't have to sleep in the same bed with my mother, for the first time the walls I stared at were my own. The door didn't have a lock, but just being able to close it made me feel more secure. And for a short time I was a little happier. I was going to college, Terry had introduced me to a few of her girlfriends, and when I came home I had my own private place. Maybe my life could get better after all.

One day I was lying on my bed, propped up on one elbow with one of my psychology textbooks beside me. A passage had caught my attention and I kept reading it over and over: *Hostages sometimes have been known to identify with their captors, a survival instinct that ironically robs them of the will to escape.* I was trying to imagine how such a thing could happen—that someone could be taken against his will and then develop an affinity or approval for his jailers, when my mother opened my door.

"I just thought I'd let you know that your father died."

Even now, at the memory, I can't think of a single thing I might have said to her. I just stared at her as if a stranger had tapped me on the shoulder and then, when I turned, had punched me in my face. "He burned up," she said. "They said he was smoking in bed. The whole house went up in flames. Anyway, he was probably drunk. Your father was always drunk. He brought it on himself if you ask me. And what are you crying about? You didn't even know the man. You don't even remember him, do you? You couldn't even remember Barbados."

She was right, of course; I didn't remember him. And I couldn't remember Barbados, either. But somewhere in the deepest part of my memory, the part with no pictures or words but only feelings, I knew I had loved him. I had always thought I would go back to Barbados one day and stand in front of him, smile at him, and instantly he would recognize me. He would call me Meg.

"Stop your sniveling, Margaret, because it doesn't impress me. I told you as a courtesy." And then she closed the door.

It never occurred to me, of course, that moving into Nick's room was one of the worst things I could have done. Now that Donald was getting a divorce and living in his new Occident Street house, he started sleeping over even more often. In the past I'd always slept with Granny, but now, in the middle of the night he'd leave my mother's room and creep down the hallway, with each creak my stomach lurching. In the light of the moon outside my window, my doorknob glistened as it turned. A moment later he was kneeling at the side of my bed, whispering, "We have time for a quickie, Margaret, but don't you be makin' any noise. It'll be your fault if she hears us."

While he was there I was terrified. I just wanted it to be

over as quickly as possible so he would leave. The only way I could shut myself off from what he was doing was to try to leave my body the way I'd read some people did when they died on the operating room table and later were revived. I imagined myself floating up to the ceiling and leaving myself behind, observing everything around me from high up in the room: the palm fronds blowing against the window, the ticking of the hallway clock, Granny's bed squeaking as she shifted in the next room.

Not long after his retirement, Donald decided to drive up to Fernandina Beach on Amelia Island, not far from Jacksonville. Back then it was just a sleepy town with little houses overlooking the ocean and ranches dotting the landscape, but I've heard it's changed. Now it's a trendy getaway for the rich and famous who want to be anonymous, and multimillion-dollar homes have replaced the bungalows along the strand. Fernandina Beach was where Donald's family was from, going way back. He used to talk about how his ancestors had a big plantation with slaves during the 1800s. ("I tell you, I *like* niggers," he'd say. "Everyone should own one. It's in my blood.") The ranch had been in the family for generations, although somewhere along the way most of the land had been sold. Jill, Donald's adopted sister, was divorced and lived with her kids in the big farmhouse. He told my mother the long trip would be hard on his back, and now that I had my license I could help him drive.

Stupidly, I assumed we would stay at his sister's house. But Donald checked us into an expensive resort called the Amelia Island Plantation, which seemed like a cross between a luxury hotel and a spa. No one at the front desk batted an eyelash when he signed us in as "Donald and Margaret Sahlman." We went over to his sister's house for possibly an hour, and then returned to the resort where he abused me for the next two days almost nonstop. I felt like an animal in a cage, let out only for its occasional walk. Donald took me to that resort at least three times that year. My mother never once asked where we'd stayed or what we did when we got there. It was obvious she didn't care, didn't want to know. That, or she already knew and had no reason to ask.

I mentioned that Donald usually never talked about private things. But one thing he did say stands out in my mind now, especially since the person he was talking about came up again right after he died. I was alone with him in our kitchen, and my mother was about to walk in the door at any moment from choir practice. I was finishing dinner when out of the blue he said, "Did I tell you I've been seeing Granny's psychiatrist?"

Donald seemed like the last man on Earth who'd go to a psychiatrist, much less talk about it. But I also remember thinking how strange it was that he was seeing Dr. Arthur. As far as I knew, Granny's psychiatrist only prescribed medication for her schizophrenia. Why choose him? And why was Donald telling me about it, anyway? As I drained a pot of pasta into the sink, Donald leaned against the counter, arms folded, and looked at me as if he expected some kind of response. Instantly I was afraid to say a word. If I asked if Dr. Arthur was helping him, he might think I was agreeing he needed a psychiatrist. And if I asked what he was seeing him for, he might think I was nosing into his business. Donald was like that—you never knew how he'd react, so usually it was safest to do nothing, to say nothing at all.

"Oh?" I said, and walked over and opened the refrigerator.

"Yep," Donald said, "and he's actually been helping me quite a bit. You know, to understand some things."

I pulled out a few radishes and a head of lettuce. I don't know why, but immediately I flashed on the "excursions" Donald recently had been taking me on late at night to the part of the Dale Mabry Highway with all the nude dancing clubs, the ones with neon signs outside that say *Live Nudes!* and *Girls Girls Girls!* Usually, not far from the parking lots out front, women would saunter in short black leather skirts and too much makeup. As we approached them, Donald would slow the car and lean over to get a better look. "Those are bad women, Margaret," he'd say, as if I didn't know what I was seeing. "I don't ever want to see you doin' anything like that." Several times he even told my mother to come along. "See that woman over there?" he'd say, and my mother would nod. "I don't want Margaret turnin' out like her."

I rinsed the lettuce leaves in the sink. "Well, that's good," I said.

"You know, Margaret, sometimes you wish you could go back in time and do things different. You think back, how somethin' might have turned out different if you'd done this or hadn't done that, and it can get to you, wonderin' like that. You get regrets. Know what I mean?" He was talking so oddly, asking me what I thought. He never did that about anything. All I could do was nod as I began chopping a radish for the salad. He exploded before I even felt it coming.

"Well, of *course* you wouldn't know! You're just a little nigger girl, aren't you? A little pickaninny! You wouldn't understand a *thing* about that yacht, how a man might feel watchin' his friend die, would you? Everythin' in *your* life has been nice and rosy and wonderful, hasn't it? What would a pickaninny like you know about anything like that?"

The yacht. He was talking about the one that sank six years before.

"And you probably don't think I notice what's been goin' on with your mother, either," he went on, as if there was some logical connection. "You think I don't know about that, don't you? What she's been doin' with that guy over at the church? Well, let me tell you somethin', Margaret. I know *everythin'* that goes on around here, and don't you forget it. Not one thing goes by with you or your mother that I don't know about. You understand what I'm tellin' you? You got that?"

Just then the front door opened and my mother called out "Yooo-hoo!" as I heard her footsteps cross the front hallway. Instantly I cringed at the cheerfulness in her voice. Even though Donald's accusation was completely ridiculous, it was just the kind of thing to confirm his suspicions. I could almost hear his brain: *You see? She's happy, and only one thing could make her that happy.*

She came into the kitchen, lifted the lid off a pot of sauce and took a deep sniff. As usual she was dressed beautifully, her short hair perfectly combed, her diamond earrings brushing the sides of her face as she bent over. Even though it was hot and balmy outside, her cheeks had the rosy freshness of someone who's just come in from a brisk wind. "I'm absolutely ravenous," she said, putting the lid back down. "Is dinner about ready, Margaret?" If she noticed Donald's black mood, she gave no sign of it.

A few minutes later we all sat down to eat. Donald didn't say another word about our conversation. He never talked about going to Dr. Arthur again, either, but the more I thought about it, the more convinced I became that he'd lied to me. That Donald had been covering his tracks. Donald wasn't seeing a psychiatrist about the yachting accident. He wasn't seeing him about my mother's nonexistent love affair, either. He had to be seeing him about me. About what he was doing to me, what he'd always done to me. He must be trying to stop it. To deal with it.

And for the first time in my life, I felt a flutter of hope it might end.

✝ ✝ ✝

From the deposition of psychiatrist Gary K. Arthur, M.D., conducted by Richard Gilbert

"What is your understanding of what this case is about?"

"My understanding is that the daughter and the son of Patricia were suing Mr. Sahlman's estate, and Mrs. Sahlman separately, regarding allegations of child abuse, sexual child abuse."

"You received a subpoena requesting that you produce certain documents in connection with your treatment of Donald Sahlman in this case?"

"Any previous records from the treatment of Donald Sahlman Sr. were destroyed because I don't keep records any longer than six or seven years. . . . They were probably destroyed before 1992."

"When was Donald Sahlman last seen by you?"

"Probably the last time I saw him as a patient would have been perhaps 1980 or 1979."

"When did you first meet Donald Sahlman?"

"I think approximately 1977. He came in for treatment basically regarding depression surrounding his marital situation to his then wife, Bette Louise."

"Can you tell me approximately how often Donald Sahlman came to see you between 1977 and 1979 or 1980?"

"To the best of my knowledge, it would have been approximately sixty to seventy individual sessions, approximately sixty group therapy sessions and maybe eight or ten family sessions."

"During the course of your treatment of Donald Sahlman, what were the issues or problems that he presented to you?"

"His initial problem was some depression and difficulty in making a decision regarding his marriage to Bette Louise Sahlman. He was actually a person of such principle that he had a great deal of difficulty entertaining the idea of divorcing his wife. He really had no other major problems to address."

"You say that he was a principled person. How did you reach that conclusion?"

"My opinion became over time that he was really the only person I'd seen that was so—the question would be, why was he so reluctant to get the divorce?

. . . He was reluctant to violate the principle that he was probably brought up with, that you shouldn't get divorced once you get married."

"Did his principles with regards to marriage include fidelity?"

"I know that he was seeing Pat Sahlman somewhere near the end of the marriage and towards the divorce. I would guess six or eight months or so [before the divorce]."

"You indicate that there were no other major problems to address. Is that your conclusion as a professional, or because Donald Sahlman didn't present you with any additional issues?"

"That's my conclusion as a professional."

"Did Donald Sahlman ever indicate to you in any way that he was abusing his stepchildren?"

"No."

"That he was a pedophile?"

"No."

"Did he ever indicate to you in any fashion that he had deviant sexual practices?"

"No."

"Have you ever had occasion to meet either Meg or Nick?"

"Yes, I think I met Meg on one occasion. My wife and I were on the Sahlmans' boat for a day fishing or boating around. And she was there with four or five other people."

"Did you have occasion to observe her demeanor?"

"Yeah. Basically she was very seductively dressed. [Her] nonverbal demeanor was more than normally seductive to the males aboard."

Eleven

By my eighteenth birthday, I realized that for the last year and a half I'd been doing nothing but killing time at college. Nothing interested me; nothing inspired even the slightest bit of curiosity. Perhaps, as my mother repeatedly told me, I was simply too stupid to have any hope of amounting to anything, which might have explained why my brain felt about as vibrant as preserved specimens in the biology lab. Whatever I did, whether it was talking with Terry and other women I'd met on campus, or sitting in a classroom, or going home and cooking for hours on end—all of it seemed to be about avoiding the other part of my life, about trying not to think about what awaited me.

It had gotten worse since Donald's retirement. Maybe it was because my eighteenth birthday had always carried with it a promise—that when I reached that age I'd finally be allowed to date and wear makeup. The latter I had taken up to the day, immediately experimenting with pale blue eye shadow, heavy eyeliner, and dark rouge and lipstick. From then on I'd never left the house without my face painted perfectly, if not, in hindsight, a trifle overdone. But I still had never been on a date. In fact, I'd never even been asked. Darley and Terry said it was because I gave off an aura of being unapproachable. "It's sure not because of how you look, Meg," Darley said. "I mean, you practically cause car accidents walking down the street. But I think they figure you're already taken. You just have that attitude."

Donald saw in every man a co-conspirator. "I saw you makin' eyes at that guy," he'd say. Or, "Don't think I didn't notice what went on between you two." It was all in his head, but nothing I said made any difference. One time he took me with him to get my mother's Maverick repaired over at the Ford dealership on the Dale Mabry Highway. The service manager was a nice-looking guy in his early twenties, and he chatted with me while Donald spoke with a mechanic. The second Donald turned around and saw us together, he marched out, glaring at me. The service manager quickly wiped his palms on his pant leg and said he'd better get back to work. As far as Donald was concerned, men were lurking and ready to damage me, ready to take advantage of me, ready to ruin me. And there was no way he was going to let that happen.

For all the years he'd gone after me and all the things he'd done to me, there still was one thing I miraculously had escaped. I still was a virgin. And now, what once had been a source of frustration for him became his obsession, something he was set on protecting. On a daily basis, often in front of my mother, he reminded me of the importance of maintaining my virginity. He warned me about what happened to girls who were "all used up" by the time they got a husband. "No man wants to think someone else beat him to it," he said.

That jarred me: Would Donald ever let me have a husband? Would he ever let me go out with a man, fall in love with someone? Or would he guard me, follow me everywhere my whole life? But then one day on the boat he answered that on his own. He told me that after I was married, after I'd been properly broken in, he'd finally be able to enjoy himself with me. "I look forward to that day," he said. And then he winked.

I'd be lying if I said there weren't men who seemed interested in me, who came up to me in the grocery store or at school, but I looked at them as if I was locked inside a phone booth. The idea of a man actually calling the house when Donald was there, or doing anything to contact me, made my stomach knot. Terry kept telling me the reason I got so nervous was because I'd been living in a cloister all my life, and that as soon as I took the plunge I'd realize it was no big deal. "You're blowing the whole thing up in your head, Meg," she said. "For Christ's sake. We're talking about going to a *movie*.

Or out to *dinner*." But she didn't understand. And neither did Darley.

Darley, who now came over to our house quite often, chalked everything up to the hold my mother and Donald had over me. I could tell she thought our relationship was strange: She looked at me oddly whenever Donald asked me to come sit on his lap and give him a hug, and she frequently remarked how jumpy I sometimes got around them. Probably, she said, I didn't even notice the change in myself. But the sooner I moved out, she said, the better. "As long as you're under that roof, Meg, you're going to be under their thumb. And as long as you're under their thumb, you're not going to have a life. That, or you'll keep on being a nervous wreck. You've got to get out of there."

Terry and Darley were both right. If I'd been wearing an electronic monitoring device, I couldn't have been watched more closely. If I came home even ten minutes late from school, Donald asked where I'd been. If I talked on the phone, he wanted to know with whom. If he had an errand to do, he took me with him and later drove over to the boat. Even St. Patrick's, the one place that had been a sanctuary of sorts, now became his domain as well. Donald had started coming to church with us and sitting in the back pew with my mother, Granny and me. After Mass he followed me outside, watching me from a few feet away. Even if I talked too long with some of the older women in the congregation, he'd make his way over to where I was standing and enter the conversation. Everyone was a threat to him; every conversation held the possibility I was talking about him. Only one person didn't seem to fall into that category, and that was Father Fausto Stampaglia.

Father Fausto had recently come to our parish from Italy and had replaced Father Obert, who unexpectedly—one day there, one day gone—had left our congregation. I always suspected that Father Obert never liked me, but Father Fausto was warm and friendly with a huge, joyful laugh. I swear to God, he had one of the kindest faces I've ever seen. You took one look at that man and your shoulders would drop an inch with some inner kind of relief. I'd never seen people react to anyone the way they did to him. Father Fausto was warm to Donald, too. He'd come up and ask him in his thick accent how he'd been, listen intently, and then turn his attention to me. Amazingly he seemed as interested in my classes and ballet lessons as he was in Donald's opinions about finances.

"Well, thatsa good," he said, patting me on my arm. "Thatsa nice. You go to da school and learn, and da world opens up for a nice girl like you! You watch!" Father Fausto's eyes peered deeply into mine. Then he looked at Donald and back at me again. I looked away, afraid of what he might see.

One Sunday I thought he'd seen the truth. Donald had stepped away from me when Father Fausto came up and said very quietly, "He hovers around you, doesn't he?" The thought of destroying whatever image he had of me with my dirtiness, with my shame, would have been like ripping the heads off flowers in the only bouquet you've ever been given. I'd thought so many times about going to Father Fausto and confessing my sins, about asking for God's forgiveness, but

Donald's words, spoken from the time I was five or six, always echoed in my head: *You'll burn in hell if you tell anyone, Margaret.*

I looked now at Father Fausto and just shrugged. In the confessional with him, I gave only fragments of the horridness I was carrying around inside me: *Forgive me Father, I've been resentful. I haven't been a good daughter. I had an angry thought about my mother. I wasn't as loving to my grandmother. I haven't worked hard enough around the house. I had a sinful thought about someone. I—I wished someone was dead. I forgot my brother's birthday.*

My mother had introduced Donald around St. Patrick's as a friend she'd met in Tampa. She had warned me to do the same. It was no one's business how long they'd really known each other, she said, and if anyone asked I was to tell them I'd met him when I was sixteen, after high school. That made no sense to me, having to lie like that. What difference did it make? But my mother was adamant. "I told you, it's no one's business!" she snapped. "And if you expect to live in this house you'll do what you're told!" So I did what I was told. Even to Father Fausto I lied about how long we'd known Donald. And if she wanted to, my mother could probably find all kinds of people who would testify that's what I told them.

From the start, Donald made a good impression at St. Patrick's. He drove up in his new Mercedes, dressed impeccably in expensive suits, and immediately started talking to Father Fausto and members of the finance committee about fund-raising strategies. People obviously saw him as one of those can-do businessmen types, the kind with a lot of clout in the community who knows how to get things done. If they knew he was in the process of a divorce or that he was a Methodist—another thing I wasn't supposed to mention—I doubt whether they even would have cared. To the outside world, he was charming and generous and rich, and practically everyone who met him at some point mentioned what a fine man he was. Whenever I heard someone go on and on about him like that, I said, "He's the best thing that ever happened to us" so they'd stop.

Even Father Fausto seemed taken in by him. Before long, he was coming frequently to our house for dinner. As I cleared the table, Mom, Donald and Father Fausto moved to the living room sofa to talk about how lovely it would be if the church got a new lawn or new window or new something or other. What I didn't know at the time was that Father Fausto was also helping Donald with another decision he'd made.

Donald wanted to convert. As soon as his nearly thirty-year marriage to Bette Louise was officially dissolved, all he needed was someone from the church to help him get it annulled. He wanted it done even if it meant that his son, Don Jr., would accuse him of having been turned into a bastard by the process, even if Don Jr. would yell that my mother was nothing but a gold digger, even if Don Jr.'s wife, Peggy, would refuse to come inside our house and sit out in the car while her husband talked with his father.

And within six months, that's exactly what happened. Father Fausto helped Donald become a Catholic. In no time he was walking down the church aisle with us, stopping to

lower himself, close his eyes and genuflect in huge exaggerated motions: left collarbone, right collarbone, forehead,
breastbone. He slid into the pew beside my mother and took
her hand, looking for all the world as if he'd just been
touched by the Holy Ghost.

Around that time, I got a phone call that put Mom and
Donald's promise about my eighteenth birthday to the test.
The person on the other end asked if I recognized the voice.
I had no intention of playing phone games with a man I didn't
know and was just about to hang up.

"I'm Mike Cobaugh, the service adviser over at the Ford
dealership, remember me? We talked while your father was
getting the Maverick fixed? Well, uh, I kind of got your phone
number off the work order. I really don't do this kind of thing,
calling women I barely know, and I wouldn't blame you at all
if you hang up on me. But, uh, I kind of wondered if maybe
you'd like to have dinner with me sometime."

My mind raced. I sure wasn't about to tell him I first
needed to get permission. "I'll tell you what, Mike," I said. "I'll
get back to you, all right? I'll call you back in a little while.
Because I have to see what I'm doing."

Surprisingly, Mom and Donald said I could go out with
him. But moments before Mike was about to pick me up,
Donald wagged a finger under my nose. "Don't do anything
naughty, Margaret. I'm telling you, because you'd better not."

I don't remember what restaurant Mike took me to or the
name of the movie afterwards. The only thing I remember
was the feeling of happiness—*I've finally taken a step*

out!—that filled me with hope. That, and Mike's look of incredulity when I told him I had an eleven o'clock curfew. "You're kidding me, right?" he asked.

When he walked me to my front door and I opened it, Mom and Donald were sitting on the sofa. "Well, did you all have a nice time?" Donald asked.

"Yes sir, we did," Mike said. "Thank you, sir."

After he left, Donald asked me if we did anything. Of course we didn't, I said. We just went to dinner and a movie and then I came straight back home. Donald nodded his head as if he was thinking it over.

"All right then," he said slowly. "Good night then, Margaret."

After that Mike and I started seeing each other quite a bit. Usually we just went out for dinner after he got off work, but one night, after we'd been seeing each other several months, he took me to his apartment over at Cooper's Pond. We sat on his sofa and kissed. It was a long wonderful kiss, and for the first time my heartbeat quickened. He was a perfect gentleman, so sweet and soft with me, and I felt incredibly happy. I can't say that I loved him, but the whole idea of finally having a boyfriend was so exciting, so marvelous, that I could have stayed there kissing him forever.

Suddenly I looked at my watch. It was already past eleven. Mike must have thought I'd turned into a crazy person. I jumped off the sofa and began hyperventilating. "Get me home," I said. I grabbed my purse and sweater, and began smoothing my long hair with my fingers. "You've got to get me back home right now. I'm late. I'm going to get into bad trouble."

"So you're half an hour late, Meg," he said. "Big deal. We'll just say—"

"Mike, listen to what I'm telling you. All right? You do not understand. Do you hear what I'm saying? Get me home right now. I mean it. Oh God, I'm going to get into such trouble."

The minute I walked in the door Donald was waiting for me. "Why are you late? What were you doing?"

I tried to sound nonchalant. "I wasn't doing anything. We just—"

"You were doing *somethin'*, Margaret, weren't you? Don't tell me you were doin' *nothin.'* What were you doin'?" He jabbed his finger at me as he talked, and my mother, her arms crossed and her brows furrowed, looked on silently.

He could tell I was nervous. I couldn't tell him I was at Mike's apartment or all hell would break loose. So I made up a story, rattling on about how the movie ran late and then we couldn't remember where we'd parked the car. He knew I was lying.

"Are you still a virgin?"

"Of course I am. I told you, we didn't do anything."

"Well, I'm going to have to check you then."

"You don't have to do that. You can believe me."

"I'm sorry, Margaret, but we have to check you."

I lay on my mother's bed, naked from the waist down. I could feel my mascara streaming down the sides of my face as Donald turned on a lamp and peered between my legs. I can't tell you how ashamed I was, how humiliated I felt. The only thing that helped me was the knowledge that I hadn't done anything wrong. *He's not going to find anything so just relax. It'll be over in a minute. Just stare at the ceiling and don't think about what's happening.*

"Just out of curiosity," my mother asked from a few feet away, "how can you tell if she's still a virgin?"

"There's supposed to be skin around the hymen. If she's not, the skin will be split on top." His fingers kept probing me. After two or three minutes he said, "The skin's still there, Pat. Okay, Margaret. Thank you."

I got up, put on my panties and went to bed. It's strange, but I don't think I cried after that. I just felt dead inside. There was no point fighting anything, and I think that's when a part of me just gave up. I guess I began to think of what they did to me the way some people think about paying the rent. An unavoidable cost of living.

Mike and I went out together for the next two years. Never once did he pressure me for sex. There were plenty of times it might have led to that, but in the back of my mind there was always the terror of being found out, of being discovered. From that first time onward, Mom and Donald checked me regularly.

It happened after practically every date.

✝ ✝ ✝

From the deposition of Margaret "Peggy" Sahlman, conducted by Richard Gilbert

"Are you the wife of Don Sahlman Jr.?"

"Uh-huh."

"When did you form the opinion that you didn't like being around [Meg]?"

"I had several incidents happen to me where she

used my name, and I had just formed a general dislike for her. She called herself Margaret Sahlman."

"Why did you take offense to that?"

"Probably because of the way she acted and the
way she looked. She looked like a cheap hooker. The
first time I really saw her up close in public, she was
hanging around a guy's neck in the grocery store line.
And her whole rear end was hanging out of her
shorts. And everybody was looking at her, and then—
and she had obviously already seen me—she turned
around like, 'This is my trophy.' And I could see the
clown makeup and the whole bit. And I just did not
appreciate somebody that looked and acted like that
telling people she was Margaret Sahlman."

"How old was she when the incident in the grocery
store occurred?"

"She was about seventeen or eighteen, something
like that."

"What other actions can you describe that produced
in you a general dislike for her?"

"I used to have men call me looking for her, thinking I was her."

"How many times did that happen?"

"Oh, goodness, over the years five or six, maybe."

"Any other actions you can describe that produced
in you a general dislike?"

"I went to the doctor once, and they told me I was
not Margaret Sahlman, that I had never been there
before, which irritated me. I went to a store and they
tried to take my credit card away, saying I was not
Margaret Sahlman."

"So you were upset with Margaret because these
people got confused with the names?"

"I don't think they were confused. She had told them she was Margaret Sahlman."

"Anything else that formed this general dislike?"

"Well, my father-in-law would frequently invite us out on the boat and to dinner, and she would make it her business to be there. We could never see him without her being there. Of course, she knew we wouldn't come if she was there. So she made it her business to be there."

"Do you know whether Don Sahlman invited her?"

"I don't know. But the relationship was such that I doubt seriously—and I could say almost positively—that he did not. I believe he told us he couldn't keep her away."

"What other times did you observe her that led to your general dislike?"

"We were at a stop light on one street and they—Mr. Sahlman, Margaret and Pat—were in the front seat of a car on one of the other streets. And when she saw us, she jumps over on him . . . and throws her arms around him and hugs him. . . . She wanted to make sure we knew that she was there and she was important to him."

"Why was it so unpleasant for Meg to hug Don Sr. in your presence?"

"Because he was married to my mother-in-law. . . . He was with his mistress and her daughter in public. It was embarrassing. . . . I mean, it was like they were a family."

Twelve

By January 1982, Donald had been divorced for more than two years. My mother, Granny and I still lived in our house on Juno Street, and Donald still officially lived alone on Occident Street. I had dropped out of school and gotten a part-time job working at a daycare center, which I figured was one of the only things I could do without a degree. But surprisingly, I discovered I enjoyed it. Whenever I was with the children, the hours flew by. Most of my free time I spent with Terry, Darley and Kathleen Macado, a woman I'd met at the community college, and occasionally I saw my high school friend, Carol Llosa. Mike and I saw each other about twice a week.

By then my relationship with Mike had turned platonic. One day I suppose we both realized it wasn't going to go anywhere, and it fizzled. Still, I cared about him a great deal, and I expect if you asked him he'd say the feeling was mutual. He came to the house often for some home cooking, and Mom and Donald were always unfailingly polite to him. In his presence, they even acted as if they liked him—although my mother never once liked any of my friends. No matter how hard my friends tried to be pleasant with her, always there was some great failing on their part: She's white trash, he's a fat slob, she's a little too prissy for my liking. It was always something. But Mike never had an inkling of who they really were when he was gone. He only saw the "loving family" show we put on for him: He saw actors.

Of all the people in my life, Mike was the only one who did finally stumble upon the truth—and in the last place I ever would have thought. When he did, he was horrified. I'll never forget the look on his face or the way his whole body shook with rage and disbelief as he approached me, or the things he said while he held the irrefutable evidence in his hands. But because that took so long to happen I can't tell you about that right now. Mike's discovery came later, and I have to tell things the way they happened first. So let me come back to that part later on.

Nick, during those years, was still living in Pensacola. Whenever we'd talked on the phone he sounded happy, even excited. At least, he did for a while. Not long after that, Mom and Donald became convinced he was using drugs again. I heard them asking him on the phone about cocaine. According to them, he didn't deny it. Pretty soon his phone calls stopped, for which I could hardly blame him. Nick obviously had demons he thought none of us could understand, and he probably got tired of hearing nothing but criticism.

Alcohol and drugs, for some reason, had never appealed to me. But on some level I think I did understand Nick's drug problems. I, too, had things that helped me lose myself: I still cooked and cleaned obsessively—even the smallest speck of dirt disgusted me—and I also had taken up running, which did for me what nothing else ever had. In the early mornings I ran through the neighborhood, passing houses that radiated normalcy: a mother through a kitchen window feeding an infant in a high chair; a lanky teenage boy stepping out the front door and yelling to his black dog to go get the newspaper; an attractive middle-aged couple, both in business attire, kissing each other in their driveway before getting into their respective cars. Everywhere I looked I saw happiness and aliveness flashing by me. And no matter how fast I ran, my own life seemed a low, dull hum in comparison. I once read a passage in the Bible about seeing the world "through a glass darkly," and that's just how it felt—as if I were inside a dark jar, and all around me was clarity and brightness and vibrancy.

I ran faster. Down Kennedy Boulevard, past restaurants and single-story office building and nail salons. The steady thunk-thunk-thunk of my shoes on the hot pavement hypnotized me, wiped my brain clean, so that all that existed was my steady breathing, the pounding of my heart, the absence of any thoughts about killing myself. Then a loop back up toward the house again, ending at the front lawn. It was a distance of more than ten miles. As I pulled off my shoes, stretching first one leg and then the other, I heard my pulse in my ears. Nothing else. Running, I thought, probably did the same thing for me that Nick's cocaine did for him, blotting out the sound of my life, the realization of who and what I was.

The possibility of ever feeling any different never entered my consciousness. The idea that the glass jar could ever be lifted seemed beyond my ability to imagine it. And if you'd told me then that in just one month my entire life would change—that suddenly I would want to feel everything, sense everything, experience everything, that the world would turn wonderful and full of possibility and joy—I would have said you were out of your mind.

In late January, Donald announced he'd always wanted to go skiing. This time he didn't even bother to ask my mother if she wanted to go. She always said she hated the cold— although I can't imagine where in her life she ever would have encountered it—and her standard answer about going anywhere was that she had to take care of Granny and the dog.

What I'm about to tell you I'm ashamed of. It's hard for me to say this, because when Donald asked me if I wanted to go to Aspen for a week, for the first time in my life I actually felt as if I had a choice. If I had told him I didn't want to go where it was cold, that I'd hate it, I honestly think he wouldn't have forced me to go. It wouldn't have been like Fernandina

Beach, where going with him was never an option. And what shames me most is that I knew there would be a price for all the expensive ski clothes he planned to buy in Tampa before the trip; I knew I'd have to pay for getting the chance to see snow for the first time.

But then I remembered the last time he'd taken me shopping at the mall. I had looked into a window and commented on what cute shoes the store had and how much I'd love a pair. "I'll get them for you," Donald had said, grinning, "but you know what you're going to have to do for them."

"Forget it, then," I blurted out angrily. "I don't want them *that* much. I don't want *anything* that much." I turned and walked away.

He didn't say a thing in the car going home. His silence, I thought, was a reaction to my anger. Maybe it had impressed him or scared him some way, especially since he'd never seen that from me. It was a side of me he didn't know I had— that *I* didn't know I had. Of course, people can mistakenly read all kinds of things into silence, and that was one of them. Without a word, he pulled into the parking lot of the Imperial Yacht Basin. He got out of the car and walked onto the deck of the boat. Then he turned and looked at me. "Come on then, Margaret," he said, holding his arms wide. He was daring me to defy him. "Come on and give your old dad a hug." I walked over without a word.

Later, after he drove me home, I had a terrible, sinful thought: *Hell, I should have just gotten those damn shoes. The most expensive ones they had. He does it to me anyway. I might as well get something for it.*

Aspen, in my mind, seemed like those shoes. The way I figured it, either he was going to go after me in Tampa or in Colorado. There was no place to hide from him, so at least I might as well get something out of it.

And so I said yes.

The St. Moritz Lodge in Aspen was a beautiful wood building with tall plate-glass windows that looked out over snow-laden pines. Wood-beamed cathedral ceilings and a huge stone fireplace dominated the main lobby. Outside one window, steam rose from a heated pool edged by snow. At night, men and women in expensive after-ski outfits roasted marshmallows around the fire or sipped hot apple cider, their tanned faces glowing in the soft flickering light. Behind them, at tables scattered about the room, others drank brandy or hot chocolate, their conversations and laughter blending into a lovely warm hum.

Donald and I sat near the fireplace with cups of hot cider. For some reason he had bought himself a pair of brown overalls in Tampa that he now wore over a bulky turtleneck sweater, and the combination, compared to the chic outfits all around us, made him look like a farmer who'd forgotten his pitchfork. I was wearing new bright pink ski pants and a cashmere cowl-neck sweater.

From where we sat, we had a clear view of the pool. It had begun to snow, and silvery flakes drifted under the beam of outside lights. Suddenly, the door to a wooden shack near the pool flung open, and several men and women bounded out in bathing suits. Laughing and screaming, they flung themselves onto the snow and then, amazingly, hurled themselves into the pool. A second later they heaved themselves out and quickly grabbed towels, shivering and laughing.

"Those people are crazy," I murmured.

Donald shook his head. "Doesn't take a genius to know that. Damn fools. They'll freeze to death."

"No, no, you should try it," a woman sitting near us interjected. "Really! You get all hot and sweaty in the sauna and then go into the snow and the pool, and it makes your skin tingle all over. I did it last night, and it makes you feel so alive!"

Alive. Oh God, that word sounded so good to me. I had such a yearning to know what that was. Was alive something you could learn? Something you could practice until it felt real? The people by the pool were still laughing and shivering and letting out loud whoops. When had I ever felt that way?

"I'm going to do it," I said and stood up.

Donald looked up at me but didn't move. "And I'm going to swallow a cow in one gulp."

"No, really, I'm going to do it. It looks like fun. I want some fun."

"That's not fun, Margaret. You said it yourself, that's crazy."

"So maybe it is. So what? Are you going, too?"

"I'm finishing my cider."

I went upstairs to our room and changed into my one-piece bathing suit, which I'd thrown into my suitcase on the off chance there was an indoor pool. *Let's see you follow me now,* I thought. Then I went downstairs. Without looking at

Donald I walked outside and opened the sauna door. There were two women on the upper bunk, and an older man by himself on the bottom. A yellow bulb made their beads of sweat look like glistening drops of honey. I closed my eyes and breathed as if through the top of my head. My shoulders dropped. My breathing became deeper. Even with these strangers I felt gloriously alone. After a few minutes, the thinner of the two women stood up. "Okay, let's go for it!" she yelled. She pushed open the door and ran out into the darkness. I followed her and suddenly let myself fall backwards into the snow, rolling from side to side and screaming with a piercing ferocity that surprised even me. Then I dove into the pool with the others.

Never before had I felt such exhilaration, such pure joy. Everything the woman in the lodge had said was true. As I pulled myself from the water and wrapped myself in a thick towel, my entire body tingled and glowed and pulsated with energy I didn't know existed. *Oh God, keep this feeling inside of me. Put it away in a safe place so I can remember it. Don't let me forget what this feels like.*

During the next two days, Donald and I skied every day from nine until three. We took lessons together with a private instructor, a young man whose face was so tanned and the whites of his eyes so bright that he reminded me of a coal miner. I was surprised, but skiing seemed to come naturally to me. While Donald was still trying to get the hang of the snowplow and falling every few feet, I already had learned how to make parallel turns. My instructor was impressed, and one time even suggested skiing down the mountain and waiting for Donald at the bottom. "You'll wait for me," Donald said to me. He wouldn't let me out of his sight.

One night we came back to the lodge, where everyone was sitting around the fireplace. We took two empty chairs and sipped hot cider. Within a few minutes, a pretty blond woman in a white sweater and black ski pants came up behind me and tapped me on the shoulder. "See that guy over there?" She looked over her shoulder at a tanned, handsome man sitting alone at a table. "He says he wants to meet you. He's a veterinarian."

"Yeah, right," I said. "He's a vet like I'm a vet."

"No, really. He's from Australia. He said he wants to meet you. Do you want me to introduce you?" Before I could answer, she beckoned him with her finger and he came over. "This is Anthony," the woman said.

After a brief silence—she didn't know my name—I said, "I'm Margaret."

Anthony sat down beside me and, a bit shyly, asked me when I'd arrived and how long I was staying. He had a beautiful accent, one you wanted to listen to all day. I thought he was gorgeous, with the most beautiful mouth and the whitest teeth I'd ever seen. He told me he lived in Sydney and was on holiday for five weeks. After Aspen he was heading to Vail. He asked if I wanted to go skiing with him the next day.

I looked over at Donald. His face revealed nothing. "Anthony, this is my father," I said, and introduced them. "We kind of stay together."

"Oh," he said. "Well, then would you mind if I joined you?"

Donald smiled and nodded in what must have seemed like

a gracious gesture. It baffled me; it was almost as if he was enjoying watching Anthony's attraction to me. "That would be fine," Donald said after a moment. "Until tomorrow morning, then." Anthony took the cue and moved back to his table.

The next day I took turns riding the chair lift with Donald and Anthony. Donald didn't seem to mind at all that I didn't always ski with him, which seemed strange, since just the day before he'd growled when the ski instructor once again had suggested it. On the way up on the lift with Anthony, the tips of our skis occasionally touching, we talked easily, effortlessly. I had the odd sense I'd known him a long time.

Anthony was in his final year of veterinary school and had been studying to get into a residency program. He said it was very competitive—loads of applicants and only a few available slots—so the ski trip was a chance to have a bit of fun before everything came down to crunch time. His dream had always been to work with animals, but he'd have to wait and see how he did on his upcoming exams. He listened while I talked about growing up in Guyana (he knew from what remained of my accent I wasn't originally from Florida), my work at the daycare center, about how I'd dropped out of school. I told him I had no idea what I wanted to do with my life or even was capable of doing. Sometimes, I said, I felt like a leaf floating on top of a strong river. "Just follow your happiness," he said. "That's where your future is. I truly believe that whatever makes us happy also will take care of us, provide for us."

I did not intentionally lie to him. At least, not in the sense that I wanted him to think I was someone I wasn't. But I did leave out huge chunks of my history that would lead to questions I could not answer. And I did continue to allow him to believe that Donald was my father. I was sorry for that part, but when I'd said it, it was because it made everything simpler. That, and I never expected to see him again. But after a few days with him, I wished I could take it back. Still, no matter how I considered it, it didn't seem possible to explain that Donald wasn't even my stepfather—*then what are you doing with him in a single room?*—without heaping upon myself immediate suspicion.

That evening, I asked Donald if I could invite Anthony to join us for dinner. Again he surprised me by saying it would be fine. For the next three nights we all ate together, with Anthony and me doing most of the talking while Donald looked on silently, almost curiously. He must have noticed something was happening to me, something he'd never seen before. I felt it, too, but had no idea what it was. All I knew was that I felt happy. When Anthony's hand brushed against mine as he reached for his wineglass, my entire body tingled as if I'd just jumped from the sauna and rolled in the glistening soft snow.

One night after dinner as we sat by the fireplace, Anthony asked if I wanted to go listen to music at a lounge not far from the lodge. Outside it was beautiful and clear, the stars more bright and plentiful than I'd ever seen them. Anthony said it was close enough to walk. "Would that be all right, sir?" he asked Donald.

Donald had to know he was not included in the invitation.

"She can go," he said. "But I want to make something absolutely clear." He pointed his finger toward Anthony's face. "You are to bring her back here the same way she's leaving—a virgin."

If the earth could have opened up and swallowed me I wish it had. I wanted to die, to sink into the ground. Any number of people had probably heard him say it. But Anthony just looked at him and said, "Yes, sir." He helped me on with my coat.

We walked along the side of the road silently, the only sound the crunching of our boots in the hard-packed snow. A sadness had come over me, as if a tiny candle inside me had been blown out. He reached over and took my hand, and without thinking I stopped and turned to him.

"May I kiss you?" he asked.

Oh God, as long as I live I will never forget the softness of his lips, how he brushed my face tenderly with his hand, how I felt myself melting. *This is heaven. I am in heaven.* Then he stopped kissing me, put both hands on my shoulders, and peered at my face—the way you do to make sure someone is all right—and smiled. A moment later, we continued walking, like very good friends, under all those stars.

We reached the lounge and he opened the door. The sound of music and loud voices and a cloud of cigarette smoke all curled out into the crisp night air. Inside, the walls were covered in red velvet, with matching red carpet and long drapes. Waitresses in skimpy skirts bent over tables, and in front a piano player was on a small stage singing Billy Joel's "I Love You Just the Way You Are."

"It rather reminds me of a house of ill repute," he said, and then quickly glanced at me. "Not that I've ever been to one, mind you." He smiled at me so mischievously that finally I laughed. And then he laughed with me, a big hearty sound that poured over me and put Donald's words behind me. We sat down at a corner table and ordered drinks. He said, "We don't have a lot of time left, do we?"

I didn't want to think about him leaving or my trip back to Tampa the next day. And I didn't want to cry, either. I had dreaded this moment, the saying good-bye. "So I need to tell this to you now," he said. "I've fallen in love with you. I never thought that could happen to me, but it has. You have such a good heart—I knew that from the moment I first saw you by the fireplace with your father. You're the most beautiful, kind woman I've ever met."

Had I dreamed those words? Or had he just said them to make saying good-bye easier on me? *No one falls in love that fast.* But if that was true, then what was I feeling for him? This beautiful, gentle man was looking into my eyes, and I knew he saw me—a *me* I hadn't known was there before. And when I looked at him I had the same sense: that I knew this man, even if I did not know the details. That I had touched his spirit the same way he had touched mine.

He leaned across the table and took my hand. "Come to Vail with me," he said. "Tell me you will."

How could I do that? Even think of it? We were flying back to Tampa the next day. Even if I could bring myself to ask, Donald would never throw those tickets away. "He'd never go straight from here, Anthony. He never does anything without first thinking it all out, without planning everything."

"Then what if you asked your father when you got home? If he'd bring you back? Do you think he might do it? He seems to enjoy skiing quite a bit."

Never, on my own, would I have considered it. But the second Anthony suggested it, I knew it wasn't as ludicrous as it sounded. It would just take some planning. All the way home on the plane, I imagined how I would ask Donald, the words, the tone of voice I'd use. The key, I knew, would be to say "we." If I asked if *I* could go, I wouldn't have a chance. As the plane touched down in Tampa, I remembered what Donald had done to me the night before, after Anthony had brought me back to the lodge. He had cared nothing that I was flushed and happy, but only wanted what he wanted. "You don't think I brought you here just for your own fun, do you?" he'd asked. He knew I hated it, but it didn't matter a bit to him. It was almost as if he got pleasure from watching me suffer.

I glanced at him in the seat beside me as he flipped through a magazine. Suddenly, I realized I was worrying about Vail for nothing. Donald would take me if I asked him. He would take me, because there was only one thing about him that was predictable.

Donald would do whatever was necessary to get access to me.

Thirteen

After Donald and I returned from Vail, Carol Llosa, my friend since high school, first wanted to see the new car Donald had just bought for me. Then she wanted to see the pictures I'd brought over to her house. So did her mother, who over the years had been very warm to me. As the three of us sat on the sofa, I showed them the two rolls Donald had taken on both ski trips. There were shots of Anthony and me outside the St. Moritz Lodge in Aspen. Of the Roost Lodge in Vail. Of Anthony in his thick sheepskin coat, sitting beside me on a double bed with a stuffed purple elephant I'd bought for him. Of the room Donald and I had shared in Vail. Another of Anthony standing beside Donald in his brown overalls.

"Oh Meg, he's *gorgeous*," Carol said, holding a picture of Anthony and me. "And a vet! If it were me, I swear to God I'd be on the next plane to Australia. What are you doing here anyway? Why aren't you in Australia with your hunk by now?"

Mrs. Llosa looked at Carol and smiled. Mrs. Llosa had always seemed like the perfect mother to me, always cheerful and involved in Carol's school projects, always friendly to all of her daughter's friends. During high school I'd wished my own mother could have been even a little bit like her, or else that Carol and I could have traded places. I watched her now as she leafed through the stack of pictures, commenting every once in a while about how beautiful the ski area was, or how happy or pretty I looked. Then she stopped at the one of our room. It was what Donald would have called a "nothing" shot: just the double bed, with an open closet and a few clothes hanging inside.

"This was your room in Vail?" she asked.

I nodded. "We took Anthony up there for a little party to celebrate his birthday. Donald let me buy him a cake and the stuffed elephant."

She looked at me strangely.

"I know it wasn't a very good present," I said, "but it was all I could find at the little gift store. They didn't really have anything. But Anthony said he liked it. He said, 'An elephant never forgets. And neither shall I.'"

Mrs. Llosa looked at the picture again. After a long moment

she said, "It was a very sweet gesture, Meg. And I'm sure that Anthony must have thought so, too."

But suddenly I wondered if that's what she'd been thinking at all. Quickly I gathered up the rest of the pictures—"The rest are all boring"—and put them away.

In the beginning, Anthony and I called each other, long conversations at night in Tampa, daytime in Australia. He told me he was studying almost constantly on top of the work he did at a clinic, but that he still thought about me all the time. The same, I told him, was true for me. Sometimes as I sat with the children at the daycare center, Anthony's face would flash in front of me and I'd feel my insides constrict, as if a warm, dark stone were weaving through my insides. There was a physical, gravitational sensation to missing him. It was as strong as being pressed against a seat in an airplane that's nosing toward the clouds.

We wrote to each other, too, long detailed letters that arrived almost every day. Sometimes we sent cassette tapes, ones he'd made in his car en route to work or that I'd whispered, beneath blankets, late at night. Each afternoon I arrived home from the daycare center and immediately asked my mother the same thing: Did anything come for me? Silently she'd hand his latest letter to me, an envelope with "Miss Margaret Sahlman" written in his beautiful writing on the front. He already called me Meg, but I hadn't yet figured out a way to explain to him that Sahlman wasn't my last name—or that Donald, technically, wasn't even my stepfather. That, I had decided, could come later. I'd disappear into my room and devour his words, hearing his voice over and over in my head. When I was done I placed his envelopes or cassettes into my "Anthony bag," a plastic sack that held everything from pictures and ticket stubs to a doily from the Roost Lodge. Anything that had anything to do with him went inside it.

One day my mother held up his latest letter. As I reached for it, she pulled her hand back a few inches. "He's writing to you quite a lot, Margaret. And actually, I'd like to hear what he says." She stared at me and then looked over her shoulder at Donald as he came into the living room. "Wouldn't you like to know what he says, Donald?"

"I would very much," he said. They both sat down on the sofa and waited without another word. I tried to put them off. "It's nothing that would interest you, really. It's just private things that—"

It was the wrong thing to say. "Open the letter," my mother commanded. "Now!"

Shakily, my index finger tore along the flap of the envelope. As soon as I saw what he'd written, I felt my face go hot.

"Go on then," Donald said. "And don't be leavin' anythin' out or I'll come over there and read it myself. And I'll know if you do, too."

In a flat voice I read to them. "My darling Margaret. I was just speaking to you, and it was so lovely to hear your voice again. I love you, miss you, and want you so very, very much. You don't know how happy it makes me to hear your voice or to receive a letter from you. I think of you during my waking hours and dream of you whilst asleep."

"He really said 'whilst'?" my mother asked. "That's rather affected, don't you think, Donald?"

"Sounds like it to me. But they do talk different down there, that's for sure. You know that Crocodile Dundee fellow on TV? 'Put anothuh shrimp on the barbie.' Anyway, go on, Margaret. Keep readin'."

I read to them how hard Anthony had been working at a clinic, and how exhausted he was on top of all his studying. He said he thought I was the most wonderful woman he'd ever met and couldn't wait to hear my voice again. He signed the letter, "All my love, Anthony."

"Is there something else at the bottom?" Donald asked.

I took a deep breath. "P.S. I'm sorry your new car got damaged. It's annoying, isn't it? But at least there wasn't a scratch on you, which is the most important thing."

From then on they made me read every letter. Donald seemed to take particular pleasure in my discomfort whenever there were passages in which Anthony told me how much he loved me. Sometimes he even claimed he hadn't heard me and asked me to read the passages once again, this time a little slower and louder. With all my might I tried to read with no expression, to give no hint of any uneasiness, but that one acting job, out of all the ones I had performed over the years, proved impossible. Donald always knew. He always focused on the one word that caught ever so slightly in my throat. Even though being forced to read my own letters to Anthony would have been difficult enough, I still would have preferred it to reading his to me. Each time I spoke his words out loud, it was as if Anthony was the one being forced to stand naked in front of them, as if Anthony was the one being made to turn first this way and then that for their inspection.

A few times I considered how I could intercept his letters. But short of appealing to the post office to alter its delivery schedule, there didn't seem to be any solution. To do so would have meant being home when the mail arrived—and that, I knew, would have required me to quit my job. As much as I loved being with the children, I would have done that in a second, except for one thing: If I did, Donald would be able to go after me even more. The daycare center, even if it was only for a few hours each day, was my only surefire escape. And the way I saw it, either I chose my privacy with Anthony or else more of Donald's abuse.

I kept reading the letters to them.

By early April, Anthony and I could barely stand being apart anymore. "Look," he said to me one night on the phone, "with all this long-distance ringing back and forth, it's costing us a fortune, don't you agree? We could have spent the same money on a ticket for you to come to Australia. So why don't you just plan to come? I'll be finished with my exams at the end of June, and you could come then."

There wasn't a chance on earth I would have been allowed to fly to Australia—or could have afforded the airfare—on my own. And I knew, too, what asking Donald would mean. Even if he said yes, how could I go, knowing what he'd do to me when Anthony wasn't with me? In Vail on our last night, while Donald had prodded me in the dark, tears had streamed down my face and I bit my lip until I tasted thick salt. For the first time I'd not only had the conscious thought of wanting to die, but also a vision—the flash of a gun—of how I might accomplish it.

I simply couldn't go through that again. Not now. Not if Anthony and I actually were together again. It was one thing to endure Donald in Anthony's absence, but something else—something I was certain I couldn't willingly bring upon myself—to go through it while Anthony was near me. My only hope was to convince my mother to go along, too.

"I don't want to fly," she said flatly. To her credit, she didn't try to convince me that the trip was ridiculous. She'd already heard enough of Anthony's letters to know how he felt about me. "You read all the time about plane crashes," she said. "And besides, who would take care of Granny? And the dog?"

"We could find someone," I said, trying to keep any hint of pleading out of my voice. In fact, I'd already talked about the possibility of housesitting to my former boyfriend, Mike Cobaugh. "Maybe one of my friends. And haven't you and Donald wanted to travel for a long time? Remember how he said that's what he wanted to do after he retired? Anthony says Sydney's beautiful."

She looked at me as if she had just stopped in front of a modern painting in a museum, considered it, and then in one instant decided it was garbage. "I don't want to go. I don't want to be on a plane that long." She turned and walked into the kitchen.

From the living room sofa where he pretended to read a magazine, Donald must have listened to her the same way he had when he'd asked her to go to the Keys, to Fernandina Beach, to everywhere else she never wanted to go. I knew that man's face so well I could tell exactly what he was thinking. *Good, Pat, because I'd rather be alone with her. You'd just get in the way. All the better for me.*

Slowly, nonchalantly, he looked up from his magazine. His expression said, *Nice try, Margaret.* "Well, I guess I could take you there," he said. "If that's really what you want to do." He looked at me with such smugness, such mirth, that a fist of anger curled inside my chest. He knew exactly how much it would cost me to go with him. But this time we weren't talking about a pair of expensive shoes or a ski trip or a car. Donald's gaze now dared me to reveal myself to him: *So just how much are you willing to pay for what you want, Margaret? Just how much is this guy worth to you?*

I wish I could tell you that I wouldn't pay the price he was asking, that I wasn't capable of becoming what he was challenging me to be—what, already, I had allowed myself in some measure to become. But the instant he offered to take me, the truth was that my desire to see Anthony was greater than my loathing of what would come with it. I would pay that price if it was the only way. And Donald, sitting there, must have known it. The second I'd said yes to the ski trip, the moment I'd stepped over that slippery slope beyond the window of a shoe store, my decision must have been a foregone conclusion to him. If the sight of snow could overcome my ethics, then Australia and Anthony, in his mind, obviously would be a piece of cake.

"Thank you," I said to him. "I'll call Anthony and tell him."

In late April, Anthony wrote that his mother was planning to stay with a friend for a few weeks, which meant we could stay at her "unit"—which I assumed was an apartment— while we were there. "There is plenty of room," I read aloud to Mom and Donald. Anthony said Australia's mid-winter climate was mild, like Los Angeles, and that his mother's unit faced northeast, so the winter sun would shine right in. He expected we would be quite comfortable there.

"Well, we're not," Donald said.

"Not what?"

"Staying at his mother's house, or whatever you call it. I wouldn't think of it."

"But he said he wants us to. He wouldn't offer if he didn't mean it. And it would be so much nicer if—"

"Frankly, Margaret, I don't care what *he* wants us to do. And if *I'm* the one takin' you all the way over to Aborigine-land, *I'll* be the one to decide where we stay. Not him. You got that?"

"But Anthony says it would—"

"Then maybe you won't go at all!" my mother yelled. "Is that what you want? You should be *grateful* Donald is willing to take you at all instead of *demanding* everything be your way! Nothing is ever good enough for you, is it, Margaret? Nothing quite lives up to your expectations, does it? Maybe you should just forget about going! Maybe *that* would teach you some appreciation!"

So that was it. Donald had just thrown down the gauntlet, and my mother was right there standing guard behind it. The trip would be on his terms, just like always. "You're right, you're right," I said, terrified now of my mother's wrath. "I'm sorry. You're right. I shouldn't have said that, really. And I am grateful he's taking me. Really I am."

"That's better," Donald said. "Isn't that better, Pat?"

She didn't answer. She walked out of the room. A few moments later she began playing her violin, a dreadful piece of furious chords followed by a few pitiful single notes that since childhood had always reminded me of a lion attacking a gazelle. Donald walked over and sat down on the sofa. He lifted a magazine from the coffee table, flipped through it, and then looked up at me and winked. He had won, just like always.

A few days later, he made arrangements through his travel agent for the two of us to stay in one room at the Hyatt Regency in Sydney. As the hotel confirmation printed out in the travel agent's office, I asked the woman if she minded printing me one out, too. Donald didn't ask why. It was for my "Anthony bag."

✝　✝　✝

From the deposition of Patricia Sahlman, conducted by Richard Gilbert

"Did Donald Sahlman take trips with Meg?"

"Yes. Two ski trips, one trip to Key West with her friends, and a couple of trips to Fernandina Beach is all that I recall."

"Let's talk about the two ski trips. Do you know how old Meg was on those two trips?"

"Nineteen."

"And do you know what the sleeping arrangements were?"

"No."

"Did you ask?"

"No."

"Where did they go skiing?"

"Aspen and Vail."

"Do you know if they were in the same room?"

"I don't know."

"Did Don take any photographs during the ski trip?"

"Yes."

"Did you see those photographs?"

"Yes."

"Were there any photographs taken inside the accommodations where they were staying?"

"No."

"How old was Meg when they went to Key West?"

"Sixteen."

"And then I believe you testified that there were a couple of trips to Fernandina Beach. How old was Meg during those trips?"

"Between the ages of sixteen and eighteen, nineteen."

"Where did they stay when they went to Fernandina Beach?"

"Amelia Island Plantation."

"Why didn't they stay with Don's sister at the family ranch?"

"Don preferred to stay in a hotel. He did not like to impose on people."

"What were the sleeping arrangements?"

"I don't know."

"Did you ever observe Donald Sahlman checking Meg's breasts, doing breast examinations?"

"Yes. She must have been about eighteen, nineteen. She had lots of very hard masses, lumps. . . . She would ask him to see if the lumps were still there, how hard the lumps were."

"What would he do?"

"He would just mash it."

"How often did this occur?"

"Whenever she was in pain."

"And how often was she in pain?"

"Quite often."

"So the examinations occurred quite often?"

"No. We didn't bother with her most of the time."

"Do you know if he ever did it in front of her friends?"

"No, he did not."

"Did Donald Sahlman express concern about Meg's virginity?"

"Sure. He told her to be careful with men, not to go sleeping around with men, to stay a virgin until marriage."

"And did he do anything to determine whether or not she had followed his advice?"

"No."

"Did he ever check Meg to determine the status of her virginity?"

"No."

"Do you recall any occasion in which Don Sahlman would have Meg remove her clothing and would manually examine her vagina?"

"No."

"You never saw that, never heard that?"

"No."

Fourteen

ou have to convince her," I pleaded with Anthony in May.
"Isn't there anything you could say to make her change
her mind?"

Anthony didn't ask why I was so desperate to have my
mother come along, too. He just didn't feel he could do or
say anything to help me. "Your mother doesn't even know
me," he said. "And it doesn't really sound as if she's all that
fond of travelling. At least, not from what you've told me."

"She's scared of flying, Anthony. She's certain the plane
she gets on will be the one that crashes. Couldn't you just try

and reassure her? Tell her how much everyone wants to meet her? Couldn't you just try?"

The next day, Anthony called my mother and read from a list of statistics about the sterling reputation of Qantas. He told her she absolutely, positively could rest assured that it was the safest airline in existence. Never in history, he said, had they ever had an accident of any kind. They were completely fastidious, obsessive even, about safety. And their record proved it. Everything would be fine. His relatives were so impressed she was a musician and couldn't wait to meet her. And if she came, he was quite confident he could get opera tickets. The city was wonderfully cosmopolitan, with museums and exquisite restaurants and millions of things to do, and he was certain she would love it. Wouldn't she reconsider?

Finally, she relented. Later that night she told me she'd go—but only if Mike Cobaugh followed through on his offer to house-sit with Granny and the dog.

"Oh, Anthony, you're so wonderful!" I told him the next morning. I was almost crying. "Thank you, oh, thank you!"

"It was nothing, really."

"No—it *wasn't* nothing, Anthony. You got all those airline records, and that's really what did it. She said that's really what convinced her. Where did you get them? How did you ever find them?"

For a few seconds all I heard was soft static and Anthony's breath against the receiver. "Well, I rather imagine you might say I stumbled across them."

"Stumbled across them? Where?"

"Let me see, how should I say this? I stumbled across them . . . in my imagination."

I threw my head back and laughed until tears streamed down my face and no sound came out. Anthony burst into laughter with me. I was so happy, so relieved, that I wouldn't have cared if he'd told her the streets of Australia were littered with diamonds and rubies and all you had to do was pick them up free for the taking.

That night at the dinner table, Donald barely said a thing. He must have been seething. There was nothing he could do about it, though; he couldn't very well try to talk her out of going now after all the motions he'd gone through pretending to convince her. He had to have known I'd won that round, that I'd gotten around him. But I was too happy to even look at him.

My mother stared at me strangely. "You know what I think, Margaret?" She took a bite of her beef Wellington and chewed thoughtfully. "I think he's going to ask you to marry him. That's what I think. What do you think, Donald?"

Donald stopped chewing mid-bite. He put down his fork and began scratching the back of his head. His expression had changed, hardened. "Might be right about that, Patricia. Maybe so."

"What would you tell him if he asked you?" my mother asked.

"Yeah," Donald said. "What would you say, Margaret?"

I took a sip of water and then a bite of food. I chewed slowly, absently, as if they'd just asked me something that never once had entered my mind. "Gee, I have no idea. I really don't." I took another bite and then furrowed my brows. "You know what? I'm really not happy with this recipe. The Wellington didn't turn out like I expected. I think it's missing something. Don't you think it is?"

Damn if I was going to tell them I knew exactly what I'd say. "Could you pass the salt, please?" I asked.

He asked me to marry him our first night in Sydney. And like the total ridiculous fool I was, I truly believed God would grant me this one thing, this one chance for happiness. I had protected my family from being deported back to Guyana all those years, hadn't I? And I had kept my mouth shut, hadn't I? Wasn't I entitled to some kind of life now? Hadn't I earned it? And that was how I talked to God. I was full of require-ments and demands and expectations, and He must have heard me and flicked me away as easily as a half-dead fly from a window sill.

Mom and Donald were exhausted from the long flight and immediately went up to our hotel room. While they rested, Anthony took me on a drive over to the harbor at Circular Quay, where a knot of skyscrapers crowded toward a vast, islanded stretch of water. The view was completely beautiful, completely magical. It was early evening, and in the distance I saw green and white ferries criss-crossing the dark blue water, heading, Anthony said, from one harbor to another. Australian taxis, he called them. He pointed out the magnifi-cent, graceful Opera House and the Harbor Bridge and then the oldest quarter of the city called The Rocks. It was where the first British had settled. The city, he told me, had begun as a prison colony in 1788, after the newly independent

America had refused to accept Britain's criminal class.

"So I'm afraid I must confess, straight off, that I'm descended from scoundrels and criminals. Just in case my lineage is important to you," he said, smiling. "Of course, I suppose you could say that about all Australians. But I did think you should be informed of my unsavory heritage."

"Thank you for telling me that," I said, smiling back at him. "I'm very glad you got that off your chest. Because now there's one less secret between us."

"Ah, secrets!" He put his arm around me and pulled me into his shoulder. "And now you must tell me one of yours."

He had parked his car near the water. I looked out at a freighter passing by slowly and a paddleboat, apparently designed for rivers, as it slapped happily through tiny waves. Everywhere I looked were boats of some kind: powerboats and water taxis and sailboats, fishing vessels chugging alongside tourist-filled cruise boats.

"You want me to tell you a secret?"

"Yes, I do," he said. "The deepest one you can think of."

"Well, then. I love you, Anthony."

"You think that's a secret?"

"Actually, I hope it isn't. I pray it isn't."

"Meg," he said, taking my face in his hands. "We don't have to have any secrets now. We're safe with each other. Nothing that has come before matters, nothing could ever change how I feel about you. I wish I could always be with you."

There was no reason for me to cry, but my eyes welled with tears. I blinked them away. "Yes," I whispered. "I want that so much. You can't know how I want that." I closed my eyes and rested my head against him. I wanted to stay there, feeling his heartbeat, listening to him breathe, forever. He pulled me closer, and for a long while we just sat there, silently. It wasn't until he moved his arm that I realized I was on the verge of drifting off.

"Oh, what a selfish person I am," he said. "Keeping you out late after such a long flight." I didn't want to go yet, but he was right. Already I'd been up for more than twenty-four hours.

At the hotel, he held my hand as we began walking across the marbled lobby toward the elevators. Perhaps he sensed my reluctance to go back up into the room, because he slowed as we came to two wingback chairs beside a table and vase filled with bright flowers. "Why don't we sit for just one more moment?" he said. That was when he told me there was no doubt in his mind. "I know it's all rather sudden, and I realize this lobby isn't the most romantic spot in the world to bring this up, but would you consider marrying me? Would you think about being my wife?"

When I opened the door of our hotel room, Mom and Donald both were sitting up in bed. They clearly had been waiting for me. "Did you all have a nice time?" Donald asked. I heard something strange in his voice, an edge I couldn't identify. Even now, looking back, I can't figure out what he must have been thinking, whether he'd known all along or still had a hint of uncertainty.

"Yes, I did. I had a lovely time. Anthony showed me the harbor, which is absolutely beautiful. He said we'll all go down there tomorrow, and he'll walk us through the old quarter. He said we can have lunch at one of the restaurants there."

Donald nodded. "Well, that's good." He looked at me a moment longer and then turned to my mother. "Well, I don't know about you, but I'm done for the day. Are you ready to sleep?" My mother nodded as I put my purse down on the second bed.

"Oh, there was one other thing Anthony said." I opened my purse and took out my brush. Slowly I began pulling it through my long hair. "He asked me to marry him."

Donald's arm, which had been reaching for the lamp switch, froze mid-air. I don't know why I told them that way, or why I waited, still brushing my hair slowly, until they were forced to ask me what I'd said to him. I didn't tell them the full truth: that I'd thrown my arms around his neck and told him I didn't need time to think about a thing, that I was just as certain as he was, just as wildly in love with him, and that we'd kissed, right there in the lobby, in front of everyone.

I looked at them and said, "Oh, I told him yes."

For at least a full minute neither of them said a word. I could feel their shock; it was as if all the air had been sucked out of the room. My mother spoke first. "Well, that's nice," she said. She adjusted her pillow, absently picked at the edge of her nightgown, and then turned her head slightly to Donald. He gave a small nod.

"Whatever makes you happy, Margaret." His eyes did not move from mine, did not blink. And then he reached over and turned out the light.

What was going on inside of them during the next few days? What were they thinking? Sometimes I wonder that; sometimes I wish I could go back in time and pay attention to their signals, to their eye movements, to anything at all that would have prepared me. At the time I was simply too happy, too full of joy to think about anything other than Anthony, anything else but being with him forever, and I took their silence as resignation. As acceptance. And Anthony and I, in turn, began to make plans.

There was no doubt that I'd first have to return to Florida while we worked out the details and Anthony found a suitable apartment. His current one was fine for a bachelor, he said, but would be no place for me. And where did I want to go for a honeymoon? he asked. Did I want to get married in Australia, or would I prefer it to be in Florida so all my friends could be there? He'd do whatever I wanted. Over the next few days, as he drove us all over Sydney showing us the sights and introducing us to his family—he had two brothers, a sister and a lovely warm mother—Mom and Donald never said a word against the marriage, never gave a hint they disapproved. They even said they wanted to go with us to Anthony's church to meet his priest.

It was a beautiful church, made of old dark stone with a little garden of rose bushes out front. The priest was a thin man with wispy gray hair, and he seemed extremely solemn—unnecessarily so, I thought—as he listened to Anthony talk about how we'd met and how long we'd known each other. I sensed disapproval in his glance when he looked at me. "Well, it won't be an easy process," he said. He told me I'd need a visa, that we'd have to apply for a marriage license, that we'd then have to find out what the laws were in Florida regarding the paperwork.

Anthony reached for my hand. He was completely unfazed. "That's all right," he said, smiling cheerfully. "We'll do whatever we need to do, won't we, Meg? We can do anything together, can't we?" From a narrow bench against the wall of the priest's office, Mom and Donald looked on without saying a word.

That night in our hotel room, I felt their eyes upon me. They were sitting on the edge of the bed, watching me as I stood in front of the mirror unclipping my hair. Beside my own reflection, in a trick of light, their two dark unmoving forms looked like the watchful animal statues you sometimes see outside rich people's houses. I imagined them as granite watchdogs guarding the gate to my future. *All you have to do is walk through the gate,* I thought. *All you have to do is pass between them and you're free.*

"You know, Margaret, your mother and I have been talking." Donald never called her "your mother," and instantly I felt a stripe of alertness up my back. "If you marry him, you need to know the consequences. Because if you do this, you'll only be able to come back to the States every five years."

"Five years?" I unraveled my braids and began brushing my hair, watching his shadowy form behind me. "Why five years?"

"That's just the way it'll be," he said. "And you should know that."

Did he honestly think the idea of not seeing them for five

or ten or twenty years would scare me? Because it didn't. Not for a second. I was ready to stay, I was ready for everything with him to end. My shoulders involuntarily gave a small shrug. And that's when I saw it: Donald's black outline moving backward and then forward as if he'd just been buffeted by the powerful gust of a passing truck.

We only had a few more days remaining. One afternoon, while Anthony and I were walking alone by the harbor, I could tell he was in a serious mood. "What is it?" I asked. "What's wrong?"

"I need to know that you'd be happy here, Meg, that you'd like living here. I'd never want to feel that I'd brought you all this way, and then was gone at work, and that you hated it. I couldn't bear it if I thought I'd made you unhappy."

"You won't ever do that. I promise you."

"Then stay now," he said, stopping and turning to me. A speedboat slapped the water as it whizzed by behind him. "Just for a few weeks, Meg, maybe until the end of August. To see if you really like it here, if you really could feel at home. I already spoke to my sister, and she said you'd be more than welcome to stay with her. Would you do that?"

We approached Mom and Donald with the idea as soon as we returned from our walk. Anthony was extremely polite to Donald; he called him "sir" and explained where I'd stay. He didn't come right out and say it, but it was obvious he wanted to impress upon them that everything would be proper, that I'd be well looked after.

I saw Donald's jaw clench. "No, I don't think that's a good

idea," he said. He put his hands in his pockets and looked away.

Anthony waited for him to say something more. When he didn't, he said, "I realize you haven't had much time to think about it, sir, but Meg and I both thought it would give her a chance to get to know Sydney better. To get a better idea of the city, the country. And my sister's home, as you saw for yourself, is quite roomy. And she's already said she'd love Meg's company."

Donald turned his head and looked at Anthony with an expression I'd never seen before. *One more word,* it seemed to say, *and it is at your own peril.* Even Anthony was taken aback. "I believe I already made myself perfectly clear," he said, as my mother moved beside him and silently slipped her hand under his arm. "And I already told you, *I don't think it's a good idea.*"

Even then I was not prepared for what happened the night before we were set to head home. The four of us were walking out of a restaurant where we'd just finished dinner, and Anthony and I held hands while Mom and Donald walked side by side toward the parking lot. Just as Anthony pulled out his keys to unlock his car door, Donald said, "We've been thinking things over." Anthony unlocked his door and reached inside to open the back door. "And we don't think this is going to work out."

Anthony stopped. He looked over the hood of the car at Donald as if he'd misheard. "We think she's too young to get married," Donald said. "This isn't going to happen."

I burst into tears. I felt as though I'd just been yanked out of a dream state. I was like the big fish Donald always let run out to sea at the end of his line, the ones he allowed to think had escaped, and then at a chosen moment reeled, in wide forceful tugs, back to the side of his boat. Anthony was instantly at my side, hugging me. I buried my head against his shoulder and sobbed. "It's all right, Meg." He rubbed the back of my head. "Love conquers all," he whispered. "Don't forget that. Love can withstand anything."

I never expected Mom and Donald to allow me to be alone with him after that, but they did. For an hour, they said, and then I needed to come back and pack. Anthony and I walked near the hotel. It was a clear night, warm enough to have worn a short-sleeved dress with no sweater.

"You are above the age of consent, Meg," he said. "You do realize that, don't you? That you could stay?"

I don't know how it's possible for time to slow to a near stop, for every moment to feel like an hour. But that's what happened as I went back and forth between picturing myself staying—and then their hatred for me if I did. I couldn't envision ever truly being free of them, not if they despised me; I also couldn't imagine standing in front of them, looking them in their eyes, and telling them good-bye forever. Anthony seemed to realize I was incapable of defying them.

"We'll just wait until you're ready, then," he said, soothingly. "And I'll write to you or call you every day, just as we've been doing. And when you're ready we'll get married, Meg. We will. We have all the time in the world."

I went back to the hotel room, opening the door quietly. One small lamp was lit beside Donald's side of the bed and my mother was already turned away from him, sleeping. Or pretending to be sleeping. "Come over here," Donald said softly. I walked over and stood next to the bed. "Did you do anything with him?"

I closed my eyes and sank down in myself. *Not now,* I thought. *Please not now.* "No, I didn't do anything. We just talked."

"How can I believe you?" I didn't answer. There was no use in answering, in protesting; there never was. He reached his hand under my dress, pulled aside the crotch of my panties and put a finger inside me. "Okay," he said after a moment. "You're still intact. Thank you very much."

We got on a plane the next day. We stopped en route in Tahiti, where Donald had planned for us to spend a few days, before heading home. The entire trip, Mom and Donald didn't mention his name again once. As far as they were concerned, it was over. To them, the chapter was closed.

It wasn't closed, though. Not for me, and not for Anthony. As soon as I got back, we wrote and called even more often than before. Mom and Donald saw his stacks of letters, but they had stopped making me read them aloud. Mainly, I think, it was because Donald seemed to consider the threat over and done with, a waste of his energy now. Instead, he took every opportunity to take me to his boat.

Within a month, I had regained some of my courage. Being so far from Anthony made me realize that I could either choose this half-life and this play-acting at being in love, or else I could take the leap and have faith. Again, Anthony asked me to marry him. He said he'd come to Florida and help me through all the paperwork. I said yes to him again. And this time, I was determined nothing would happen to unhinge me.

As if on cue, about a week later Donald said he wanted to hear Anthony's latest letter. It was almost as if he'd been reading my mind, waiting for the correct moment to intervene. As I pulled it from the blue airmail envelope, I pictured Mom and Donald again as granite guardians at the gate, and I remembered how I'd steeled myself in our hotel room to walk through it, to pass between them. This time I would.

"My darling Meg," I began reading. It must have seemed odd to me, he wrote, that he sounded unhappy when he had just found out that he had passed his exams. But he was just so lonely not having me with him to celebrate. It is the sort of time, he said, when you need to be with the one you love. His job interview was on Monday, but he was fairly confident he'd get it. When he eventually set up a practice, "it means we will be more than comfortably well-off."

The letter was shaking in my hand. I looked up at Mom and Donald on the sofa, and then took a deep breath and read on. What really was going to make his life complete, he wrote, was for me to be his wife and to have our children together. He said he never imagined that he could love anyone so much.

I folded the letter and put it back in the envelope. They were staring at me, waiting for me to say something. Suddenly I was terrified, like an animal that all at once realizes it is completely exposed to predators. What would they do to me?

"He's talking mighty serious," Donald said. I looked at my feet. "And I thought we already decided you were too young. Didn't we already decide that?"

My twentieth birthday was in less than a week. That was exactly how old my mother had been when she married my father. But right then I didn't feel twenty; I felt like a little girl still missing her two front teeth. Quietly I said, "He wants to come here."

"What's that?" Donald asked. "I didn't hear you."

"I said, he wants to come here." I looked up at him. "To Florida. He wants us to get married here. The first week of January." Donald and Mom looked at each other and then back at me. At the thought of Anthony getting on a plane, of his coming for me, I felt emboldened. "I love him, and he loves me. And we want to get married. It's what I want, and I am old enough to decide." They kept staring at me as if I was a space creature, as if they simply could not believe I was talking to them this way. "It's what I want," I said. "It's what he wants, too."

Donald got up from the sofa first. My mother stood next to him with the same scrunched expression she always got whenever Donald said how bad I smelled. Why did she hate me so much? What had I ever done to make her hate me that way?

"Well, far be it for us to stand in your way, then," Donald said. "You go ahead. But when the whole thing collapses, when you're stuck over in Australia with nothing and no one, don't come looking to us to help you. Because you won't find any help, Margaret. You remember that. You'll be totally on your own."

Anthony and I moved ahead quickly with our wedding plans. In mid-October, he wrote that he'd gotten the job he'd applied for and had a good prospect of getting an apartment nearby. He asked me about my dual American and British citizenship so he could get the paperwork moving with the immigration department, and then said he was hoping to arrive in Florida in January so we could be married the following week. He wrote out the proposed dates. He'd wait to hear back from me before he actually purchased the tickets, he said, but he thought it would be a good idea if we left for Australia the day after the wedding. That way we'd have a week together in Sydney before he started his new job.

It was the last letter, the last communication, I ever had from him. At first I thought there must be a problem with the mail, but after a few weeks went by with nothing I became desperate. "Are you sure nothing came?" I'd ask my mother as soon as I came home. "Sorry," she'd say. I tried several times to call him, but there was never an answer. By mid-November I could barely eat, barely get up in the mornings. I sobbed myself to sleep, and then woke in the middle of the night drenched in sweat.

Ever since his last letter, Mom and Donald never once mentioned Anthony's name. They never asked anything about how our wedding plans were progressing, or even if we'd changed our minds. It was almost as if they knew all along. They went about their business as if nothing strange was happening, and only one time, when I asked again if anything had come for me, did my mother say anything about him. "It should be obvious to you by now that he's lost interest in you, that he's moved on to someone else," she said. "Sometimes you can be such a stupid girl, Margaret."

I never found out what happened. All I knew was that my life felt over. By December I had stopped writing to him, stopped calling, and accepted the truth of what my mother had said. He'd lost interest in me.

Not long after Christmas, Donald asked me to drive with him to the market. I didn't care anymore what I did, where I went. I was numb. I sat next to him on the front seat, and as he drove he began grinning and tapping the steering wheel with his thumbs. "I've got something to tell you," he said.

I looked over at him, at his bald head, his thick black glasses, his gash for a mouth. I did not care, whatever it was.

"Your mother and I have decided we've been goin' on like this long enough. You know, that it's time we made everything legal."

"Really."

"Yep," he said. "We're goin' to pick a day."

What difference could that make to me? They'd been together nearly twenty years. How could it change anything? But I was wrong about that. And I also didn't realize what day they'd chosen.

Mom and Donald were married in a small ceremony at St. Patrick's church. Nick had come from Pensacola, and for practically the first time in his life had worn a suit and tie. I sat beside him, wearing a cream-colored dress, with my friend Mike Cobaugh. I felt as though someone surely would put a hand on my shoulder and wake me up.

It was the same day—in the same church, with the same priest—that Anthony and I had planned to be married.

From the deposition of Katherine Mann Beville, conducted by Richard Gilbert

"Are you related to Donald Sahlman Sr.?"

"He was my uncle."

"And who is your mother?"

"Jill Durham."

"What is her relationship with Donald Sahlman?"

"Brother and sister."

"And how much do you know Margaret?"

"I have had a lot of interaction with her through the years . . . family functions, family dinners, family excursions, birthday parties, Christmas, holidays, etc."

"Do you have any conclusions or opinions about Meg, Margaret?"

"I think she was absolutely the daughter that Uncle Donald never had. I think she was loved. I think she was looked after like every other child of a . . . normal home. I think they had the same concerns that I had when I raised my children: Were they getting enough, too much, not enough care, love, religion, guidance. If anything, maybe she was spoiled."

"Any other conclusions you have drawn from having observed her and her family relationship?"

"She loved Uncle Donald. There's no doubt about that. She was a very attentive daughter. If there's going to be a negative, it's that there was a little jealousy there with her mother. Donald was probably one of the most considerate, kindest men I've ever met in my life. . . . And Donald obviously had just about everything that money could buy. And the one thing he didn't have—I'll use his words. He told me one time, 'You know, I just want somebody that will go buy my underwear.' Pat was that person in his life . . . and he would have done anything for her. Nicholas and Margaret reaped the benefit of that love, of the devotion he had for Pat."

"You indicated there was a little jealousy. Who was jealous of whom?"

"When you take someone that is young and impressionable, sometimes their exposure to a lot of money and the things money can buy—it's like that television show, 'The Rich and the Famous.' I was raised around boats, and very nice big boats. But she wanted to be on the bow pulling it to the pier. You know, like, 'Here I am.' That type of thing."

"Was Margaret jealous of Pat or—"

"Yes. I think she would have liked to have been the object of that devotion, that attention."

"Did you ever see photographs that Donald Sahlman took of Margaret when she was in various states of undress?"

"Various states, no."

"Partial nudity?"

"That was sort of her typical mode of dress for quite a number of years."

"Did you ever observe Donald Sahlman manually examining Meg's breasts?"

"Yes. Margaret had a series of breast problems. I came to visit her right after her surgery, and she was sitting on the sofa in shorty pajamas. It was a very open household, but my house was, too. My kids would do the same thing. You know, 'Here, Mama, look at this. Here, Daddy, feel this. . . .' And one time, like I said, [she said] 'Does it feel like it's gone?'"

"Meg is the one who asked Don Sahlman to examine her breasts?"

"Right. She showed him."

"Physically, what did he do?"

"Touched the spot. . . . She was very much an attention-getter. She demanded that. That was a real big deal during that period of time."

"What was a big deal?"

"Margaret. Anything that she could have, or anything to bring into the focus—Margaret was very much a center-of-attention-type young lady."

"Did you ever become aware of Don Sahlman checking Meg's genitals for cleanliness?"

"No. I've heard that story lately, but I know nothing about it."

"Who did you hear that story from?"

"Pat."

"What did she tell you?"

"That it was one of the allegations."

"If you found out that it did in fact occur, would that surprise you about Donald Sahlman?"

"I'm going to have to be very honest with you. A lot of things I've heard surprise me. The validity of them—you would have to go a long way to convince me of that. None of this is representative of the man that I knew. . . . And the man is dead. I guess it's pure speculation at this point."

Fifteen

om, Granny and I moved into Donald's canal-front house on Occident Street, my mother and I both quit our jobs, and Nick returned to Tampa to marry a woman he'd never mentioned and none of us had met. Those were the outer changes, the visible ones, but over the next two years there were others as well. Flourishing in her new life of leisure, my mother threw herself into music, playing both violin and organ at St. Patrick's in addition to singing in the choir. She gave me the responsibility of taking care of the house—"You have nothing better to do"—and ever since Anthony's sudden silence had relegated to me all of the cooking, cleaning, shopping and gardening. The only life I had outside the house, outside of my almost daily trips to Donald's boat, consisted of daily runs through the neighborhood and occasional visits with friends. It wasn't much.

The truth was, I had succumbed to him. Donald was stronger, his will far more insistent, and I no longer had the strength to fight him. He monitored my whereabouts, abused me at home as soon as my mother left for church, he even followed me into the bathroom. His newest obsession, besides the status of my virginity, was my diet. He forced me to sit on the toilet and urinate in front of him; he put his fingers under my stream and then placed them in his mouth, informing me he could tell by the taste if I'd eaten sugar. Whenever his presence made it impossible for me to go, he turned on the bathtub full blast, as a kind of suggestive catalyst, and waited.

The biggest change in me was a loss of hope. Somewhere in some tiny crevice I'd always carried the belief that it would end one day, that something would happen to save me. But I no longer believed that. I was too depressed to even go to a job I'd once loved. Ever since Anthony's disappearance—which more and more I thought Donald had somehow engineered—I had come to envision myself in that house forever, scrubbing countertops and washing Granny's laundry and preparing gourmet meals: I saw the shadow of a life passing in front of me, the life of a stupid little nigger girl who was dependent on her parents' good graces to define her. My future, as far as I could see, had been obliterated.

Mom and Donald now decided what my day would be like, what my life would be like. And as a result, my greatest terror became of displeasing them, of angering them in the slightest way. I learned to be quiet when it suited them, perky and affectionate to them in front of guests, ever obedient. I sat on Donald's lap and hugged him; I started calling him "Daddy Donald" and my mother "Mommy." I was, finally, their perfect daughter.

No one, including my friends, knew what was truly happening to me. Over the years I'd become adept at putting on my cheerful face, at closing inner doors on command, and so they had no hint of my growing helplessness. They knew nothing about the nightmares that made me scream myself awake, or my fear of leaving the house alone during the day. In fact, if any of them had been told what I did one day, I'm quite sure they wouldn't have believed it.

Mom and Donald were away from the house. I was so damn tired of the abuse, I just wanted it to end. That's all I could think of. As I poured bleach into the washing machine, it struck me that maybe, in that pile of laundry, was my solution. *If you were blind he wouldn't want you anymore,* I thought. *If you couldn't see, he'd have to take pity on you.* I stared at the plastic bottle, and that's when I decided to do it. I dipped my fingers into the bleach and tilted my head back, letting it drip off my finger into my eyes. It burned horribly. *Good,* I thought. *It's working.* I stood there letting it burn, forcing myself not to flush it out with water, and started to see white spots. By the time Mom and Donald came home, my eyes were swollen shut. I opened a cabinet to clean, I told them, and bleach accidentally spilled into my eyes. They took me to an eye doctor, who told me I was going to be all right. *Damn,* I thought as we drove home. *Damn, damn, damn.*

A couple of weeks later I tried it again. This time I used lye. It was like having hot coals pressed on your eyeballs, but I did the same thing—just stood there, waiting for it to work. And then Mom and Donald came home again and took me to the same eye doctor. I made up another story. "Boy," the doctor said, "you're a regular Calamity Jane when it comes to your eyes, aren't you?" As soon as he said that, I knew I had to figure out something else. I was afraid they were onto me.

Nick was now living in a nearby apartment with his new wife, but the two of us were no closer than we'd ever been. When he started coming over to the house practically every day, throwing himself down on the sofa to watch television with Granny or rifle through the refrigerator, we barely said a thing to each other. Nick didn't look good. He was thin and acted strangely, chewing constantly at the skin around his fingernails, and I had no idea who he was anymore. "How's it going?" he'd ask. "Pretty good, Nick, how about you?" "Not bad." That was the extent of our exchanges. After a few months, he told us his wife was pregnant. After their son was born, once again he stopped coming over. None of us saw him again for another year.

In the summer of 1985, a few months before my twenty-third birthday, Donald decided to take Mom and me to Europe. Mike Cobaugh offered to house-sit with Granny and my mother's dog, just as he'd done when we went to Australia to see Anthony.

By then Mike and I had known each other nearly five years. He still worked at the Ford dealership, still was as responsible and grounded as ever, and we'd kept in touch through occasional dinners or movies together. Mike meant a lot to me. He cared about me, and our friendship was as important as the ones I had with Darley or Terry or Kathleen Macado Murphy, who'd married shortly after we were in college and already had two children. Even Mom and Donald seemed to understand the nature of my relationship with him, which is probably why he'd long ago ceased being a threat to them.

As usual, Donald wanted only the best. He booked us on a top-of-the-line tour through Germany, Austria, Switzerland, Italy and France, with accommodations in five-star hotels. The tour bus was comprised of all Americans, mainly retired couples or elderly women with lacquered blue-gray hair, and with the exception of the driver, a German man named Hans Meixner, I was by decades the youngest person on the bus.

Donald seemed to like Hans Meixner. When the bus stopped at a Hofbrauhaus for lunch along the Rhine or a restaurant in Vienna, Donald sat next to him and got into good-natured debates about the stock market. Hans was in his thirties, from a town called Augsburg, and conducted the tours for Olsen Travel in Tampa. As he drove he spoke into a microphone, telling us in sometimes fractured English about the historical sights outside our windows. Sometimes, from where I sat beside Mom and Donald in the last row, I saw his eyes watching me in his rearview mirror. Donald saw it, too.

The first hint of problems came in Zurich. A woman at the hotel's front desk informed Donald that it wasn't possible to get a third bed into a single room. The instant I saw a flash of anger cross his face, I walked quickly across the lobby and sat down with several other members of the group so I wouldn't have to hear what he said. Later that night, Hans showed up at our hotel room. As soon as he saw the small cot that had been brought up, he apologized to Donald and said he'd just learned of it. There must have been some oversight, he said. He'd get a second room for us at no cost right away.

At first Hans seemed confused when Donald turned him down. Then he assumed he'd been misunderstood. "Mr. Zallmann," he said in his thick accent, "ze room, it is free to you. No charge to you for ze room. Ze tour pays. I take care of it right now, yes?" I went into the bathroom. Even with the door closed, I could hear Donald saying something angrily and then the slam of the hotel room door.

Hans clearly liked me. Whenever we were sightseeing he walked beside me whenever he could, and at dinnertime, whenever I came down the hotel's wide staircase in one of my long gowns, he told me how lovely I looked. But I didn't always come down for dinner. Some nights Donald told my mother to go down without us. "Make our excuses, Pat," he'd say. "I'm not hungry." She never asked why I had to stay, too. One night after my mother left me alone with him, I went to the window, pulled the curtain aside and looked down onto the street just as the group was leaving the hotel for a nearby restaurant. At that moment Hans looked up. I waved and smiled, and he waved back. But a baffled look crossed his face. "Get away from that window," Donald said.

In Venice, Hans asked whether I'd like to go with him on a gondola ride that evening. I was dying to get away from the hotel and almost told him yes on the spot, but there was no question of not first getting permission. "Just make sure you're back by eleven," Donald said. "Not a minute later."

Hans was a nice man, self-assured and almost overly polite, although I sensed in him the kind of strong will that could bulldoze over someone like me. He had dark blond hair, a high forehead and an aquiline nose, and in profile he reminded me of an ancient Roman coin. As we floated down the canal and listened to a mandolin on another gondola nearby, he leaned over and kissed me. He told me over and over how beautiful I was, how he'd never met anyone like me, and that maybe he would come visit me in America after the tour was finished. Would I like it if he did that?

My first thought wasn't whether I truly would want that: It was of Donald's face when Hans showed up in Tampa. And that was when I looked at my watch. "Oh God," I said. "We have to go back. Make him turn around."

Hans reacted to my curfew the same way Mike Cobaugh had the first time he'd taken me to his apartment. The difference was that Hans protested a lot longer and made no attempt to communicate my plight to our gondolier. "What does zis matter if you come five minutes late?" he asked. "You are a grown woman, yes? I do not understand zis, you have to be at zis time home. Why you so afraid? Why you get worried like zis? Explain to me." There was no time to explain, I said. The gondola continued to move down the canal as if through molasses.

When I opened our hotel room door, Donald was waiting with the lights on. My mother, her back to him, was lying on her side. He told me to come over to the bed and slip off my slacks, and then inserted his finger into me. "You're wet!" he yelled. "You've been having sex with him, haven't you? Tell me the truth!" Even though I could hear her shallow breathing, my mother didn't move.

Nothing I said to him made any difference. "Go to bed, Margaret." There was something in his voice that made me know he wasn't done with it. I lay on the narrow cot, trembling. All through that night, any time their mattress moved, I was certain he was getting out of bed to come over to me. I couldn't sleep at all. I had one thought: *Something bad is coming.*

From Venice we traveled to Monte Carlo. It was there that Donald walked up to Hans and tapped him on the shoulder. I was too far away to hear, but Hans kept shaking his head and gesturing with his hands. Later, in a rare moment when I was alone, Hans whispered to me that he'd been warned to stay away from me. "I hate him!" I hissed. "He's not even my father! I don't care what he says!"

"He seems very angry," Hans said. "Maybe we should not cause trouble."

For the next few days, Hans kept his distance from me. I thought it might blow over if I did the same thing, but I was wrong. Our first night in Paris, the entire group went on a dinner cruise on the Seine River. We were all seated at one long table under a string of lights on the upper deck when Donald suddenly pushed his chair back and walked over to Hans seated near the end. He leaned over and said something in a low voice, and Hans said something back to him. Suddenly Donald yelled, "I know you fucked my daughter! Don't tell me you're not fucking her! Because I *know* you're fucking her!"

Hans looked as if he'd been slugged in his face. The entire group was instantly silent. They all stared at Donald, forks held mid-air, and watched as he marched over and grabbed my arm. "Come on," he said, yanking me from the table. "Right now! We're not sitting here!" My mother followed as he led me to the bow. I was so mortified I wanted to drown myself in the river right then and there. The three of us stood, our backs to the group, until the boat docked.

At the hotel, Donald threw his suitcase onto the bed and began tossing clothes into it. "Go on, get your things," he growled, balling up a cashmere sweater and stuffing it under a pile of shirts. "Hurry up, both of you." Wordlessly my mother and I retrieved clothes from the closet and then carried our haphazardly packed suitcases down to the lobby. No one from the group had returned yet. Donald went up to the man behind the reception desk and asked him to call us a taxi to take us to the airport. We needed to go home right away.

Our dog, he told him, was very sick.

My mother's dog, of course, was fine. It was Mike Cobaugh
who looked sick when we walked in the door. At first I
thought he was just thrown off-guard by our unannounced
arrival. "What's the matter, Mike?" I asked. "Is everything
okay?"

"Everything's fine." Mike stood in the entryway with his
hands clasped behind his back, awkwardly shifting from one
foot to the other. "I guess I got the days mixed up. Anyway,
Granny's asleep and the dog's out back. But why don't I talk
with you tomorrow, Meg, all right? I'm kinda tired. And you
must be, too."

Mom and Donald were standing right beside me and so I
just nodded. "Sure, Mike. We are kind of tired, actually. We
had to wait at the airport."

"And thank you so much for everything," my mother said
as Mike walked outside. "We couldn't have taken the trip
without your help."

"That's right," Donald drawled. "We really 'preciate ever-
thin' you did." Mike turned and looked at them as they stood
in the doorway. He had an expression I'd never seen on his
face—disgust mixed with disbelief. I had no idea what he was
thinking, or whether Mom and Donald had noticed it, but a
chill went through me all the same.

The next day Mike came over to the house while Mom and
Donald were out doing an errand. While Granny watched
television in the living room, we went into my bedroom and
sat on the edge of the bed. "I need to talk with you," he said.
Slowly he reached into the pocket of his jacket and pulled
out a thick envelope. He didn't look at me—he kept staring

at his hands. For a long while he didn't say anything. "I—I want to ask you something, Meg."

"Sure, Mike."

"I don't know how to say it. This isn't easy for me."

"Just say it." I leaned over and smiled at him. "It's me, okay? Just say it."

"Meg, is your father having sex with you?"

I can't tell you how many times I've played that moment over and over in my head: how my heart seemed to stop beating, how my body went numb, how my cheeks felt implanted with hot embers. I've gone back and thought: *What if I'd been able to let it all go right then?* What would Mike have done? Would my life from then on have been different? It's the same thing I've done hundreds of times about Anthony: Who would I be today if I'd stayed with him in Australia, if only I'd had the courage to watch them board the airplane, if only I'd grasped the lifeline when it was tossed out to me?

But as Mike waited, staring down into his hands, I couldn't see that far. The only thing I could think of was what Donald had always told me, the years and years of warnings he'd issued: *Bad things will happen if you tell anyone, Margaret. Very bad things. And you know that's true, you know it. You'll burn in hell. . . .*

"That's crazy," I stammered. "Why would you say something like that?"

Finally he looked up at me. "Because I found these." He raised the envelope a few inches and then let it fall back in his lap as if it was too heavy to lift. "I was up in the attic. And

I found these pictures, Meg." He was shaking; he was terribly upset. "And Meg," he said, his voice trembling, "this isn't right. This isn't normal. A father . . . it's—it's—"

"It's nothing, Mike. So you found pictures. They're just a bunch of—"

What? What could I tell him? Donald must have taken thousands of pictures of me over the years. It didn't matter which ones Mike had seen. They were all bad, all horrid. And Mike had to think I was filthy and horrid, too. He had to feel disgust for me. I couldn't bear the thought of his having seen me that way.

I bolted into the bathroom and locked the door behind me. *Oh God, oh God, oh God. What am I going to do? He knows. He knows!*

"Meg," he said softly. "Open the door, Meg. Please open it."

I crumpled to the floor. *Make this not be happening, God. Please make this go away. Donald will think I told him. He'll never believe me. . . .* With my head on the floor, I could see the tips of his tennis shoes in the slat above the tiles.

"Meg, I'm your friend. I want to help you. I'm not judging you. Please believe me. Please. Open the door."

"Go away, Mike."

"Meg, I know how difficult this must be for you, but—"

"Go away, Mike! I don't want you here. I mean it. Leave me alone. Just leave!"

For a few seconds, the only sound was his breathing, a creaking floorboard. And then silence. The tips of his tennis shoes moved away from the door.

Mike would never have anything to do with me again after

that. All those years I'd kept the ugly truth from him, concealed it as certainly as if I'd lied to him. And now that he knew who I really was, what I was, he'd run from me as if from a dreaded disease. The idea of it had to be totally repulsive to him. How couldn't it be?

At least, that was what I'd assumed. And that was why I was so stunned when he called me only a few days later. "Don't hang up, Meg," he said rapidly. "Just listen to me for a minute, Meg. I know what's been going on, and I'm not judging you for it, you have to believe me, but you can't pretend like this hasn't happened. I'm just trying to help you. What your father did—"

Donald had just come into the kitchen and was now standing next to my elbow. It was as if his internal radar system had switched on the minute I picked up the phone, as if he'd known instantly that whatever I was hearing from Mike concerned him. He glared at me as if he'd already heard every word Mike had said. Silently I handed the phone to him.

"Hello?" he said.

For a few seconds, Donald just listened. "You've got the wrong idea about that, Mike," he said. In a reasonable tone of voice he started talking about how normal it was, that Mike obviously had misconstrued everything, that these were just pictures and all families did this, no no no, Mike was wrong. But Mike wasn't buying it. "How dare you make such an insinuation!" Donald yelled. "How dare you!"

My mother, who had been listening from the doorway, disappeared into the next room. A few seconds later I heard her screeching into the extension phone. "You swine!" she screamed. "You disgusting swine!" And then Donald slammed down the receiver. He was shaking with rage.

My mother came marching back into the kitchen. "You see, Donald? I told you we never should have kept those pictures around," she said. "I told you someday somebody would find them, didn't I?"

"Who does he think he is?" Donald bellowed. "Just who the hell does he think he's talkin' to?"

That was nearly eight years ago. I never saw or heard from Mike ever again.

Sixteen

Father Fausto once told me that God never closes a door without also opening a window. I wasn't sure what he meant. At the time I imagined it had something to do with always having enough air or being given at least the bare minimum you needed to survive, but later, after Mike disappeared, it struck me that maybe he'd meant something different. Maybe Father Fausto was saying that God always leaves you an escape route, even if it isn't the one you might have imagined. That sometimes you have to climb through a window instead of walk out a door.

I missed Father Fausto. He'd been with our parish for several years, but then he got transferred to another parish in St. Petersburg. Later on he got moved again to another congregation down in Sarasota, which meant I saw him even less often. He was in great demand, and people loved him. Still, even though he got moved around a lot, we'd always stayed in touch. We talked on the phone, and every year on my birthday we had lunch together at a restaurant. It was a ritual we had managed to maintain for several years, and September 1986, the year I turned twenty-four, had been no exception. Over salad and pasta we talked about Mom and Donald's health, the renovation at St. Patrick's, how everyone at church was doing—easy subjects that couldn't cause any trouble.

I never came right out and said it, but I think Father Fausto knew how I felt about the priest who'd replaced him. Father Venard Moffitt had always been cordial to me, but there had always been something about him that made me uneasy, something I didn't quite trust. Maybe it was the way Father Venard and Donald looked so much alike—they were both the same height and build, both bald with thick glasses—or because the two of them had become such instant friends. Within just a few months of his arrival Father Venard had begun coming regularly to our house for dinner, and not long after that he appointed Donald to St. Patrick's finance committee. Just about everyone at church could tell they had a deep connection, the kind you don't see very often in grown men.

There were times when I thought about calling Father Fausto and telling him the truth about how I was doing,

about asking for his guidance. But unless I told him everything, it would have been like giving him just the first page of
a book. I could hardly say I thought about killing myself
every day without saying why, and if I didn't, what use would
his counsel have been to me then? You can hardly take someone's advice if they don't know all the facts, and no one knew
the facts about what Donald did to me. And so no one, in my
mind, could help me.

But maybe that's where God's window came in.

In October, Darley and her boyfriend convinced me to go
with them to a Halloween party. I'd never really liked being
around lots of people, but Darley kept saying it would be fun.
"Doing something new is good for you, Meg," she said. "You
can't be a nun forever." I ended up going as a harem girl, with
a translucent scarf over my nose and mouth and a red rhinestone glittering in my navel.

The party was held in a large house on a lake. The house
was packed, the music vibrating the floorboards, and people
were spilling out from the living room onto a dimly lit balcony. After a while Darley and her boyfriend disappeared
among the dancing throng. Alone, I made my way over to the
refreshment table. It was there that a nice-looking guy came
up to me and introduced himself.

Right off the bat, I could tell Tom Cassedy was one of those
super-responsible types who takes care of business first and
plays later. Even before he told me he was a stockbroker, I figured by his neatly trimmed mustache and perfect fingernails
that he'd be something conservative like that—a banker or
insurance agent, maybe—and when he told me he played

sports at his club every day after work, it didn't surprise me one bit. Somehow I got the courage to ask if he wanted to play racquetball with me the next day, and immediately he said yes. From then on we saw each other nearly every day.

I'm not going to lie and tell you I fell madly in love with the man. Besides, whatever part of me ever had been able to feel that was probably long gone, long dead. So was the stupid girl who went to Australia and believed those whispered words about love conquering all. Love didn't conquer anything. What mattered to me was that Tom was sensible and self-confident. Even Mom and Donald said he seemed like a nice young man after the four of us went out on the boat one weekend, a trip Donald had suggested to meet this new person in my life. They still checked me after practically every date—at one point, my mother asked Donald if I wasn't getting too old for it—but at least they didn't object to Tom the way they had to Hans. Tom was educated and well-spoken and obviously successful, and to me he was attractive in a predictable, grounded kind of way. I liked the idea that there wouldn't be any surprises, that what you saw would be what you got. But most of all, I liked it that he was crazy about me.

After a few months Tom and I began going over to his house in the evenings, where we kissed and got excited and then had to calm down before I went home again. As long as I remained a virgin, Donald could keep inspecting me until hell froze over. I hated it as much as ever, but as long as he never found anything I'd be all right. *But what,* I wondered, *would happen if that ever changed?* And just as important, what if that never did? If I let things go on as they had for seven months now, I saw Tom going the way of Anthony, the way of Mike. Something would happen to make him disappear. I couldn't let that happen; Tom was my only hope, my only chance of getting out.

I lost my virginity much in the same way I had dashed from the sauna in Aspen years earlier and jumped into the snow, my brain overriding every rational instinct that told me not to do it. I didn't allow myself to think about what would come afterwards; I blotted it from my mind. I concentrated only on the fact that Tom was tender and sweet, that there was very little pain. After it was over I lay on his bed and stared up at the ceiling and could not stop the thought that came: *That was it? That was the big huge deal?* Tom reached over, stroked my hair and smiled at me. "You're so beautiful," he said. "I wish you could stay here forever." I smiled back and kissed him.

And then the shock came. It was as sudden as if I'd just plunged into ice water. I pictured Donald hovering between my legs: *She's not intact, Patricia! Look here!* and my heart felt as if someone had stomped on my chest. If Mom and Donald told me to strip down, I'd have to do it. And Donald would know, instantly. *Oh God, oh God, oh God . . . help me God.* I looked at Tom's bedside clock. The later I arrived home, the greater the chance they'd inspect me. That's always how it worked: *Why are you ten minutes late, Margaret? What have you been doin'? I'm sorry, but we have to check you.*

My only hope was to get back to the house right away. It wasn't 10:00 P.M. yet; I could walk in and pretend as though I'd had a terrible time. Or maybe a fight with Tom. Stomp around, act mad. That would put them off, that would throw them off the track. *That's it. You can look like you asked him to bring you back early, that you wanted to come home. Donald taught you to act, and you're good at it. So act. You can do it, Meg.* Tom had no idea why I ran into the bathroom and began soaping myself to get his smell off of me, or why I ran back into the bedroom and began pulling on my clothes like a crazy woman.

By the grace and mercy of God, they went to bed as soon as I got home and left to do errands early the next morning. As soon as they were gone I leaped out of bed and paced through the house like a frantic zoo animal, back and forth, trying to figure out what to do. I couldn't stay, that was certain. They'd find out. I had to get away. There was no other choice.

I called Tom at his office and told him I was moving in with him. He had to come over right away. I was already gathering up my things; he had to hurry because my parents couldn't find out. Tom must have heard the panic in my voice. He didn't say a word about being in the middle of a trade or that he'd just arrived at the office or anything else like that. "You're sure you want to do this?" he asked. "You're positive you want to do it this way?" I almost screamed yes. He said he'd be right over.

Next I called Darley and told her the same thing. By the time she arrived I already had two trash bags filled with clothes and haphazardly was throwing the contents of my closet into a third. I nearly jumped out of my skin every time I thought I heard Donald's Lincoln coming back, but I kept moving. Darley and I hauled the bags to the front door just as Tom drove up. We carried them outside and threw them into the trunk of his car.

"You did it, Meg!" Darley said. "You go, girl! You finally did it!"

I couldn't answer. My heart was beating too fast. I jumped into the front seat of Tom's Mercedes and adjusted the side mirror. My hands were trembling. It wasn't over yet; Donald's red Lincoln could turn the corner at any second.

"Drive, Tom!" I didn't take my eyes off the mirror. "Go! Get me out of here!"

Part II

Refuge

I have long time holden my peace; I have been still, and refrained myself: now will I cry like a travailing woman. . . .

—Isaiah 42:14

. . . *A*nd he that departeth from evil maketh himself a prey: and the Lord saw it, and it displeased him that there was no judgment.

—Isaiah 59:15

Seventeen

CLIENT FILE: Margaret "Meg" Cassedy
INTERVIEW: Second Session; February 1993
SUBJECT: Client's Background Statement, Continued
ATTORNEYS PRESENT: Richard Gilbert, Lynwood Arnold

I was too frightened to stay at Tom's house on West Angeles after we dropped off my things and he went back to work. Mom and Donald knew where he lived, and I was certain they'd come looking for me. Tom didn't believe that—it was obvious he thought I was being paranoid—but finally he gave in and drove me over to a friend's house. He told me he'd come back for me as soon as he could.

All day long I stayed in a chair by a window, thinking about what I'd done, picturing their faces when they discovered I was gone. There was no going back now. Not now, not ever again. I'd finally broken out, finally gotten away. And once they realized where I was they'd—what? What would they do? *I can't think about that now. Don't think about that, Meg, think about something else.* From now on, Tom would be my only source of security. But he'd take care of me, I was sure of that; he'd do for me what my mother never had. Tom would protect me from Donald; he'd be my watchdog at the gate. Never again would Donald touch me; never again would I have to endure one more second of it. *It's finally over,* I thought. *Over, over, over.*

I stayed curled in the chair and stared out the window until the sun went low in the sky and the light turned egg-yolk orange through the curtains. Finally, Tom came back to get me. I huddled next to him in the front seat as he drove and glanced at every red car that went by. Only as he approached his house did I ask him to slow down in case they were there. Tom didn't say anything, but I know he thought I was just acting crazy. "Don't worry, Meg," he said. "Everything's fine."

And then we pulled into the carport and walked toward the front door. It was Tom who first saw what Mom and Donald had done. Strewn across his front porch were my clothes I'd left behind, shoes, old stuffed animals, as if a cyclone had touched down just at his house.

It's strange: I can remember the license plate number of Donald's white car in Guyana, but I can't remember much about the next few weeks. I remember lying in Tom's bed and staring at the ceiling; Tom calling up to me from downstairs, telling me to pick up the phone; my mother's voice, screeching horrible names, unspeakable names. Curling into a ball. Tom soothing me, telling me it was all right.

But it wasn't all right.

After the phone call, we didn't talk to them again. Not for what seemed like ages. Still, in my mind they were always there; they might as well have had their noses pressed up against Tom's windows, watching me. The moment Tom left for work each day I locked the doors and pulled the curtains closed. *Stay upstairs, Meg, they can't see you there. And don't think about them. I can't read, can't pay attention to the words. So watch television, Meg. Yeah, that helps. But maybe I'll turn out like Granny, staring at the screen all day, shuffling to the bathroom and back. You'll be okay, Meg. How many days has it been now? Day thirty-two. Day thirty-three. Don't count. Are you feeling a bit better? I think so. I only thought about them four times today.*

And then the nausea. Huge waves of it that sent me spinning, reeling, into the bathroom. *Oh God, this time it's not them doing it to me. I know what it is. Please don't let it be that. But my breasts are big and sore, and I can't stand even the smell of food. Oh, God, this is worse than losing my virginity. They're going to kill me. They can't ever know about it.*

"What do you mean we can't tell them?" Tom said. "You think you're going to hide a baby from them? How long do you think you can do that?"

How could I ever make him understand? He couldn't, ever. "I don't know, Tom, but you have to promise me you won't say anything, promise me! Just not now, Tom, please don't tell them now, promise me you won't. I have to do it when I'm ready."

"Then can we at least tell them we're getting married, Meg? Will you at least let me call them up, maybe invite them to dinner somewhere? See if we can all call a truce? We're going to have to talk with them sometime, you know."

"You can't tell them about the marriage. Not yet. Do you promise me? You have to let me do it my own way. Please don't tell them."

Tom shrugged. "Whatever makes you happy."

Mom and Donald agreed to meet us at a restaurant in St. Petersburg. Tom did all the talking. He handled them politely, firmly, as if they were prospective clients. It must have been obvious to them that Tom wasn't going to be like Anthony, that he was used to taking control of things; and with Tom acting so sure of himself like that, there was really nothing they could do. So they put on their best faces for him. Tom said later in the car that he thought everything went well, that he was glad we'd patched everything up.

For the next few weeks, Mom or Donald phoned me almost every day. They both acted as if nothing at all had happened, as if my living with Tom was no longer something that concerned them in the slightest. "I just wanted to see how you're doing," my mother said. "So are you ever going to come over and see us again?" Donald drawled pretty much the same thing. "We sure miss you," he'd say. "You know, we should all go out on the boat again. Why don't you ask Tom about it?" I wanted to believe so much they'd let me go, that they were going to allow me to go on with my life, but I couldn't. In the back of my mind was the memory of Australia, of how they'd told me I'd only be able to come home every five years; and their silence, their watchfulness, while Anthony and I wrote about our plans to be married. Maybe they were doing the same thing now. Maybe they were waiting for just the right moment to ruin my life again, and I just couldn't envision how they'd accomplish it. Tom kept telling me everything was going to be fine, but I kept thinking, *You just don't know them.*

One afternoon I heard a car pull into Tom's carport behind my Camaro. Even before I pulled aside the curtains I knew what I'd see, but the sight of the red Lincoln still made my heart thud. He knew I was home. "Well," Donald said, grinning at me as I stood in the doorway. "I was just in the neighborhood, just coming back from the office." He'd been doing that for some time now—going to Sahlman Seafoods for an hour or two a few times a week, although I had no idea what he did when he got there. I kept my hand on the doorknob and smiled as if nothing could have made me happier than to see him. "Anyway, I thought I'd stop in and see the place. So aren't you goin' to ask your old dad inside? Or do I have to stand here all day?"

He stepped inside the hallway and casually asked if Tom was home. I told him I expected him at any moment. Tom, in fact, was probably already on his way home. "Really?" he said, glancing around. "He gets home this early, does he?"

"He does today," I said. "His schedule's always different."

He smiled. "Is that so? Then we just have time for a quick one."

"Tom's on his way home, really he is. He could come in any second."

"Then we have to hurry, don't we? Unless you want him to see? Do you want that?" He stared at me a moment, and then walked over to the bottom of the stairs. "Do I take it correctly that the bedroom's up there?"

He walked up the stairs in front of me until he reached the landing. He turned and looked around, as if he expected me to give him a tour of the house. "Well?"

Finally I said, "It's over there."

"Well, come on then, Margaret. Let's see this bedroom of yours."

He did everything quickly. He washed me as I sat on the edge of Tom's bathroom sink, laid me down on Tom's dark green sheets, did what he'd always done. The whole time I was straining to hear Tom's car, petrified. When it was over he pulled on his clothes. "That's all we have time for now," he said. But he didn't leave right away, not even when he saw me trembling. He had to go through his ritual: running his fingers in short jerks down his cheeks, and then spitting into the bathroom sink. "Gotta always milk the saliva glands. Get the germs out, you know?" He winked at me. "I don't want to catch nothin' from you, Margaret."

When he left the house that day, I had, for the second time in my life, the most sinful of thoughts. As I watched him climb into his Lincoln and back out the driveway, a small voice rose up in me. *I wish you were dead,* it whispered. *I wish you'd just die.*

I drove over to their house one day in August. I was better; I had the courage to tell them now. Tom and I have decided to get married, I said. We don't want to wait any longer. "Really," my mother said. "Is that so?" Donald added. Yeah, and we want it to be in October, I told them. Tom and I were thinking we probably should go over and talk with Father Venard about the ceremony. Did they maybe want to come, too?

Donald took two steps toward me and jabbed a finger at my face. "So that's what you all were thinkin'? Let me tell you somethin'. Because you're not getting married at *our* church, Margaret. Not where our friends could see you, not after what you've done. Everyone knows about it, I can tell you that, and if you think you're wearin' white when everyone knows what you are, you've got another thing comin'. You're goin' to have to wear a black dress to your weddin'. Only *virgins* can wear white."

I ran out of the house in tears. When I told Tom what they'd said he put his arm around me and said, "Then they just won't come, Meg. That's their choice."

From then on, I let Tom take care of everything. He did better with them, made them at least pretend to be reasonable, and somehow he convinced them that St. Patrick's was the only logical place to have the wedding. Tom and I took everything in small steps, and every time things were going well he said not to worry, that we'd have a beautiful wedding. I didn't even care about it, really; if someone could have stamped my hand and pushed me through a turnstile I would have done it.

A few weeks later, when things had calmed down again, I mentioned to my mother that I was thinking of calling my grandmother and tracking down some of my cousins. My father's mother had kept in touch with me over the years by sending birthday and Christmas cards, and maybe she'd have some addresses. "I'm not goin' to pay for one cent, or walk you down the aisle if you invite even *one* of your nigger relatives," Donald said, stomping into the kitchen. "I don't want one nigger face at the church, Margaret. You got that?"

That night, Tom asked me where I wanted to go on our honeymoon. We hadn't discussed it, and until then I hadn't even given it any thought. But now I didn't need to. It was Donald who'd made me realize where I needed to go.

"Can we go anywhere, Tom?"

"Anywhere you want. Name the place."

"Are you sure? We can go anywhere in the world?"

"Meg! I love you! Just tell me where you want to go!"

"I want to go to Barbados, Tom."

One of his eyebrows lifted quizzically, but Tom didn't ask me why. "You want to go to Barbados?" He smiled. "Then that's where we'll go."

All my life, my parents had told me never to reveal I was half-black to anyone. And so, of course, I'd never told Tom anything except that I was "from the islands." I have no idea what my husband of two days thought of me as we stepped off the plane in Barbados, or when three of my father's brothers and two of his sisters embraced me, or when I asked to be driven to my father's unmarked grave at an over-grown cemetery at the top of a lush green hillside. Maybe Tom was thinking about the baby inside me, and whether it would have the dark mocha coloring of my relatives. Maybe he was listening to my Aunt Louise when she put her hands on my face and told me I looked just like my father, that it was as if she was seeing her brother's tiny ghost.

All I know for certain is that while I laid flowers on the patch of ground my aunt had pointed to, a narrow strip of earth with a small wooden cross I easily could have walked past, Tom waited in the car. He might have seen me kneel, but he couldn't have heard me tell my father how I wished to God I'd known him, or how I prayed he wasn't ashamed of me now. Tom couldn't have seen the tears on my face, and he didn't hear me whisper how sorry I was it took me so long to come home.

✝   ✝   ✝

From the deposition of Thomas Cassedy, direct examination conducted by Charlie Luckie

"Did Margaret ever tell you that Donald Sahlman had abused her in any way?"

"No."

"Did she ever express to you during the marriage that she was fearful of him in any way?"

"Her relationship with her father was very strange. She envisioned him or saw him as an extremely pow-erful man. She said that to me on quite a few occasions."

"Powerful in what way?"

"Just like omnipotent, like he was God or something. Yes, he had money and that sort of thing, but she treated him like he was God. It was a difficult thing, and we ran into a lot of problems in the marriage because of this. She would do things and make decisions in reference to how her father or mother would look at it, rather than make her own decisions. . . . She was in awe of the guy. I told her, 'Sometimes I feel like I'm married to your dad.'"

"Has she, since this lawsuit has been started, talked to you about her relationship with Don Sahlman?"

"No. I personally don't want to have anything to do with this lawsuit. The whole thing disgusts me. I think it's despicable, and I just don't want to talk to her about it. I don't really want to talk to anybody about it."

"You supposedly may testify about Margaret Cassedy's emotional and psychological dysfunctions."

"Well, the more I've gotten to know her, I think she definitely had some psychological problems, or seems to. One of the problems with Margaret is that she has a problem telling the truth. It's something that I experienced in the marriage, something I've experienced after our marriage. And she has a hard time dealing with facts and reality. I'm not really sure what caused that. Maybe self-denial in her past."

"You said that Margaret considered Don Sahlman to be sort of godlike. Did she appear to be afraid of him?"

"Sometimes she was terrified of the man, and sometimes he was the greatest thing in the world. I mean, that's the way the relationship was. He was like her darling and that sort of thing sometimes. He was cuddly and lovely with her, or she was terrified of the man."

"In what types of situations was she terrified of him?"

"A perfect example was when she moved out. That one day she was absolutely terrified of him."

"Any time after that?"

"Yeah. At a time when she did something that she thought might displease him, that's when she was terrified of him—if it was something she thought he might think was not the right thing."

"How would you describe your relationship with Don Sahlman?"

"Friendly. I mean, Don and Pat were strange in certain ways. Sometimes I got along with them, sometimes I didn't."

"How about your relationship with Pat?"

"I had an okay relationship with her. We weren't close. I had never really gotten along with them that well. I thought they treated Meg very, very poorly."

"In what way?"

". . . They did some very, very ugly, mean things to her. I thought they were more concerned about what appeared good to the community than what was best for their daughter. . . . And I don't think they were very honest and direct with people. A perfect example is the time we told them that Meg was pregnant. I was the one who had to tell them because she was too terrified. . . . We told them after the wedding. They were like, 'Oh, that's great, congratulations, that's just wonderful, we're so happy for you.' Then they didn't talk to us for two months."

✝ ✝ ✝

Deposition cross-examination, conducted by Richard Gilbert

"Mr. Cassedy, you talked about Meg being terrified and you related one incident of that as an example when she moved out of the house. Were you with her when she moved out of the house?"

"Yes. I actually physically went over to the house and helped her move the stuff."

"How did she arrange for that to occur?"

"She called me on the phone. She told me she was going to move out, and she said, 'I don't want my father or mom to know, so come over here right now.' It was kind of, Boom! It was very clandestine. She was terrified. It was like a person running or escaping from jail."

"What did you all do?"

"I went over there. Darley was there, and we loaded up my car. We took it to my house and put it inside the house, and then she would not stay at the house. I said, 'Look, you can lock the door.' She was afraid her father was going to come get her. . . . I said, 'He's not going to break down the door,' but she would have nothing to do with it. It was like her life was going to end. She was just whacked out."

"What did you do then?"

"I left her at a friend's house. I had a meeting with a client at five o'clock that evening. I went out and saw him, came back, picked her up at the friend's house, and then we went back to my house. We drove up in the driveway and there was stuff all over my front porch. Meg was very upset and cried. The whole thing. I said, 'Don't worry about it.' We took the stuff and put it in the house."

"Did you have any conversations with Don or Pat about Meg's coming to live with you?"

"Not immediately, not within the first day or two. But there was a time, about a week later, of trying to get them back together. Her brother Nicholas called the house, and I talked to Nicholas. I wouldn't let Meg answer the phone."

"Why not?"

"She was just so upset. I wanted her to calm down a little bit. She was really unstable."

"This is a week after she moved?"

"Yeah. Nicholas had called and said, 'Hey look, Tom. You know, I think Mom and Dad have calmed down a little bit, and I'm going to call and get them to talk to Meg.' So one night I was at home. The phone rang. I picked it up . . . [and] Don and Pat got on the phone. I was downstairs on the downstairs phone, and she was upstairs in the bedroom. I called up to her and said, 'Meg, pick up the phone. I want you to talk to your mom and dad.' So they started talking. Don was a little calmer of the two. Then they had a conversation that lasted a few minutes. And then it got pretty ugly, to say the least."

"What was said as best you can recall?"

"Don got on the phone and said, 'Hi Meg,' and they were talking. Then Meg's mother started saying some things that were—she called Meg a whore and a bitch. And to be honest with you, some much uglier words than that. A cunt. I don't think she knew I was on the phone. I hung up and went upstairs and told Meg to get off the phone. There was no point in her getting all upset again. She had calmed down a little bit—this was a week or two weeks later—and here her mother was just reaming her out again. I just said, 'Look, Meg, you don't need this.' I told her to get off the phone. All I know is that the conversation started out okay, and then it went downhill real fast."

"Did Meg say anything to cause the conversation to go downhill?"

"No. Meg is like this terrified little child, you know. And she could hardly talk on the phone, much less say anything ugly. She was the one who supposedly had done so wrong. She didn't say anything, hardly."

"Describe her ability to express her feelings."

"She was good at doing certain things and she could act—she was a great actress in the sense that she could act certain ways. But I think she had a difficult time expressing herself."

Eighteen

I knew, as certain as I'm sitting here today, that Mom and Donald would see my pregnancy as a sin. It didn't matter that I was married or that Tom, holding my hand, had been the one to disclose it. To them the news was the same. Donald didn't move, but my mother leaned back on the sofa and crossed her legs. As her lips curled into a tight, pursed smile, her eyes narrowed just as I'd seen them do hundreds of times before. It was the same expression, the same squint, she got whenever Donald examined me and told her how bad I smelled. She despised me, I could tell. I didn't believe one word she or Donald said after that, about how thrilled they were for us, because it didn't change a thing. I just wanted to get out of there as soon as I could. Only Tom was stunned when they wouldn't talk to us after that.

Nick reacted oddly during that time. For some reason, their refusal to talk to me seemed to represent some kind of personal crisis for him, almost as if he considered it his duty to act as peacemaker. It was a role he'd played when I first moved in with Tom, when Nick intervened and convinced them to call me; and now he was doing it again, conveying to me things they said and, presumably, vice versa. "They really do care about you, Meg," Nick said. "They're just still hurt about the way you left. Maybe if you called them and—"

"Then they'd better get over it, hadn't they?" I didn't want to get into it with him. And what made Nick think he was the sudden expert about having a good relationship with them? "What's done is done, Nick, and it's too late for them to do anything about it now. I'm married, and it's too damn late. You don't have to tell them I said that. And I don't want you getting in the middle anymore. All right? If you say anything to them, you just tell them we're busy renovating the house, redoing the kitchen, stuff like that. You don't have to tell them anything else I said."

"You know, Meg, maybe you should give them a chance. I mean, you have to expect they'd be upset after you—"

"What is it with you, Nick? How come you care so much all of a sudden what they think? You sure didn't care what they thought all those years you were in Pensacola. Or when you announced one day you were married. Why do you care so much now?"

"I don't know," he said. "I guess I just do."

I have no idea what he said to them. But a few days later, Donald's red Lincoln pulled into the driveway. Two carpenters were putting up new shelves in our kitchen, and Donald parked behind their pickup trucks. When I opened the door, he acted as if it had been two days since we'd seen or talked with each other instead of two months. He glanced at my huge stomach, and then nodded at one of the carpenters who came out of the kitchen and walked past us on his way outside to his truck. "I'm headin' over to do some work on the boat," he said as a greeting. "I really could use your help, Margaret."

I don't know how long I stood there, saying nothing. Donald didn't move from the front porch; he just glared at me as my thoughts went into a whirl. "Well, come on, then," he said. "I don't have all day." It was no use. Nothing was ever going to change. I was too frightened of him to say anything. Silently I walked outside with him and got into the front seat of his car.

When the carpenter looked at me as he began walking toward the house, I said, "I'll be back in a little bit." I looked straight ahead of me then, afraid to look into the man's eyes. "Yep," Donald added. "We gotta do an errand." And then he backed into the street and headed for the harbor.

Nick and his wife, by then, had already divorced. He and his new girlfriend had recently moved into an apartment about twenty minutes from where Tom and I lived in Hyde Park. Nick was working part time at night as a steakhouse chef, and sometimes, in the afternoons, he came by to visit me. Sometimes I had the feeling he wanted to say something to me, that he'd be on the verge of revealing something to me, but didn't know how. We ended up talking about surface things: Money was tight, and he needed another job; my back had really been hurting me, and maybe I'd have to see a doctor. Both of us were good actors in that respect: Nick obviously didn't feel any safer revealing secrets to me than I did to him.

Sometimes Nick brought along his nearly two-year-old son, Daniel. I'd never imagined Nick as being a good father, but as soon as I watched the way he pranced around with Daniel on his back or hoisted him up onto his shoulders, I realized how wrong I'd been. Nick loved that little boy. He doted on him. Daniel brought out a quality in my brother I'd never seen before, a tenderness I never would have thought possible. That made me wonder: *Where did that come from? Was it something Nick had learned?* I was very afraid of what kind of mother I'd be, of turning out like my own mother. What if it was something genetic and there was nothing I could do about it? The idea of breast-feeding already repulsed me—just imagining it disgusted me. So what if that was just the beginning? What if the process had already begun? I prayed hard: *Please God. Please don't let me turn out like her.*

I was now eight months pregnant. Donald hadn't gone after me since that last time on the boat. Still, he couldn't keep his hands off me completely. Several times a week his Lincoln appeared in the carport, even when the workers were there, and often he came inside the house just long enough to grab at me. He was nervous, though, as if the possibility of Tom coming home unexpectedly somehow had become real to him.

In reality, Tom was almost never home. Most nights he worked late, and usually he came home just long enough to change his clothes and head off to his club. On weekends he played sports with his friends—tennis, golf, you name it. He told me he loved me, and I tried to believe it, but we argued terribly about how often he was gone. Tom said I was being unreasonable to expect him to change now that we were married—hadn't he told me right from the start about the basketball and golf and everything else?—and I didn't have the courage to tell him why it was so important. Granted, Tom could hardly protect me if he didn't know what I needed protecting from, but I thought it should have been enough that I'd told him I needed him.

Tom did go over to my parents' house when I asked him to, I'll give him that. And mostly, he got along well with them, usually by keeping the conversations light. There was only one disagreement I can remember. One time my mother said offhandedly that my father hadn't been black. Donald was standing there, and Tom looked at her as if he couldn't believe what he'd heard. "Pat, I met his brothers," Tom said. She immediately got very angry. "You don't know what you're talking about, Tom. Margaret's father was not black." Tom shook his head. "I was in Barbados, Pat. And Meg's uncles are black." She kept up with it, telling him he was wrong, and so finally he gave up. "Why would she say that?" he asked me later. I told him I had no idea.

Finally, in April 1988, our son Cameron was born. His skin was as white as Tom's, his hair the same light brown. I had spent months worrying about how I'd respond to him, but from the first moment I laid eyes on him I fell madly in love with him. The only thing I wanted to do was hold him against me, touch his satin skin, feel his tiny puffs of breath against my face. And all through that summer and into the fall, taking care of him was the only thing I could think about, the only thing that mattered.

✝ ✝ ✝

From the letter of referral by clinical social worker Stephen D. Csizmadia, Ph.D., written to psychiatrist Charles Deminico, M.D.

Re: Margaret ("Meg") Cassedy

Margaret was seen in an initial session on March 9 in my office. Margaret relates a long history of extreme and sustained sexual and emotional abuse by her stepfather.

Margaret recalls that she began to be sexually molested by the stepfather shortly after her arrival [in Guyana]. When Meg was twenty-three years old she met her future husband and thought that by marrying him she might be able to secure protection for herself from Don. . . .

The impression that Margaret has been emotionally severely damaged is particularly strong. She appears consumed with guilt; her self-esteem is very greatly damaged, and her perception of reality can be tenuous.

For example, she wondered if she might have caused Don's death. . . .

✝ ✝ ✝

From the deposition of psychiatrist Charles Deminico, M.D., conducted by Charlie Luckie

"I understand that Margaret Cassedy has consulted you with reference to the claims that she has in this litigation?"

"Well, she actually first saw me on a referral by a therapist, Dr. Csizmadia, who wanted a second opinion from me. . . . The initial evaluation took place on April 8, 1993."

"What happened that day?"

"I did my usual formal psychiatric interview, and at the same time did what we call a mental status examination."

"Did you conduct any formal testing of her on that date?"

"Not on that date. She came back on the 17th for the MMPI, the Minnesota Multiphasic Personality Inventory. Then she came back on the 19th and did a drawing test."

"What was your interpretation of Margaret Cassedy's MMPI?"

"It was an invalid report. The complaints and

symptoms were so exaggerated that they cannot be put in the context of a readable profile. It's what's called overreporting."

"So are you saying that you did not place very much credence or reliability upon [it]?"

"Well, yes. [But] it doesn't have to be valid. . . . A profile of this type, which is so highly elevated, could be that the person was confused; it could be a matter of repression or blanking out of ideas; or it could be a total lack of insight. The other thing that could be indicative here [is] . . . a plea for help, where people want to be sure that the person reading this understands how much they're hurting."

"All right. Did you later conduct another MMPI?"

"Yes. About a year later—April 7, 1994."

"Did you tell her you thought she had exaggerated?"

"No. What I explained to her was my feeling that she was scared, she didn't know what to do. She was looking as though she didn't believe whether I would believe her. So what I wanted her to do was, don't worry about what the results are going to be."

"What was your interpretation of the second one?"

". . . This is typical [of] . . . a borderline personality disorder. That's a pretty severe personality disorder. The reason it's called borderline is because it goes so far of extremes of neurotic thinking and behavior that there are times where the person may even be on the borderline of a severe mental disorder such as a psychosis. . . ."

"What other conclusion did you arrive at from studying [the last] MMPI?"

"She was very self-critical and had a very poor self-concept. There was an indication of a great deal of anxiety. . . . She's shy, avoids deep intimate social contacts, and has bad feelings about herself. She's self-alienated . . . [has] a tendency toward obsessiveness . . . [and] an element of cynicism that had developed in her. . . . In other words, this would be a difficult person to treat."

"You say that even to this day—the day you signed the affidavit—Margaret lacks insight into her psychological and emotional condition, and the cause of that condition. What does that mean?"

"She has no insight into how she behaves. . . . She is not an analytical-type person. Things are seen in terms of black and white and without the fine shades of gray."

"On paragraph three, you say, 'Margaret Cassedy is naïve and simple-minded, and Donald Sahlman was able to control her mind.' How did you arrive at that conclusion?"

"By the very fact of how she would behave. . . . If she said something and then I wrote my remarks down, she said, 'Did I do wrong? I bet you hate me for this.' There was always this plea of the need to be accepted, the need to be believed. I used to get the feeling that I was dealing with an eight-year-old kid."

"What was Donald Sahlman's control over her, if you know what it was?"

"The control would have been the matter of which happens in about every case of child sexual abuse I've seen. . . . The perpetrator uses threats of either harm, doing harm to the rest of the family, doing harm to the person, or taking away whatever they can provide."

"You are aware that she left the home of Donald Sahlman and her mother when she was about twenty-five years old and went to live with a man named Cassedy and then married him? And then she really never returned home to live after that time?"

"Not to live, but she did return on and off."

"You don't feel that Donald Sahlman had control over her after she left the home and went to live with Mr. Cassedy and married him, do you?"

"Psychologically, yes."

Nineteen

Now that Donald is dead, I understand why Nick and I kept secrets from each other all our lives. But until Cameron was about six months old, I didn't realize that Nick had probably been trying to reach out to me for help all those afternoons he came over with Daniel. For whatever reason, he hadn't been able to confide in me. That, or maybe he just couldn't bring himself to tell anyone what he was going through.

Anyone, that is, except one person.

One day my mother called and told me that Kim Hourigan,

Nick's girlfriend, had just been over at their house. Kim was extremely worried about Nick and hadn't known what else to do. He was out of control, completely irrational. He'd been bingeing on cocaine and alcohol for weeks—Kim was afraid he might overdose—and nothing she said did any good. Kim told my mother she'd spoken with a drug addiction counselor at a rehab hospital in Clearwater. The counselor had given her advice on how to get help for him. "Kim wants all of us to go over to the apartment and confront him, get him to check himself into the hospital," my mother said. "Do an interruption, something like that."

"An intervention?"

"Yes, that's it. The counselors are expecting him, and so we're all supposed to go get him and take him to the hospital together. Donald and I talked it over, and we decided that if he won't go on his own, then we'll beggar ax him."

"What's that?"

"What?"

"Beggar ax?"

"No, *Baker Act.* It's some kind of law. Dr. Arthur explained it to me. A person can legally be committed against their will if they're a threat to themselves or others. Anyway, Margaret, we need you and Tom to come over here. Donald wants us all to go over there together, see if we can talk some reason into him."

Nick, it turned out, didn't require much reasoning. The moment he saw the four of us at his apartment door and Kim told him why we were there, he sank back onto his ratty, thrift-store sofa and put his hands over his face. He looked horrible—emaciated, sunken eyes, as if he hadn't slept in days. At first he insisted he was fine, that he could stop on his own, but after just a few minutes of Donald telling him how screwed up his life had become, he broke down and agreed he needed help. With Nick sandwiched between Kim and me, all six of us rode over in Donald's red Lincoln to the Suncoast Hospital in Clearwater. As soon as we arrived we were led into a therapist's office at the end of a hallway. There was a sofa and several chairs, and all of us sat down, silently, waiting to be told what to do. Kim sat in a chair next to Nick, who was nervously jerking one foot in the air while he stared at his hands, and Mom and Donald sat beside Tom and me on the sofa.

The therapist, a woman who looked to be in her early fifties, started out by telling Nick that he should be very proud of himself because he'd just taken an important first step in his recovery. She thanked us all for coming along and being so supportive of him. Often, she said, it was exactly this kind of participation and willingness that made all the difference for someone struggling with drug addiction, because drug addiction doesn't come out of nowhere. Very often, she said, it's linked to unresolved issues in the person's family, and if the entire family participates the chances for recovery are a lot greater.

"Well," Donald said, "we sure want to help the boy any way we can."

The therapist looked at Donald and nodded. In that one second—just the way her eyes focused on him—I got a very bad feeling. A feeling of fear. I have no idea why, but suddenly

I wanted to bolt, to get out of there. It made no sense to me, though, and so I stayed exactly where I was, not moving.

After a few minutes of describing the recovery program at the hospital, the therapist asked us if we'd each be willing to talk about how we saw Nick's drug use, and how we thought it affected him and the family. That was difficult for me, since Nick had always kept things hidden. Mom and Donald talked briefly about his long history of drug use and their efforts to help him stop in the past—something I hadn't been aware of—but when it came to Tom and me, we both said we didn't really have anything to say.

It was Kim's turn. Strangely she didn't look at any of us. After a moment she reached into her purse and pulled out an envelope and handed it to the therapist. "This explains things," she said.

"You want me to read this?" the therapist asked. Kim nodded. We all watched the therapist as she read the first page, and then the second. My heart instantly thudded as she folded the letter and put it back into the envelope. What if it was about me? Once, sometime when I was a teenager, my mother took me to a gynecologist, but I ran out of his office and refused to be examined. What if that doctor had figured it out and told someone? What if Mike Cobaugh told someone about the pictures? My brain raced through possibilities. Out of the corner of my eye I saw Donald's chin go up just a fraction, his shoulders stiffen and go back, and right away I knew he was doing the same thing. He knew the letter was trouble the same way I did.

The therapist looked up at Donald and then Kim. "Well,

Kim, maybe we can discuss some of what's in this letter today. But I don't know about all of it." She started to turn to Nick when Donald leaped out of his chair.

"We don't need this crap," Donald said. "We don't need any of this crap." He grabbed his jacket. "We don't need to sit here and listen to this . . . this *garbage*. Nick's the one with the problem, and I'm not goin' to sit here and listen to this New Age trash." He jerked his head at us. "Y'all comin' with me? Because I'm leavin'. Right now." All of us, including the therapist, were too stunned to move or say anything. "Y'all comin' or not? 'Cause either y'all come this instant or else y'all can walk home." He flung open the door and stormed out.

Without a word the four of us got up and followed him. Nick stayed behind. No one said a thing on the way home, and it wasn't until Tom and I were in our own car that Tom started shaking his head. "What the hell was that about, Meg? Did you get any of that? Because I sure didn't. Do you have any idea what went on in there?"

"Beats me," I shrugged. "Your guess is as good as mine."

After that, no one mentioned the incident again. It wasn't until a few days later, when my mother called to talk about Granny's cold, that I got an idea of what had been in Kim's letter. After rattling on about how bad Granny was feeling, my mother, without warning, changed the topic. "Listen. I want to ask you something. Did Donald ever do anything bad to you?"

She meant to throw me off that way. If she'd really wanted to know, she would have led me into it. Instantly a chorus of voices went off in my head: *"Bad things will happen if you tell anyone, Margaret." "Meg, is your father having sex with you?" "You're a very dirty girl, Margaret." "Who do you think anyone would believe—a rich man like me or a nigger girl like you?" "Donald has been very good to us. You'll go to that boat when he asks you, and I don't want to hear any more about it." "I don't enjoy this, Patricia, I really don't. I wish there were an easier way." "He hovers around you, doesn't he?"*

She didn't want to hear it. Deep down she knew, but she didn't really want to know. "Of course not. Why would you say that?"

"Because Kim just came over again telling a bunch of lies. She said Donald did stuff to Nick. When he was little." I didn't say a thing. "She said Nick told her that. Anyway, I knew it was all a bunch of lies. I don't want her coming here anymore."

No one seemed terribly surprised when Nick checked himself out of the hospital a few days later and announced he was better, that he had a handle on things now. This time, he was absolutely sure he could stay clean on his own and put his life together. For some reason, Donald believed it. Right after that he gave Nick enough money to open his own restaurant, which had been Nick's dream for as long as he could remember. When Tom heard about it, he just shook his head in disbelief.

"Let me see if I've got this straight," he said. "A month ago Nick was a hopeless drug addict who'd have to be committed if he wouldn't go into detox on his own. And now he's shown he has the responsibility to own and operate his own restaurant. Is there a piece in this I'm missing?"

But Nick's problems soon seemed less important than my own. One morning I woke up and realized I couldn't move an inch without excruciating pain. Tom was already at work and Cameron was screaming in his crib, but I couldn't even roll over. Ever since I was a child I'd had back trouble, but since my pregnancy it had gotten even worse. And now I was completely immobilized.

It was very strange, said the doctor who reviewed my X-rays. I had two crushed disks near the base of my spine, something that usually occurs only in much older or extremely overweight people. That, he said, or in people who have been involved in serious car accidents. My mother, who'd brought me, stood mutely as the doctor shook his head. Was I sure I hadn't been involved in some kind of accident? Nothing I could recall? A few days later I went in for surgery to have one of the disks removed and spent the next several weeks in bed. On a daily basis I thanked God for my friends. If it hadn't been for Darley, Kathleen Murphy and Sue Sparks, another mother I'd met at St. Patrick's, I had no idea who would have taken care of Cameron while Tom was at work. Mom and Donald had made it clear they wanted nothing to do with babies.

I recovered, and fairly quickly. Within a few months I was able to bend and sit without pain, and I even felt well enough to help Nick a few evenings a week at his restaurant. Nick had said he couldn't afford to pay me to be a hostess, but just the way he'd asked made me think of what my mother once said about my father being able to charm the skin off a snake. "You know, I really could use a gorgeous woman to add some class to the joint," he said. "If I could, I'd have you stand out in the parking lot. That would bring them in." For the next six months that's what I did: I smiled and showed people to their seats and welcomed them to Nick's Café by the Bay. I did it even though Tom told me it wasn't right for me to be gone so much, that I had a child to take care of, that it wasn't *at all* the same thing as his playing sports with his friends. And I probably would have gone on being a hostess a lot longer, too, if Nick hadn't come to work one day and told me to go home.

The restaurant was bust. He'd run out of money. He was closing the doors.

And right after Café by the Bay went bankrupt, Nick went right back to the drugs.

From the deposition of Nicholas Clairmonte, conducted by Charlie Luckie

"Have you ever received any psychological or psychiatric counseling?"

"Yes, I have. It was at the Suncoast Hospital. I stayed there for about ten to twelve days."

"What were you there for?"

"Drug rehabilitation."

"What drugs were you being rehabilitated from?"

"Cocaine."

"Do you still use cocaine?"

"On occasion."

"Have you ever used crack cocaine?"

"Yes, I have."

"Are you now a crack cocaine user?"

"I was up until two months ago."

"You have not used any type of cocaine in the last two months?"

"Yes, I have, but I'm not a daily user."

"Has any therapist, psychologist or psychiatrist ever tried to get you to recall the abuse that you say you received from Mr. Sahlman?"

"They tried at Suncoast, but that's when I left. I couldn't get into it. I couldn't face it."

"Well, you've known about the abuse for a long time, but you're just now recalling the specifics? Is that what you're saying?"

"Yes, sir. I've had a mental block from age five, maybe, to age fourteen."

"Did you ever talk to your mother about it?"

"Once. It has to have been at least three years ago. I told her if she knew how many times he abused me she wouldn't feel the same way about him."

"Where did this conversation take place?"

"Her bedroom."

"What did your mother say to you?"

"She denied it."

"Did you ever talk to [Donald Sahlman] about the abuse?"

"Yes, sir. After I came back the first time from Pensacola. He tried to start abuse with me on the boat, and I told him that I was too old for that. 'It's wrong, and you've done it to me all my life, and I'm not going to turn out to be a bad product.' And he said, 'Well, you don't love me anymore, do you?' I said, 'No, I don't like the abuse anymore.'"

"Why have you sued your mother?"

"My feelings—just as far as her not believing me. And I would like her to try and seek some help and therapy with me. I'd like to be back together as a family."

"Is that the only reason you sued?"

"Yes, sir."

"Then you don't believe that she knew that you were being abused, do you?"

"I—I—I have mixed emotions on that. One half of me says she knew it, and one half of me says she didn't."

"Do you have any evidence that she knew it?"

"Yes, sir."

Twenty

Darley once told me she got divorced because she woke up one day and realized she and her husband were strangers. For me, the process was more like a wall being built, and each day that went by another brick or two got mortared in. The first few bricks were Tom's sports club, his tennis, his golf, his basketball. Then it was the realization that Donald knew how much I was always alone and nothing I said to Tom made any difference. And then there were specific things: the way Tom saw what went on at Suncoast Hospital but never tried to put anything together; the way he responded when I asked him if he couldn't *please* just stay home with me in the evenings. Maybe it wasn't fair of me, especially since he didn't really know what he was dealing with, but before Cameron was even a year old I'd built up the Berlin Wall inside of me.

Tom's a good man, a good person, don't get me wrong. But sometimes I think he just didn't want to see anything. Maybe it was easier for him to think of our life as perfect than to put anything together, to understand what was going on all that time. For Tom, everything was like one of those connect-the-dot pictures that you can't see the shape of until you draw all the lines. But he didn't want to do that. As far as he was concerned, we lived in a nice house in one of the trendiest neighborhoods in Tampa, he had a great job, a nice car, and my life as a stay-at-home mom wasn't bad at all. So what more did I want? There was only one thing I wanted, but Tom didn't seem to be able to give it to me. Tom just wasn't there for me when I needed him. He couldn't protect me. And that was exactly what went through my mind the day I frantically called him when Cameron got locked in the spare bedroom upstairs.

I don't know how it happened, but one moment Cameron was crawling around beside me as I folded laundry and the next he was gone. Suddenly I heard his screams from the other side of the door. I jiggled the doorknob and pounded on it, but it was locked. Cameron could get into all sorts of things in there, and what was I supposed to do? "I don't know, Meg," Tom said. "Just handle it, all right?" He was in the middle of something and couldn't leave. I begged him to come home, but he couldn't for another few hours. "Why don't you call your dad? He's always around."

I slammed down the receiver.

Donald did come right over, and he brought along his tools to take off the doorknob. But nothing with him was ever free; no matter what it was, he always had a price tag attached. "Aren't you goin' to give your old dad a hug?" he asked. In the upstairs hallway, with Cameron at my feet, he extended his arms. He slipped his hands down my pants and reached between my legs. "Tom's coming home," I said. "He'll be here any minute."

"Is that right?" he asked. He didn't believe me for a second.

"No, really. He is, Donald. Really."

And just then, God answered my prayers. The front door opened and in walked Tom. Donald looked as if someone had just walked on his grave. I scooped up Cameron and ran downstairs. I wanted to throw my arms around Tom, but I stopped in my tracks when I saw his face. He was angry. "Looks like you didn't need me after all," he said.

"I did, Tom. Really I did—"

Donald walked slowly down the stairs. "Thanks for helping her, Don. And I'm sorry for dragging you over. If it's not one thing it's another, right?"

"No problem," Donald said, smiling at me. "Didn't mind it a bit."

Tom and I did try to work on the marriage, and a few times we managed to get away for the weekend. By the time

Cameron was a year old, Mom and Donald were willing to take care of him, and during the summer we even took a week-long trip without him to the Bahamas. But even on vacation, nothing really improved. As far as I was concerned I could have lived without sex for the rest of my life, which didn't exactly please Tom. He told me he thought I should see a sex therapist.

"I don't want to do that," I said, "and I don't need to do that."

"Well, I think you do. You've got some problems you should talk to someone about. And you obviously don't feel you can talk to me about them."

"It's not that. It's just—I'm like my mother, Tom. Okay? It's that simple."

"What do you mean you're like your mother?"

"Well, Donald told me she doesn't like sex either, and I'm the same way."

"Are you telling me you discuss your sex life—our sex life—with your father?"

"Look, Tom. I'm not going to any sex therapist. So can we drop it?"

At the end of the summer, Tom decided it might help things if we moved and got a fresh start. Sometime near the end of 1989 we bought a new house on Davis Island, which was just five minutes from Tom's work downtown. It was a beautiful two-story house on a canal, larger than our last one, but to me it made no difference. The old house hadn't been the problem, and so the new one wasn't going to fix it.

The problem was that the man was always gone, and even when he wasn't I still felt alone.

The following spring, Tom suggested another trip, this time to England. He knew how much I'd loved seeing my Uncle David and Aunt Louise in Barbados, and both of them lived in London. He bought two tickets and then, at the last minute, announced he couldn't get away from work after all. "Well, do you mind if I go, then?" I asked. Never in my life had I gone anywhere alone. The idea thrilled and scared me at the same time.

"Alone?" he asked. "You want to go without me, alone?"

"Okay, then I'll take Darley. She'd love to go. Why should I cancel the trip just because you can't go? And we have to use the tickets, Tom. You don't just want to throw them away, do you?" Tom finally agreed—as long as I could arrange child care.

For the first few days I was gone, Cameron would be looked after by my friend Sue Sparks, and after that, Mom and Donald agreed to watch him for the rest of the week. My mother never pretended to like young kids, especially since she had so many beautiful things in the house she was afraid would get broken, and mostly she interacted with Cameron by telling him not to touch this and not to touch that. But Donald was a lot better with him. Even though I didn't like it that he insisted Cameron shouldn't wear a diaper in the pool or hot tub, Donald took him swimming every day and loved to follow him around with his movie camera. He took him down to the boat and carried him around on his shoulders, and really seemed to like having him at the house. I never once had even the smallest hesitation about leaving him there.

Darley and I boarded the plane as if we were headed off for the biggest adventure of our lives. It wasn't until we'd left the ground and the flight attendant brought beverages that I realized how free I suddenly felt. For the first time in my life, no one was watching me. No one was controlling me. Even though Donald had said some ugly things about my visiting my nigger relatives, no one would tell me where to go. And most of all, no one was going to be bothering me for sex.

"Have another Pepsi, for England," Darley said, raising her glass to me.

"Don't mind if I do," I said, grinning. "To the queen!"

I called Mom and Donald to let them know I was back from London, to thank them for watching Cameron and tell them about everything Darley and I had seen. I had just started to describe to Donald the site where Anne Boleyn had her head chopped off because she couldn't give Henry VIII a son, when he interrupted me.

"I got somethin' to tell you first," he said. His voice was strange, strained. I knew straight off he was going to tell me something bad, because I could read that man better than myself. "Remember that lump I told you about in my mouth? The one I told you I was goin' to the doctor about?"

"Yes. I remember."

"Well, this might interest you. Guess what, Margaret?"

"What?"

"Well, looks like I didn't do a good enough job."

"Good enough job of what?"

He didn't answer straight off. "I've got cancer," he said slowly. "Of the saliva gland, is what they tell me. I just thought you might like to know."

I put down the phone and walked outside. The night was alive with chirping and whirring insects, a buzzing I usually didn't pay attention to anymore. As I stood there I remembered a sermon I once heard about how God gives every creature something it can defend itself with, that even the lowliest insect has something to use as protection. I thought back to something I read in college about insects that could paralyze potential predators with one bite, and spiders with poison so powerful it could kill a man in three minutes, and then I remembered Donald: the years and years he'd cleaned me, the years and years he'd tugged on his cheeks, the years and years he'd gargled and spat to no avail.

I had done it. It had been me. It was my body that had poisoned him, as surely as if I'd put strychnine in his coffee or poured rat poison on his cereal or baked cyanide into his beloved Key Lime pie. All those years I wished he'd die—and it was my fault. It was just like the time in Guyana when I imagined his boat sinking, and then it really did.

"You okay, Meg?" Tom had come outside without my hearing him.

"Don't do that! Don't sneak up on me like that!"

"I'm sorry. I didn't mean to scare you. I thought you heard me." He came up beside me and put his arms around me. "I missed you, you know. I didn't like having my wife gone so long. Our bed was very, very empty without you."

I let him hold me like that a few moments, with my head against his shoulder, until his hands began moving in their familiar pattern up and down my thighs. I couldn't stand the thought of it, of his wanting me; my insides felt draped in spider webs.

"I'm going inside," I said, breaking away. "All of a sudden I'm kind of cold."

For the next few months, I waited. I can't tell you what for, only that I had a kind of inner certainty I'd never known before. *Something's going to happen,* a voice said. *And when it does, you'll know when to go.* Sometimes I felt like the egret that swooped down every evening and stood along the edge of the canal in our backyard, his reflection so still that sometimes he looked like a photograph until the water rippled. Suddenly his beak pierced the water in one smooth, beautiful movement—*got it!*—and he swallowed whatever it was he'd known all along would come his way. That's how I would have to be, too: completely still until the water rippled.

But it wasn't a ripple, or any one event for that matter, that ended up giving me the answer I needed. It was Donald. Donald, and the realization that nothing was ever going to change. His mouth cancer had put an end to the one thing I had always hated most—whether it was out of consideration for me or his fear of getting something worse, I don't know—but he still made me touch him. He did it at our house when Tom was at work, he did it on weekends when Tom was playing sports. And one day I woke up and understood something I never had: that I hadn't failed the marriage, as much as the idea of marriage had failed me.

When Tom came home that night, hot and sweaty from his workout at the club, I met him at the door. Cameron, who was two-and-a-half, was playing with toys in the corner. "I've thought it over, Tom," I said to him. "I want a divorce."

Twenty-One

I do not know the answer to this: If I could gather the strength to leave Tom, why couldn't I get away from Donald? If I had the courage to close that door, why couldn't I lock the one that followed?

In September 1990, I moved with Cameron into a tiny apartment at Lookout Point on South Westshore. Basically I took out of the marriage what I'd brought into it: a few bags of clothes and my fear. I had no idea how I was going to support myself or even, for that matter, how I'd manage to buy necessary things like dishes, but I did my best not to think about the future, to tell myself I'd figure things out later. The most important thing, as Darley reminded me, was that I was free.

Tom, meanwhile, was being amazingly decent about everything—even though he told me repeatedly he didn't understand what had gone wrong, that he'd always thought we'd had a good marriage, that nothing made sense to him. It was obvious he was hoping I'd change my mind, but he still immediately offered to give me enough money each month to make sure Cameron and I were all right. Tom could have been nasty, could have done all the things I'd heard some husbands do in the midst of a divorce, but he didn't. It was almost enough to make me regret having left him.

Mom and Donald, of course, wanted to know what the problem was. I couldn't very well tell them the truth—that there was no point being married if Tom couldn't protect me—and so I told them the same flippant phrase I'd said to all my friends: that I was tired of being a sports widow. For some reason this seemed as acceptable an answer to everyone as when I'd explained my heritage by saying I was from the islands, and generally was met with knowing nods.

At first Mom and Donald didn't say anything either way. But after Tom went over to their house one night without me, Donald told me we should at least go to a counselor. To this day I have no idea why he said that to me. "He wants to work on it, Margaret," he said. It was pointless, but I still went through the motion of calling Father Fausto just to say I'd tried.

Father Fausto was very sad, and probably also a little

surprised, to hear what I'd done. Only a few weeks earlier I'd gone to lunch with him for my twenty-eighth birthday, but I'd neglected to mention how unhappy I was or what I was planning to do. I sensed now that he was hurt I'd withheld such important information from him. On the phone he told me he'd always liked Tom, that we'd always seemed like such a nice couple. Of course, he added, it was impossible for anyone to ever see into another person's heart, but had I at least sought guidance from Father Venard? Or anyone else at St. Patrick's? When I told him I really didn't want to do that, Father Fausto gave me the name of a counselor and urged me to talk with him. Tom and I went to see the man for one session, but after that no one mentioned trying to save the marriage again. Even Tom must have realized it was hopeless, because the next day Donald told me he'd go with me to all my legal appointments to make sure I didn't get hurt in the divorce.

For the next several months, I clung to my friends for moral support. Of everyone, though, Darley was probably the greatest comfort. Practically every day she came over to the apartment and talked with me, made me laugh, and just about every weekend she and her boyfriend took me places "so you won't sit around and dwell on things." Having experienced a divorce herself, Darley said she knew what I was going through. She said it was normal to feel depressed—even if I'd been the one who wanted to leave—and she assured me that pretty soon I'd be open to things again. It might take time, she said, but I just had to have faith. Slowly, I began to believe her.

After about six months I started to run again. I began slowly at first, afraid I might reinjure my back, but pretty soon I was jogging each morning at a good clip along Tampa Bay, feeling happier and healthier than I had in years. Now that Tom took Cameron on weekends I also had free time, and so I even went out on a few dinner dates. Most of the men were vaguely terrifying to me and I only saw them once or twice, but one man I met through a mutual friend made me feel comfortable right off the bat. That was Ernie Haefele.

Ernie's probably as different from Tom Cassedy as any two men could ever be. The first time I was introduced to him at a restaurant in Hyde Park, he told me about the pawnshops he runs in Tampa, along with a fill-dirt lot and a fish farm. I'd never heard of such things, but he told me there was a huge market for dirt ("People are always going to have holes, Meg"), and tropical fish for people's aquariums, he said, can cost hundreds of dollars apiece. Ernie told me he'd gotten a college degree in business, but he seemed more like the kind of guy who'd graduated from the school of hard knocks. He's street smart and a wheeler-dealer, always looking for a new "investment opportunity," and whenever one project doesn't work out he just goes on to the next idea. Mostly, though, he does pretty well. He took me to nice restaurants, or I'd fix him dinner at his house on Robin Hood Drive, and a few times he even went with me to Occident Street for dinner. After I'd been going out with him for a few months I invited him to come with me on Donald's boat, even though I knew what Mom and Donald thought of him. Neither of them said anything against him, but they didn't have to. It was obvious by the way my mother squinted at him that she despised him from the moment she set eyes on him.

By mid-1991, Donald had finished his radiation treatments. Until then he'd been leaving me pretty much alone, but now, once again, he started dropping by my apartment unannounced just as he'd done while I was living with Tom on Angeles Street and later on Davis Island. The apartment had no garage, and he always knew when I was home. A few times I tried parking around the corner or several blocks away to throw him off, but it didn't work. One day he came in and asked me if I'd been having engine trouble. "No? Well, I saw your car in the alley, so I thought maybe it broke down on you." And then he winked at me, letting me know he was onto me. "So why don't you come and give your old dad a hug, Margaret?"

Darley, gratefully, was sometimes at my apartment when he came by. The instant I heard his red Lincoln pulling up outside or his familiar two raps on my door, I'd beg her not to go, to stay with me until he went home. Darley was the truest friend I could have asked for. She never once asked me why I went into such a terror. She stayed with me even when it ran her late with something else she'd planned, and even when Donald sat on the sofa and looked at her as if he wished she'd just hurry up and die. Darley stood her ground like a pit bull. "Would you like another cheese wedge?" she'd ask, offering him a plate and smiling her sweetest smile. "Or maybe some more crackers?" Donald just glowered at her and shook his head.

The news that would change my life didn't come until the

end of summer. It was the time of year when the sweltering heat and drenching humidity feel as though they'll never end, when anywhere in the world seems preferable to Tampa. I have a vivid memory of the flowered dress I was wearing when the phone rang, the way one sandal slipped off my foot as I went to answer it, the blue stuffed animal Cameron was holding while I listened to my mother's voice. "It's Donald," she said. "His cancer's back."

Oh, how I wanted to scream for joy at that news! To say, *Good! Now he'll leave me alone again!* But I was too good an actress to show her even one speck of the elation surging through me. "Oh Mom, that's too bad," I said. "I'm so sorry."

"It's not his mouth this time," she went on. "It's gone to his lungs. It's very, very bad, Margaret, extremely bad. He's going to have chemotherapy, but the doctors said it's not—" She broke off. For a moment, I thought she might cry or tell me how worried she was. "Anyway, I need you to come over right away and do some things for me. I've got too much on my mind now to worry about them."

From that day on I went to their house practically every day. I went when she took Donald to the doctor and needed me to watch Granny; when she had to take Granny to get more medication from her psychiatrist, Dr. Arthur; when she had to go to St. Patrick's and didn't want to leave Donald alone; when she needed me to cook or bring groceries or do laundry or clean up. It was always something. Still, I went because it gave me a chance to see for myself how he was doing, to see if he was getting sicker. Donald had already gone into remission once; what if that happened again? The only way to know was to watch him.

God forgive me, but I prayed for the cancer to spread. This is horrible of me, but I prayed for it to eat away at his insides like black acid, to choke the life out of him like a powerful creeping vine. I fluffed his pillows and rubbed his neck and asked if he was comfortable, if I could get him anything else, and all the while I was listening to his coughs, to the rattle in his chest, and asking myself, *Is it worse? Has it spread any more today?* I paid attention to other things, too. For God knows what reason he had started wearing a toupee. It sat ridiculously askew on his head like a dead rodent, and I took it as a good sign. There had to be something bad underneath it.

I cooked soups for him, practically the only things he could eat now. Sometimes while I worked in the kitchen I chatted with Carmen, the Hispanic woman Mom and Donald had hired to come in a few times a week. Carmen was in her fifties, had a thick New York accent, and had gone to Mass at St. Patrick's for years. Of all the people from St. Patrick's who came by to pray for Donald, Carmen was probably the most distraught.

"It's such a tragedy he's so sick," she said one day, shaking her head. "Such a terrible tragedy, if you ask me. He's the most generous man I've ever known, and I mean that, Margaret. He lent me money when my daughter got married. Did I ever tell you that? Never once asked me when I'd pay him back. I did—you can be sure of that—but there was no hurry with him. 'Pay me back when you can,' he said. If you ask me you've got a saint for a father, Margaret. A real saint."

"You think so, Carmen?"

"Yeah, I do," she said. "I really do."

I nodded, and then reached for another carrot and sliced it in half.

Out of all the people in my life I could have told about Donald, why did I choose Ernie Haefele? Even now, I don't know the answer. It wasn't that he seemed more trustworthy to me than Tom, who probably loved me as much as I was capable of being loved by anyone. But one thing I do know: Ernie immediately made me regret I'd ever said a thing.

Tom was keeping Cameron for the weekend, and Ernie and I decided to get away for a few days. We were driving to Port Canaveral in his black Ford Bronco, listening to the radio with the windows rolled up, neither of us saying much of anything. In Florida, you can go for miles and miles and see nothing but flat highways and a blur of green trees and bushes along either side, not a hill or bump in the entire state, and so there wasn't much to look at. After a while, I turned down the radio.

I was just thinking about a friend of mine, I said to him. A really good friend, actually. And I'd been wondering something.

"Yeah?" he said when I didn't go on right away.

Well, what would a man like him think about someone who'd been sexually abused by her father for a long time? From the time she was a small child into her being an adult—but she'd never told anyone? See, this friend of mine had kept it hidden her whole life and never had been able to stop it, even though she'd always wanted to, even though she always hated it. Even after she had a child it still went on. What would someone like him think of someone like that?

"Well," Ernie said, shrugging and keeping his eyes on the road, "I don't really know. I guess it would kind of depend on the person."

I didn't say anything right away. Well, I said slowly, what if it were me? What would he say if I were talking about something that happened to me?

Ernie jerked his head. "Is this a hypothetical question, Meg? Or was it really you?"

I shoved my feet onto the floor of the car, my whole body tense. And then I closed my eyes and nodded. I couldn't look at him.

"You and Donald? You're telling me that you and Donald, Donald and you—?"

I nodded again. And then there was silence. It seemed as if it lasted for miles. "I don't know, Meg." He knuckles were white on the steering wheel.

"What? What don't you know?"

"Well, why didn't you ever tell anyone if it was really that bad?" He didn't take his eyes off the road. "I mean, if it really was as horrible as you say, then why didn't you stop it when you were eighteen? When you were an adult? The way I figure it, you must've kinda liked it. You know, to keep doing it. That, or maybe you're as perverted as he is."

I couldn't breathe. It was as if I'd been kicked in the chest. I sank down so low in the seat that I could barely see over the dashboard. I was struggling not to let him see what he'd done to me, that it was as if he'd reached into my soul and then plucked my greatest fear, word for word, out of my brain. I wanted to crawl into a hole and pull the dirt in on top of me. As Ernie drove in silence, Donald's words, spoken one day when he took me from Tom's house to the boat, reverberated through my head: *You passed the point of no return a long time ago, Margaret. It's too late now, don't you know? No one would ever believe you didn't want it; they'd never believe you didn't ask for it.*

The rest of the trip, Ernie and I avoided the entire topic. In the back of my mind, though, his words were always there. And from that point forward in the car, I vowed I'd never bring it up to another person for as long as I lived.

Ernie's not a bad guy. He just didn't know how to take everything at first. By the following June, what I'd told him must have sunk in, especially when certain things he'd do— the way he tried to touch me sometimes—got me upset. "He did this to you, didn't he?" he said one time. "It's because of what that bastard did to you that you're like this, isn't it?" After that, Ernie sometimes lay in bed and yelled at the ceiling about how crazy it made him to imagine what Donald had done to me, and he'd pound the mattress and breathe heavily through his nostrils like an overworked horse. "The man's a sicko, Meg," he said one night. "And you know what? I guarantee you're not the only one. You're probably just the tip of the iceberg. I'll bet you anything he did it to other kids, too."

I didn't believe that for a second, but it did make me feel better to hear him talk like that. Ernie got a lot better about everything, a lot more understanding, as time went on. Even though I hadn't told him everything, any of the details, it still meant more to me than I could tell him that he had sympathy for me, that he wasn't judging me anymore. The only thing that upset me was the way Ernie went on being pleasant to Donald. It felt like a betrayal, I told him, the way he could keep on being polite after everything he knew.

"Well, what do you expect me to do, Meg?" Ernie said one day in frustration. "Punch him in the nose? I already told you what I think of him, but how's it going to help anything if I let him know that, too? I mean, the man's already got one foot in the grave. He'll get what's coming to him soon enough, don't you worry about that."

That startled me. No one had ever said those words out loud. "You really think so, Ernie? You really think he's dying?"

"Oh come on, Meg, don't tell me you haven't noticed the way he looks? I mean, the guy looks like death warmed over. In the last month alone he's probably lost twenty pounds, maybe more, and not even that stupid-looking toupee he's been wearing can hide what's going on. Why's he wearing that thing anyway? You told me he's been bald all his life, so who does he think he's fooling? Like he really thinks people will believe he gets lung cancer and suddenly grows a mop of brown hair?"

"He went into remission before, Ernie. Maybe he'll do it again."

"Meg, I'm telling you, he's not going into remission. You watch. I give him six months, tops. And you remember what I told you, too. I'll bet you anything there's gonna be a slew of people lining up to spit on his grave." From the moment Ernie said that, something lightened inside me, as though someone had just taken away a hundred-pound backpack I'd been carrying all my life. If Ernie was right, it really was over. It would just be a matter of time.

A few days later, I decided to take Ernie up on his offer to move in with him. I knew Mom and Donald would scream at me, hate me—but as it turned out, Mom needed me to help out around the house too much to do anything more than tell me I was acting like a slut and that all of their friends would be shocked. She didn't speak to me for about a week, and then she called me at Ernie's house to give me the latest news.

"Well, Margaret. The doctors have given up hope," she said flatly. "They say his cancer is terminal. I hope you're very happy that you're doing this to him now, shaming him at the very end of his life, after everything he's done for you, done for all of us. Because it's tearing him apart, Margaret. Just destroying him. I hope you're very happy."

I wanted so badly to say to her, *I'm very happy, Mother. I can't tell you how happy I am.*

✝ ✝ ✝

From the deposition of Carmen Clift, direct examination conducted by Richard Gilbert

"Where are you employed?"

"St. Patrick's Church and Target department store and Pat Sahlman's domestic work."

"What do you do for St. Patrick's?"

"I work with the priests at the friary. I do house-keeping and cooking and animal tending at the pet center."

"Any particular priest that you work with there?"

"All of them."

"What do you do at Target?"

"I unload trucks and stock shelves."

"And what do you do for Pat Sahlman?"

"I do domestic work. Housekeeping and odds-and-ends jobs."

"How long did you know Donald Sahlman?"

"A little over five years. From the time I started [working for the Sahlmans] until he deceased. . . . I met him through the church."

"And what was his involvement with the church?"

"Something to do with the finance committee. I served meals for the finance committee."

"How did it come about that you began working for Donald and Pat Sahlman?"

"He gave me a call at the friary one day and asked me if I would like to do that. . . . I did it for other people and he knew that."

"Had Margaret already moved out of the house?"

"Yes."

"You've been listed as a witness in this proceeding. Do you know what you're going to be called upon to testify to?"

"Not really."

"What do you know about Donald Sahlman Sr.'s relationship with Margaret?"

"Very loving, sweet, nice happy family."

"And what is the basis for your opinion about that?"

"I'm a good observer myself, and I've had a family. And I just used to watch them. I thought it was cute because [Margaret] used to call him 'Daddy Donald' all the time. . . . She was there all the time. Every day she was there, her and the child. Before the baby she was there, and then after the baby she was there all the time, just hanging out with the family and stuff. . . ."

"Do you know if Donald Sahlman invited her over?"

"No. She just popped in like any kid to a parent's house. Sometimes she would come over on her bike because she was into working out, you know, fitness and all this stuff. . . . She would say, 'Do you want to go and have lunch?' And Don and Pat would say, 'Where do you want to go?' She would name the place and they'd go there. Or, she'd say, 'Do you want to go to the boat? Let's go out on the boat.'"

"Did Don and Margaret hang out together by themselves?"

"Well, Pat was always around the area in the house. But sometimes Don would be in the back doing something and she would say, 'Where is Daddy Donald?' And I would say, 'Back there.' And she would cruise down there and go see Daddy Donald. I would just hear muffled conversation. . . ."

"Are you a good friend of Pat's?"

"I love her dearly because she's a good lady. She's a wonderful woman. She's very involved in my church, and I think highly of her. . . . She may have bucks, but she's not like some of the people I know that have money. She's down-to-earth. These other people, they have a façade, they're big phonies. . . ."

"Did she ever talk to you about this lawsuit?"

"Not really in detail. Just that she couldn't believe it happened. Because I read it in the paper and I called her. I said, 'What the heck is the story there?' And she just cried and felt hurt and was angry, and I couldn't believe it had happened. I felt sorry for her, but I felt more sorry for Don, because Don wasn't around to defend himself. It pissed me off, if you want to know the truth. . . . It was such a shock. Because all I ever saw was kindness and family and love, and it blew me out of the water. . . ."

"So you don't believe the allegations?"

"No, I don't. I was mad at Meg when I read the paper and saw what she was doing because it's dirty pool. If there was such a thing going on, why in the hell didn't she bring it up sooner when somebody was around and not dead so they could defend themselves?"

"Anything you can tell me about your conversations with Meg?"

". . . She would tell me about her conquests, how good [various men] were in bed. She compared them to her ex-husband. At the time he was still her husband, she wasn't quite divorced. . . . And then she told me about when she met this other guy, Ernie. He was hot. He was really hot, the best. . . ."

"She said Ernie was hot?"

"Yes, hot, and she was referring to in the sack. . . . The first time I met Ernie I thought he was a shyster. From the minute I saw him my hair went up on my neck. I kind of stayed clear because I was leery of Ernie. I didn't trust him. He looked like the type of people you see on 42nd Street in Manhattan."

"Is that the way you still feel about Ernie?"

"Yes. There was nothing to change my opinion of him."

"Any other incident with Meg that you can tell us that demonstrates either her behavior or personality or her relationship with Don Sahlman?"

"Well, just that when Don got sick—even before Don got sick—she was very doting. She was a doting daughter, doting on her mother. They hugged a lot. She called her Mommy. . . . She loved Don. Excuse me, I thought she loved Don. Because she'd say, 'Is there anything I can get for you, Daddy? Do you want this?' She'd go to the refrigerator and get something. 'Do you want something to drink?' And when he was feeling badly, when he was sick and had a lot of pains and aches in his back, she would say, 'Do you want me to rub your back? Come sit down in the recliner. . . . Are you feeling all right? Is that better? That's much better.' Just like a daughter would do to a father that's not well."

"Would your perception of Pat Sahlman change if you were to find out that she participated with Don Sahlman in checking Margaret's genitals to determine their cleanliness?"

"It's not true. It would never be true because that's not the type of person Pat Sahlman is."

"But if—"

"Don't 'but if,' please. Because whatever poppycock concoction stories you have, it's a bunch of crap. Okay? I don't know anything about what this is all about, and now you're bringing all this trashy crap up. . . . Whatever stories you hear, it's bullshit. I'm sorry. I'm from Brooklyn. I'll tell you like it is."

✝ ✝ ✝

Deposition cross-examination, conducted by Charlie Luckie

"I just want to ask you one question. Would it shock you—and it's true—that Margaret Cassedy has testified under oath that she hated Don Sahlman and is glad that he's dead?"

"No, no way. She wouldn't say that."

"She did say that. Does it shock you?"

"That's a crock of shit. Because if that's the truth, she's the best actress. The broad ought to get an Academy Award."

Twenty-Two

God forgive me, but I wanted him to die. By August I wanted
it so badly, so consumingly, that I consciously had to make
certain my expression around my mother was always solemn,
that my voice didn't betray any excitement or cheeriness, that
everyone from St. Patrick's who came by the house with
prayers or casseroles or offers of support thought I was just
as sad and distraught as anyone about his sickness.

There were only two things that frightened me. The first
was the nagging fear that despite his doctor's pronounce-
ment, Donald might experience a miracle and recover. Surely

praying for him to die was a sin, and what if God punished me by making him healthy again? But my second fear filled me with even greater dread. What if Donald went ahead and got worse but didn't give me what I needed? What if he went to the grave without telling me what I deserved to hear?

Ever since I'd realized that Ernie had been right—that Donald was going to die any time now—there was only one thing I could think about. It was the one thing I needed in order to go on with my life, the one thing I knew I had to have in order to truly put what Donald had done to me behind me, to heal.

Donald had to tell me he was sorry. He had to tell me he had loved me, that he was truly sorry for hurting me. He knew what he'd done to me was wrong; otherwise he never would have threatened me all those years or been so afraid I'd tell someone. And now I needed for him to tell me that before he died. I didn't care what words he chose, or where he said it, but he could not die without apologizing. He could not, because I wasn't going to let him. I would go over to the house every day for the rest of his life and wait, if that's what it took. I'd sit by his side, do whatever I had to do, and I'd make sure I was there whenever he finally decided to say those words to me. *Forgive me, Margaret.* Donald was not going to rob me of it. He was not going to withhold this one thing from me.

And if he asked for the forgiveness, I would not withhold it from him.

Each and every day I went over to Occident Street and busied myself. I listened for changes in his breathing; I watched his face; I was constantly ready to bend over and put my ear close if he needed to whisper it. Sometimes I wanted to scream at him: *You son of a bitch! Say you're sorry to me!* But I held it inside, just as I'd always done about everything.

If it counts for anything, I did wish I could feel sorry for Donald's suffering. That was especially true whenever my mother talked and talked about all the wonderful things he'd done for our family—as if she already was thinking about him in the past tense and trying to build him up even bigger in her mind. The sicker he got, the more she went on about all his good deeds over the years: how he paid for us to move from Guyana, how he helped us become U.S. citizens, how he rented us our first apartment, how if it hadn't been for him we never would have had that house on Juno Street. She'd remind me, as if somehow I'd forgotten it, that Donald paid for everything since we came to America—for Nick and me to go to the best private schools in Tampa, for all those beautiful clothes and cars, and don't forget all those vacations he took you on all over the world, Margaret. "Because of that man," she said one afternoon, her index finger pointing toward the bedroom where Donald was sleeping, "we've never wanted for a *thing!* You owe everything you are to that man!" She said it as if I'd told her any different.

The truth was, Donald had done all those things. He'd saved us from poverty; he'd made us into who we were as surely as if he'd pinched our forms out of warm wax. But there was so much more to the version of the story she was telling; and she and I both knew, without a word passing between us, that there was the huge price that had been paid for his generosity. The knowledge of that cost was between us each day as Donald sat propped in his lounge chair or lay sedated in the bedroom or sat next to Granny on the sofa in front of the television; the knowledge of it flashed before me every time I saw her diamond rings sparkle under the chandelier, each time she straightened one of her expensive paintings on the wall, each time she slid into the leather seats of her new car. *I hope you're happy,* she had said to me. *I hope you're very happy.* Was my mother happy? Had it been worth it for her?

For the past several weeks Donald had spent most of his time propped up in a lounge chair in the living room. His head drooped to one side, his arms and legs were thin and gangly, and he looked as if he'd aged twenty years just since June. His shoulders were bony and stooped, and his stubbly chin jutted out over his collarbone because his neck was so weak. His eyes, sunken and dark, reminded me of a blind person's. As usual, I had gone over to the house this one day to stay with him and Granny while Mom went off to do an errand, and I looked at him as if I were seeing an odd species at the zoo. *This,* I thought, *is not the same man who did everything to me: This is a skeleton, a shell, a shadow.*

But then the shadow raised its head and spoke. "Margaret?" he asked in a raspy voice. I stepped closer to his chair. Donald's thick glasses magnified his eyes so they took over his entire face. With his long nose and thin lips and wrinkled neck he reminded me of an old buzzard, one that's been plucked of feathers with the smell of death on him. The top of his head was covered with large dark splotches—obviously what the toupee had been meant to conceal—and the same blotches, only smaller, covered the tops of his hands. *Say it to me, you bastard. Say it while you still can.*

"I have to pee, Margaret. Get me the bedpan, will you?"

I reached over and handed him the metal bedpan. Then I stepped back as he reached under his robe and pulled out his thing. It was shriveled and gray, like something dead. He held it between his thumb and forefinger, considering it, and then looked up at me. He smiled. "Why don't you hold it for me, Margaret? I wouldn't want to mess up the chair, you know?"

Oh God, how I hated him at that moment. How he made me sick just to look at him. Forgive me for saying that, because I know you're not supposed to say bad things about the dying or the dead, but I did hate him, I couldn't help it. I had come over there for one reason only, the same reason that had been bringing me over every day, but obviously nothing had changed. Nothing was any different than it always had been.

Actually, that's not accurate. One thing had changed: He was too weak to do anything to me. He couldn't hurt me now even if he tried. It hit me just like that: *Damn! You're nothing but an infant now! You can threaten me, you can say anything you want, but you can't do a damn thing about it!* And for the first time in my entire life, I wasn't afraid of him. His power over me was gone. I looked down at him and real slow—so he knew exactly what I was doing—I shook my head.

He couldn't believe what I'd done. "I need you to hold it

and help me pee!" he yelled. "I'm sick! Aren't you even going to help me?"

I don't know how long I stood there and stared down at him. My jaw was clenched and my insides were trembling. I was feeling something I'd never felt before—the word "No!" echoing inside me as if my brain was nothing but a big dark tunnel someone had shouted into. *No! I won't help you! No! I won't do what you say, ever again!*

Finally, in a firm voice that surprised even me, I said, "Mom will be home soon. She can do that for you." And then I actually walked away from him to the other side of the room. Out of the corner of my eye I saw him shakily put the bedpan up to his lap and then I heard a tinkling sound against the metal.

"Damn it!" he screamed. "Look what you've made me do!"

I looked at him from across the room. He'd peed all over himself and the chair. And then the words came: *He's never going to say it to you. You're wasting your time because he's never going to say it to you.* I knew that then as certain as I've ever known anything in my life. Donald was going to go to the grave with what he'd done to me.

"Come help me clean it up!" he bellowed.

I took a few steps toward him and then stopped. He looked at me, perplexed. "Mom will be home soon," I said again, not moving. "*She* can clean you. That's *her* job. It's not mine."

I turned and walked outside by the pool. Sunlight through the palm fronds flickered long-fingered shadows onto the pale aquamarine water. On the other side of the house, out of view, was the canal that led to Tampa Bay. Every once in a while I heard the sound of water lapping gently as another one of Mom and Donald's neighbors steered a boat or yacht up to a backyard dock. My mother had certainly gotten what she'd always wanted. She had her lovely house, her beautiful furniture, her clothes, her furs, her jewelry. It was everything she'd collected to shield her from the life she left behind in Guyana, the life she probably had no idea how close she'd always been to resuming. But if she'd ever had even an inkling of how often Donald threatened to send her back, she'd never have to worry about that now. She and Donald's son would have everything—his millions, his house, his yacht. I looked up at the sky, to the thick dark thunderclouds that rolled in every afternoon during the summer, and wondered: *What have I ever wanted so much that I would have done what she did? Had there ever been anything or anyone in my life—even Anthony—I could have wanted so much?*

It was hot and humid outside and difficult to breathe. Still, I didn't want to go back inside. The only thing I wanted was for my mother to get back so I could leave. All I wanted was to get out of there, to never come back, to never see Donald's face ever again.

Two weeks later I drove over to Bennigan's restaurant on the Dale Mabry Highway. As I pulled into the parking lot and got out of the car, I remembered some of the words I'd said the night before on the phone. *Too late to take them back now.* Inside the restaurant, as I scanned the noontime crowd, I realized I was trembling.

Father Fausto was sitting at a corner table and stood up as

soon as he saw me. He was dressed in casual clothes without his clerical collar, and as soon as I reached the table he put his arms around me. "Meg," he said, hugging me. "I am so very glad to see you. So glad." His voice was heavy with emotion.

"Oh Father, I'm so glad to see you, too." He motioned to the chair and we sat down. "Thank you for meeting with me, it means so much to me." He smiled and shook his head as if I'd just said something ridiculous.

"But it's your birthday today, is it not? Your thirtieth birthday?"

I nodded. Suddenly I felt on the verge of tears. I couldn't remember everything I'd said to him the night before. The words had just shot out of me, tumbling out as if they were on a barrel going over Niagara Falls. But whom else could I have told it to? Whom else could I trust? Ernie was doing his best, but it wasn't enough. And how could I tell Ernie every-thing—that it had gone on even after I met him?

Father Fausto reached across the table and wrapped his fingers around my hand. "I am so shocked by everything you said to me, Meg." He let his hand rest on mine as if he was trying to figure out what to say to me. "I must tell you, though, that many things, they make sense to me now. Things I didn't understand before. There was this way he always was near you, watching you. I did always see that, but you know, I never could put something like this together. But now it makes sense to me."

I believed him when he said that. I never thought anyone who knew Donald—especially anyone from the church— would ever believe me. But Father Fausto truly had seen what was happening, even if at the time he hadn't known what it was. I remembered how he had quietly commented to me one Sunday that Donald hovered over me. And now he was looking at me from across the table with such great compassion that I knew he didn't doubt me, that he didn't judge me either.

I opened my mouth and the words poured out. Fury raged inside me. I told him everything—how Donald had abused me in Guyana and growing up, as a teenager, while I was married to Tom, after my divorce. Everything spilled out in a torrent of words. I was talking a hundred miles a minute, as if there wasn't enough time to say everything, as if the only way to be rid of it was to say aloud everything he'd done to me. Father Fausto's eyes were locked on mine, his jaw clenched, and I was so furious I didn't even care if anyone in the restaurant heard me. He was mad—I could tell by his face he was extremely upset. It must have been hard for him to hear the part about the flashlight, because he winced when I said it.

"Meg, this checking . . ."

"It was to find out if I was a virgin. He had to make sure no one got to me."

Father Fausto seemed as if he was struggling to find the words. Maybe he was wondering how Donald could have abused me all those years if I was a virgin, or maybe how I'd let it go on that long. After all, that's what Ernie had said when he first heard it, wasn't it? That I must have liked it or been just as perverted to let it go on that long.

"Your mother." It came out almost as a whisper. "Were you ever able to tell your mother, Meg?"

"My mother?" I almost spat out the word. "My mother was *there*. She watched it. She allowed it. She told him he could do it."

Just then the waitress came up to the table. Both of us ordered something without paying any attention to what it was. When she left again, Father Fausto looked at me again as if he had no idea what to say to me. "What do you want from this man now, Meg? What do you need for him to do?"

"I—I want him to apologize to me." I tried to blink it back, but a tear rolled down my cheek before I could wipe it away. "I want him to tell me he's sorry for what he did to me, I want him to tell me I was more than a. . . . I want him to say those words to me. He has to say that to me."

"Maybe he will, Meg. It's possible he will."

I shook my head. And then I told him what Donald had done to me with the bedpan. "He's not changing, Father Fausto. Nothing is different for him, even now. How can I get an apology if he's still going after me?"

"You need to tell him what he has done to you. You need to ask him for the apology."

Again I shook my head. It couldn't work that way. It had to come from Donald on his own. It wouldn't mean a thing if I put the words in his mouth; it would be like a script that way. Still, if Donald didn't say those words, I didn't know what I'd do. I couldn't get better without them. My whole being was focused on that apology the way a choking person can't think about anything but air.

"Maybe he will say it on the deathbed, Meg. Maybe it will come at the very end. That happens sometimes. I have seen it. Some people realize what they have done and the pain they have caused, but not until the very end."

I wanted so much to believe he was right, and I tried to picture it, too: Donald asking everyone to leave the room except me, and then the sound of his voice as he struggled to begin, struggled to reach down inside himself and find the right way to tell me how sorry he was for everything. I tried to imagine what his face might look like, how it would heal me to hear those words right before he gasped his last breath and. . . .

And then a terrible thought struck me. "If he apologized, he'd go to heaven, wouldn't he?"

Father Fausto tilted his head slightly to one side. "Well, if he asks for forgiveness for his sins, then yes, he would."

I sat there shaking my head at the thought of it. Not burning in hell was one thing. But home free, off the hook completely—that was something totally different. "Well, isn't that something?" I said. Father Fausto had never seen me so angry, never heard such bitterness in my voice. "So even the bad ones get up there if they ask for forgiveness. Is that what the church says? So it's okay for them to do all these horrible things on Earth and then, *poof!* they say they're sorry and it's all wiped clean? I've never heard anything so wrong in my life, and that seems so wrong to me, Father, so wrong that it could be that easy, that one person could do so much bad and then go on to the next life with no final judgment, no nothing. It's so unfair."

He looked at me sadly, his elbows on the table and his fingers laced under his chin. Just then the waitress arrived and put down our food. I was so grateful she left without saying anything bright or cheerful, because I certainly would have burst into tears. I picked up my fork, even though the last thing I wanted to do was eat.

"It just seems so unfair," I said again, "so very wrong."

"Meg," Father Fausto said softly. "We have a very forgiving Lord."

Ever since Donald's request of me with the bedpan, I had avoided going over to Occident Street as much as possible. Ernie told me it was best for me. "You don't need to deal with that shit anymore, Meg," he said to me. "That man's going to be a sicko until the day he dies. It's better for you to just stay away from him."

Ernie's support meant so much to me that sometimes I felt like crying with gratitude. Still, staying away from Mom and Donald's house wasn't as simple as Ernie thought it should be. Several times a week Mom called me to tell me I needed to come right over and sit with Donald while she did an errand. Now that Donald was dying, she seemed colder and more demanding than ever before. I couldn't say no to her.

Sometimes Nick was at the house when I drove up, working in the garden or hauling lawn bags or doing some other task he'd been summoned to do. We didn't say too much to each other those times; both of us just jerked our chins at the other and smiled, and then did whatever needed to be done before going our separate ways. Nick and I hadn't had much of anything to say to each other in a long time, not since his restaurant closed and he'd disappeared once again into whatever world gave him comfort.

One night in late September Ernie and I invited some friends over for dinner. Just as we were sitting down to eat, Mom called and told me to go shopping for her. She said she didn't want Granny and Donald to be alone and needed some eggs. "Well, I've kind of got people here for dinner," I said.

"I don't care, Margaret. I need you to come over right now." There was a long pause. I could hear her impatient breathing into the phone.

"Tell me you're not going over there now, Meg," Ernie said after I hung up and apologized to our guests. "Please tell me you're not going over there." He didn't understand. It wasn't as if I could tell her no. "Why can't you?" he asked, following me out into the driveway.

"Why can't I what?"

"Just tell her no, Meg? That you're busy?"

I shook my head, got into the car and started the engine. It wasn't that simple. And right then, I didn't have the energy to explain it to him. Maybe the truth was that I couldn't have explained it, even to myself. "What is it with you?" he asked. "They say jump, and you jump. When are you going to stop?"

At least when I did go over there, Donald wasn't going after me anymore. Maybe the way I'd refused to help him pee had actually had some kind of effect on him. That, or else he was too sick and weak. But it didn't matter to me which one it was. The only thing I cared about was that it had stopped, that it was never going to start up again. I know this sounds so mean, and I hope God forgives me, but the sicker he got, the more relief I was getting. Every day that went by and he got skinnier and paler than the kitchen walls, I grew stronger.

It was almost as if all of Donald's power was draining out of him and going into me. I could feel it, too: a life force coming into me as if through a blood transfusion.

Finally, in the middle of November, Mom called with the news I'd waited for. Donald was going to the hospital. The ambulance was on its way. "I really think this is it," she said. "I don't think he's ever coming back." I told her how sorry I was, but deep down the little girl inside me was singing and dancing on a tabletop. *Never coming back! Left step, right step, rock step! Never coming back!*

A few nights later, Mom called again. "Come over right now," she said, with no greeting. "I need you to stay with Granny while I visit Donald in the hospital. I need to leave right now." There was nothing more; she hung up.

Ernie said he'd stay with Cameron, and so I drove over alone. When I got there I was surprised to see Nick spread out on the living room sofa. Why did she need two of us there? What possible reason could she have had for calling both of us? Nick jerked his chin at me and went back to staring at the television. Granny was sitting beside him in her lounge chair, for all purposes oblivious to us. "Hi, Granny," I said. She didn't move her head. After a while, Nick got up, stretched, and walked out the front door to the driveway. For lack of anything better to do I followed him and stood beside him as he leaned against Donald's red Lincoln. He reached into his shirt pocket and pulled out a cigarette.

It was a warm, clear night, and the sky was studded with stars. Above the roof, Orion was watching over us with his three-studded belt and sword hanging down. The only sound was the gentle lapping of water in the canal behind the house. Nick struck a match and held it up to his cigarette, the light casting shadow on his sharp chiseled features. Instantly I was reminded of the only picture I had of my father, the one taken with his friends and family in Barbados.

"Oh, I wish he'd just hurry up," I blurted out. "Why doesn't God just hurry up and take the man?"

Nick's eyebrows went up a little, but he didn't seem too surprised I'd said that out of nowhere. He nodded, as though he was thinking it over. "You sure don't seem too sad about it," he said. He took a deep drag on his cigarette and blew out a thin stream of smoke toward the stars. "Aren't you even sorry he's dying?"

I wished I hadn't said anything. "Well," I said slowly, "he did things to me." I didn't want to go into it. Still, the way Nick had said it made it sound more like curiosity than an accusation.

"Yeah?" he said. He turned to look at me. "For how long?"

I shrugged. "You don't want to know." I was about to go back inside. But something stopped me. "Hell, I don't care anymore. For most of my damn life, Nick."

Nick dropped his barely smoked cigarette and ground it with his foot. "Well, guess what?" He shoved his hands into his pockets. "Donald did stuff to me, too. For years and years."

You want to think that when you find out something important in your life, it'll sink right in. That once you know the truth of a thing, everything that never made sense before will fall right into place, that the pieces will fit nice and snug. But the fact is, some things don't have a place to go inside you right away. Sometimes your mind can be like bone-dry, rock-hard soil when it's first rained on: The details flash flood over the surface of your brain. I suspect God does that for our own protection so we can get used to horrible things slowly, so everything doesn't soak us down so fast we can't move, so we don't end up not being able to breathe and just drown on the spot.

I didn't think straight off about what Nick had just told me. I thought instead about Ernie. *You're probably just the tip of the iceberg, Meg.* Ernie had been so sure I wasn't the only one, but I hadn't believed him. How had he known it? And how could he have known something in just a few months that I hadn't known my entire life?

But then, slowly, awfully, things started to make sense. There was the way Nick always disappeared as soon as school was over, which was when Donald took me to his yacht. There was the way he never was around when we lived on Juno Street and was always off somewhere with his friends. There were all those times I blamed him for what was happening to me, because if he'd been at home he could have protected me. But right then I started to understand. Nick had been trying to run away from it. He hadn't known what he was leaving me to deal with.

I looked over at my brother's profile, suddenly picturing his face when he was younger. Years before it would have been shyness and gentleness you saw there instead of the bitterness and anger etched there now. Neither of us had ever known what was happening to the other. The only person had been Donald—and he had made certain it stayed that way.

"When did it start with you?" From the tone in my voice, I could have been asking him, So how did you like living in Pensacola?

Nick pulled out another cigarette and lit it. "Guyana," he said. He looked away. "With the washing. When I was about five."

I nodded and then looked away, too, back up at Orion's belt. I remembered those baths in Guyana at the flat, and later at Bel Air, but I never thought about what Donald might have done to Nick. *Men who like little girls don't like little boys, too.* Where had I learned that? Why had I been telling myself that my entire life?

"Then a lot more after we came to the States," Nick said. "On the boat, you know? He'd do stuff to me there."

I didn't want to hear anymore. It's terrible to say, but right then I was thinking, *Oh my God, he put it in Nick and then put it in me, in my mouth.* It was so nasty and horrible to think about that I wanted to clasp my hands over my ears and vomit at the same time.

I leaned against the red Lincoln and closed my eyes. *Don't think about that now, Meg, think about something else. Think about anything else. You'll go crazy if you think about that now. Oh God, oh God, oh God . . . please help me to not think about that now. . . .*

We both went inside. Neither of us said anything more about it, and we both left as soon as Mom got back from the hospital. But that night, I told everything to Ernie. "I told you so," Ernie said, slapping the kitchen counter. "Donald's a perverted son of a bitch. I wonder who else he did it to? Not just the two of you, that's for sure. I'll bet you anything he even did it to other kids, too."

I gasped. It was like ice water thrown in my face. *Other kids.* If he'd do it to Nick, then why not Cameron, too? Whenever I had changed Cameron's diaper after we'd been over at Occident Street, I'd always checked him, looked there carefully without any awareness of what I was looking for. It was as if somewhere in the back of my mind the thought had been trying to make its way into my head, but I wouldn't let it in. I remembered all the times Donald insisted Cameron shouldn't wear a diaper in the pool. How he'd taken pictures of him naked. How he liked to hold him on his lap in the hot tub. And suddenly I was so frightened, so terrified at the thought of what Donald might have done to my child that I couldn't even speak.

Maybe it wasn't true. Oh God, it couldn't be true, could it? But I'd left Cameron there overnight before, and Donald might have been alone with him. Was it possible I'd missed the signs? I'd missed them with Nick, my own brother, and they'd been right there under my nose. All those years, right under my nose!

Ernie reached out his hand and grasped my arm. "Meg, are you all right?"

I squeezed my eyes shut and violently shook my head. "No," I whispered. "No, Ernie, I am not all right. *I am not all right.*"

Twenty-Three

What better day to die could Donald have chosen than Thanksgiving Day?

Ernie and I had driven over to Occident Street early that morning—Cameron was spending his first holiday away from me with Tom—and my mother already was at the hospital when we arrived. She had asked me to fix the dinner while she was gone, and Kathy Mann, Donald's niece, was helping me in the kitchen when the phone rang.

"He's slipping fast," my mother said. "The doctor says he's almost gone. Leave Ernie there—I don't want him here. Come right now with Kathy."

Kathy and I drove in her car to St. Joseph's Hospital and took the elevator up to Donald's private room. Instantly we were greeted by his gaunt face, his hollow cheeks and sunken eyes, while Mom stood beside him stroking his forehead. Don Jr. and his wife, Peggy were at the foot of the bed, and Nick was leaning against the wall. No one said a thing. All of us just stood there, waiting.

I didn't actually see Donald die. I always thought the moment of death would be something you'd know or feel right away, like when someone leaves a room and slams the door. But it wasn't like that at all. It wasn't until I heard someone say, "He's gone," that I realized it was finally over, that I'd never again have his flesh anywhere near me. My mother burst out sobbing and climbed into bed with him. She kissed him on his forehead, on his cheeks, on his half-open mouth—more affection than I'd ever seen while he was alive—and then she put her head on his shoulder like a scene from one of the stained glass windows at our church. "I'm going to miss you so much!" she wailed. "So, so much! Oh, but you're in a better place now, you don't have to suffer anymore! You're in heaven now, Donald, you're with God now."

Don Jr., who resembled a young version of his father, looked on without a speck of emotion on his face while Peggy dabbed at her nose with a tissue. But when I looked over at Nick, tears were streaming down his face. I couldn't believe that. Nick was actually crying for him. I wasn't crying, that's for sure. When Mom said Donald was in heaven with God it took all my strength to say, *That's what you think. He's probably in hell for all the torture and torment he put me through. At least I hope he is, burning in hell!*

It seemed to me there was a very good chance of that. After all, Father Fausto had been wrong about a deathbed confession; there hadn't even been a priest near him when he died. But then a terrible thought occurred to me: Donald had never asked me, but what if he'd asked God for forgiveness? What if he silently had confessed his sins to God and repented? There was always that possibility. And right then I knew what that meant: I'd never be able to be sure where Donald had gone, up or down. I'd never know if he ever got his final judgment.

Don Jr. and Peggy turned down my mother's invitation to come home with us for Thanksgiving dinner. The rest of us went back to the house, where the aroma of turkey wafted through the rooms. As my mother sat quietly next to Granny, Nick and Kathy on the living room sofa, I went into the kitchen and brought out the stuffing, broccoli, potatoes and cranberry sauce. Then I set the table. When I realized I'd grabbed one too many sets of utensils, I tossed the extra fork and knife onto the counter. "Guess who's not getting any dinner tonight?" I said softly.

It was Kathy Mann who said the blessing. "We thank you Lord for the love that is here among us and for your strength." I sneaked a look at everyone praying, their heads bowed and eyes closed. "And please bless Donald and watch over him and keep him with you always. Amen."

Everyone lifted their heads and pulled their napkins onto their laps. It was then that I bowed my own head. "Thank

you, God," I whispered. When I looked up, Kathy was staring
at me strangely.

Donald's wake was scheduled for Sunday evening at a
funeral home on MacDill Avenue. His funeral, at St. Patrick's,
would be the following day. On Sunday morning I drove over
alone to stay with Granny while Mom went over to the
funeral home to make last-minute arrangements. As usual,
Granny was staring at the television. For not the first time I
wondered what it was my mother thought might happen if
we ever left her alone.

After a while, the phone rang. It was Jeanne Becker, the
adult education director at St. Patrick's. Part of Jeanne's job
was to reach out to people in the congregation whenever
they were having any kind of trouble or needed spiritual
guidance, but I also knew that Mom and Jeanne were close
friends. They went out to dinner, and sometimes they went
to the symphony together. Jeanne recognized my voice
immediately.

"Hello, Margaret. How's your mother? Is she home?"

I told her Mom was doing all right, but that she'd taken
clothes over to the funeral director. "And how are you,
Margaret? How are you doing through all of this?"

"I'm fine."

"Are you?"

"Yes."

"I can tell you, Margaret, that Donald is going to be greatly
missed. He was such a good, fine man, and this world just
won't be the same without him. It's hard for me to think of

going to St. Patrick's and not seeing him there with you and your mother, because he was such an important part of the church. He was such a good person, Margaret, and so greatly loved by so very many people. I hope you know that."

That was it. It was as if a two-by-four inside me snapped in half like a toothpick. Fury shot through me. "Let me tell you something, Jeanne. Donald was not the man you or anyone else thought he was, okay? Let me tell you a few things that went on, okay? Because I'm tired of people telling me how good he was, because he wasn't and I'll tell you a side of him no one knew and no one saw but I saw it all the time. . . . I saw it my whole life." And then I told her what I'd told Father Fausto, everything coming out a hundred miles a minute. Jeanne didn't say a word while I was going on like that. "And I'm sick of everyone saying how fine a man he was, and it bothers the hell out of me if you want to know the truth and now that he's dead I can tell everyone how he really was whether they believe it or not because I don't give a damn anymore and I don't care who believes it because I'm glad the man is dead and I couldn't be happier about it."

When I was done there was a long silence. Then Jeanne said, "That must have been a very hard thing you went through. I'm so sorry that happened to you, especially starting at such a young age. You must be very angry, and now that he's dead you must be very relieved it's over."

"Yes, I am." I was breathing hard and shaking. "I really am."

Jeanne told me she was there to help me if I needed anyone to talk to. She gave me her phone number and told me I could call her any time, day or night. I wrote the number down, not thinking I'd ever do that, though later I ended up calling her several times. Jeanne was the only person I told about Ernie's gun, how I wanted to use it on myself.

"You need some counseling," she said, "someone to help you through this. I'm here for you, Margaret, anytime you need me, but can I find you the name of a good counselor? Would you let me do that for you?"

I told her she could, that she was probably right. I did need someone to talk to. "And tonight, at the wake," she said, "you just look over at me if it gets too hard. I'll be right there for you, and I'll help you get through it if it gets too difficult. All right?"

I thanked her and hung up the phone just as my mother walked in the door.

That evening the funeral home was filled with people. Some I knew from St. Patrick's and others were people I'd never met from Donald's company. Everyone milled about, talking softly, and right then I wished Ernie was with me. He'd gotten mad that my mother said he wasn't a polished enough person to ride with us in the limousine—something, in hindsight, I shouldn't have told him the truth about—but I also think the idea of showing any respect for Donald was more than he could take. As I walked toward the back of the room I looked around for Nick but didn't see him anywhere.

Donald's blue marble casket, the one my mother told me he'd ordered from Italy just a few weeks earlier, was closed. As I looked at all the flowers and wreaths propped against its base, it struck me how typical that last gesture of his had been. Flaunting his money right to the end. As if anyone really cared whether he rotted in marble or wood. When I turned away I spotted Father Fausto in the middle of the room. He was dressed in his clerical collar, talking with several people, and not far from him was Father Venard. For a moment, looking at him was like seeing Donald's ghost.

As soon as the people Father Fausto had been talking to moved on, I walked over and gave him a kiss on his cheek. "Meg," he said warmly. "How are you?"

I leaned forward and smiled. "Better now that he's dead," I whispered.

"Yes, I know," he said quietly.

"But the son of a bitch died without giving me my apology."

He took my hand and stepped closer. "How is your mother holding up?"

"Fine." In fact, she hadn't cried once since the hospital room. At the same moment Father Fausto and I looked over at her, surrounded by her friends. As usual she was perfectly put together: Her dark hair was immaculately styled, she wore a pair of her beautiful earrings and a tasteful designer dress with high heels. She looked rich and well-kept. In contrast I had worn a pair of black slacks and a plain white blouse.

After a while everyone moved toward the chairs lined up in front of the casket. Jeanne Becker sat in the middle of the front row and began by leading the rosary. From my seat beside my mother I had a clear view of her as she bowed her head and moved her fingers over the dark red beads. After she finished, she looked up and met my eyes. She smiled at me softly as if to say, *Hang in there, it'll be all right.* After what I'd said to her that morning, she probably thought I was on the verge of doing something crazy.

What do you wear to the funeral of a man when you're glad he's dead? I've never seen that question asked in any fashion magazine. But now I have the answer: the brightest outfit you own. I wore a slim-fitting neon pink suit with onyx earrings. If anyone dared to ask, I'd say that Donald sure wouldn't have wanted me to go around looking sad on his account. Which, technically, was true. Hadn't he always told me he wanted me to look cheerful, that as soon as I walked through a door he wanted me to look happy?

My mother, dressed in an elegant black dress with beautiful diamond earrings, sat on the pew beside me. Then there was Nick, in a suit and tie for perhaps the second time in his entire life; Don Jr., sitting ramrod straight next to his wife, Peggy; and Kathy Mann. As Father Venard walked slowly past Donald's marble casket to the pulpit, the choir in their orange robes sang "Let There Be Peace on Earth," Donald's favorite hymn.

The choir stopped singing and Father Venard lifted his head. He gazed out on the congregation and stretched out his hands, palms upward. "Let us pray," he said. There was a collective dropping of heads and closing of eyes. I waited for the rise of his voice, the pause that signified it was over, and then joined the congregation in unison: "Amen." My mother's hands, with her perfectly manicured nails, were folded demurely in her lap. Her face could have been carved from stone. *How dignified she is in her grief,* people must have been thinking. *What a tragedy, losing a man like Donald Sahlman, and after just a few brief years of happiness.*

Father Venard struggled to begin the eulogy. "Donald Sahlman—" Everyone could tell his cracking voice was real, that he wasn't just eulogizing a parishioner but also a close friend. "Donald Sahlman was a good, kind, generous man who gave freely of himself to everyone who knew him." And then he launched into it: how he was a loving husband, a loving father and stepfather, a dedicated member of this congregation. He recited a few psalms and then on and on he went about Donald's greatness, his huge generosity to St. Patrick's over the years, until I thought he couldn't possibly say more. But I was wrong. He started all over again, as if he forgot he'd already said what a kind, generous man my stepfather was, and it was Donald this and Donald that, on and on, until I was digging my fingernails into my palms and I thought I might scream.

Finally, Father Venard stopped talking and took a step back. He looked at my mother and nodded, and she rose slowly and walked over to where her violin lay in its case. As one of the orange-robed choir members moved in front of the casket, my mother put the violin under her chin and began playing "Ave Maria" while the soprano sang. Slowly people rose and began making their way to the front of the church for communion. The thought of accepting the host when God knew there was such hatred in my heart felt like a terrible sin, but I knelt and cupped my hands like everyone else.

That night Ernie didn't know what to say to me. He didn't have the tools. I was like a walking human nuclear spill and all he had was a mop.

"What did you expect him to say at the funeral, Meg? That Donald was a son of a bitch and a pedophile? At least it's over now. At least you don't have to go through anything with him ever again."

"It's not over, Ernie. Donald may be dead, but I'm still here, and I'm the one who has to look at all those people while they tell me how wonderful he was, what a saint, and it drives me insane, Ernie! It just totally drives me insane!"

"Then maybe you should tell it to Father Venard," he said finally. "Go tell him everything, spell it out for him."

"I can't do that."

"Why not, Meg? Why can't you?"

"Because he and Donald were best friends. He thinks my mother is wonderful. He used to come over to Occident Street all the time for dinner. He and Donald were like this." I crossed my fingers. "He'd never believe me."

Ernie leaned back against the kitchen counter, looking down at me. He's more than a foot taller than I, so I had to tip my head back to look up into his face. "Listen, Meg. I really think you should go to Father Venard. Tell him the story."

"What good will it do, Ernie? The man's dead now."

"Well, you don't know what good it'll do, do you? And the way I figure it, anything's better than how you are now. Look at you. You're a mess."

Ernie was right. I thought I'd be fine once Donald was dead and buried, that the weight would be gone and I'd feel relieved, but I was jumpy and I couldn't sleep at night and I couldn't remember when I last ate something. It was as if Donald was there in the room with me, watching me.

"Then come with me, Ernie. I can't do it alone."

"You have to, Meg. I can't go with you on this one. You have to do this alone."

No matter what I said, Ernie wouldn't change his mind.

The next day I drove over to St. Patrick's to pick up Cameron from the church school. He was in pre-kindergarten, which I sometimes thought must have been invented so parents could have a few hours to themselves. As I walked across the parking lot my eyes automatically went over to the Aegean Towers on the other side of the chain-link fence. I almost expected to see the ghost of myself as a twelve-year-old girl in an upstairs window.

I walked across the lawn. As I passed the rectory, Father Venard came out the door into the sunlight. He squinted, and then nodded when he recognized me. "Hello, Margaret."

"Hello, Father."

Sometimes I think my world can be divided into two sets of people: the ones who call me Margaret and bring out the person Donald always wanted everyone to see—the well-mannered, perfectly groomed woman who does what she's told and never talks back; and the handful who know something closer to the truth, the real Meg who rarely gets out. The real Meg is angry and so damn tired of everything and can start talking so fast she almost forgets to breathe. That Meg scares me sometimes.

"And how are you today, Margaret?" he asked.

I was about to give my standard reply, the answer I've been giving all my life. But when I opened my mouth, it wasn't Margaret who was there to answer "fine": It was that other Meg, and she had taken control of my mouth. "You know what, Father Venard? I'm not doing very well. I'll tell you, I'm really not doing well at all."

"Oh?" he said. He wasn't expecting that. The anger.

"No, I'm not. And you know what? I need to talk with you. Because there's some things you need to know. Some things I need to tell you."

"I see," he said. He waited there and then after a long moment said, "Is it something about the funeral? About your stepfather's death?"

"Yeah, you could say that. You could say it's about the funeral."

Father Venard was looking at me strangely. For years, I had sensed he didn't like me: I felt it when Tom and I went to talk with him about our wedding, while he was performing our ceremony, and I most definitely felt it after Tom and I got divorced. It was a chill, something that always made me feel like putting on a sweater, but my brain had always out-talked my gut. What kind of priest would dislike you for no good reason?

"Well," he asked, "is there perhaps something I can do for you now, Margaret?"

"No, not here. Not now. I need to talk with you in private."

One of Father Venard's eyebrows rose behind his thick aviator frame glasses, the same type Donald wore at the end. Then he looked at his watch. "I'm a bit pressed for time today," he said, "but what about tomorrow? Would tomorrow be all right?"

I shook my head. Or rather, that other Meg shook my head. Tomorrow, I knew, would be too late. My courage would be gone by then. "Today would be better, Father."

"All right then," he said slowly. "Tonight at seven o'clock, if that's not too late?"

"No."

"No?"

"No, that's not too late. That'll be fine, Father Venard. Thank you very much."

He gave me a tight smile, and then turned and walked toward the front of the church.

It was dusk when I returned to the church later that evening. Pink and orange clouds surrounded downtown Tampa in the distance. Even in November it was too hot and humid for a jacket, so I had dressed in a long flowered summer dress and carefully reapplied my makeup. I had a sick sensation, a feeling of dread, as I approached the rectory doors. My knees were shaking, and I did not want to go inside. I wanted to turn and go back to the car and tell Ernie I couldn't go through with it, but something—I can't tell you what—propelled me forward. I knocked on Father Venard's door and opened it.

He rose from his desk but didn't make a move toward me. "Hello, Margaret," he said. He waved one hand toward a chair. "Please," he said, motioning for me to sit down.

My purse was on my lap. As I looked around his office I

opened it and closed it, opened it and closed it. My fingers were moist and trembling, and they slipped off the clasp. I was too afraid to look into his eyes.

"Well, Margaret, you said you needed to talk about something. I don't have a lot of time. What is it?"

I wasn't ready for him to be so brusque, so suddenly businesslike. By his tone it was obvious he wanted me to go, that he had no interest in anything I had to say. He already knew he wouldn't like it, whatever it was.

"I—I . . . I don't know if I can do this."

He breathed deeply through his nose and expelled the air impatiently. "Come now," he said. "If you need to talk about something, you certainly can do it here. There is no one else in this room. Just the two of us."

"But it's . . . it's just that I. . . ."

"You're worried? You're afraid that whatever you tell me won't be safe?"

I nodded and then burst into tears. *Oh God, I can't believe I'm crying. No one ever sees me cry.* "Yes," I said between sobs. "Yes, I am, Father. I'm very afraid of that."

"Margaret, you know that as a priest I am forbidden to repeat anything you tell me in confidence. If I tell you that this conversation will be under the seal, if I assure you of that, will that help you?" I nodded and took the Kleenex he handed me. "Well, then. You have my word of it. Now, what was it?"

"It's about Donald. About all those things you said about him yesterday."

"Yes?"

"And you said what a wonderful man he was and how

good and kind he was to everyone, but there's something you don't know about him, Father Venard, there's a side of him you never knew, that no one knew. I'm not saying Donald didn't do all those things you said, because he did have a good side, but you don't know what he's done to me, you have no idea. He abused me, Father Venard. He abused me from the time I was four years old in Guyana. He abused me when I was a teenager growing up, he even abused me when I was married to Tom and after Cameron was born." I was shaking so intensely my purse fell off my lap.

"Margaret," he said, leaning forward. "Are you talking about Don Sahlman, your stepfather? You cannot be talking about the same man."

The second he said that, a shaft of anger shot through me. "Yes, I am! You know what he did to me? What he and my mother did?" And then I told him what Mom and Donald did after every date I had with a boy, up until the time I married Tom, and how Donald took me to his boat and everything he did to me.

He was staring at me as if I was mad. And then he leaned back in his chair and began shaking his head. Father Venard and everyone else at St. Patrick's thought my mother met Donald in Tampa when I was sixteen; that's the story they always were told. But Father Venard didn't ask me about any of that. He didn't say, *Wait a minute, how could this have happened when you were four? I thought you met Donald Sahlman here when you were a teenager?* In fact, he didn't ask me a thing.

"I must tell you that I find all of this very hard to believe," he said. "I knew Don Sahlman, and this cannot possibly be the same man. I know your mother, too, and I simply cannot imagine her doing what you have told me. Don Sahlman was one of the finest men I have known, a pillar of honor in our community—"

"But it's true, Father Venard, all of it's true. Everyone thinks what a great man he was, but they didn't know him. And they don't know my mother, either!"

He dropped his shoulders and sighed, as if the conversation was pointless. Finally, in exasperation, he said, "Then may I ask you something? If what you say is true, can you tell me why you would have permitted such a thing to go on for so long? You say it has been happening all of your life, and happened even during your marriage. You are, what, nearly thirty years old now? So can you explain to me how you could have let something like that go on for so long?" He stared at me, as if he didn't think I would answer.

"He threatened me."

"Don threatened you? With what?"

"With all kinds of terrible things. He said I'd burn in hell. That if I told anyone, all kinds of bad things would happen."

"He said you'd burn in hell if you told anyone?"

"Yes."

"And you believed that?"

"He said he'd send my mother back to Guyana, that he'd brought her here to America and he could send her back to the slums where he found her. He said he was rich and powerful enough to do it to all of us, to Nick, me and Granny, that we'd all get sent back."

He folded his hands on his desk. "I'm sure you can understand how difficult all of this is for me to take in. And I must tell you that I don't feel equipped to deal with everything you have said. I believe you need a counselor, a professional. May I ask if you have told this story to anyone else?"

I knew how he meant the question—if I'd told anyone at all about it, and not just a counselor. I knew I should tell him the whole truth, but right then I didn't trust him. "Ernie knows."

"Ernie. And this would be the man with whom you are cohabiting?"

"We live together."

"Yes. And what does Ernie say about all of this?"

"He said I should come and talk with you."

"Ernie said this? He suggested it?"

"Yes."

"I see. And should I assume it is for the purpose of a lawsuit?" That word—his suspicion spoken out loud like that—jolted me. I knew I shouldn't have come, I knew I shouldn't have listened to Ernie. Father Venard kept staring at me. "Your stepfather was a very wealthy man, Margaret. So I have to wonder if somewhere that plays a role."

I shook my head. "I just came here because . . . because I need to heal. I need to get better. I kept waiting for Donald to apologize to me for what he did. I kept thinking he'd tell me he was sorry for it before he died, but he never said it. I kept going over to Occident Street to do things for them, and I kept hoping he'd say it to me but he never did. It was the only thing that mattered to me, my only goal."

"But now that he's dead, Margaret, it must be obvious to

you that your goal is gone now, that your goal is no longer possible. You must realize that, don't you?"

Father Venard stood up and looked at his watch. He was done with me. Disgusted. "I am very sorry for you, Margaret, because it is clear you are a very troubled woman. If it's all right with you, I would like to find you the name of someone who might be able to help you better than I can. May I find someone within the church?"

I nodded and stood up. He didn't show me to the door. He stood behind his desk, his hands at his sides, and as I went to leave I felt his eyes boring into the back of my head. In the doorway, I turned to look at his face one more time. His jaw was clenched, his lips pressed tightly together. "Well, you know what they say, Margaret," he said sarcastically. "The truth shall set you free."

It was exactly what I told Ernie would happen.

Father Venard thought I was lying through my teeth.

Twenty-Four

In early December—just six weeks before I first walked into Lynwood Arnold's office and began telling you this story—my mother asked me to move back into the house with her. She didn't say she was afraid to be alone or needed some company, just that she needed help with all the errands. Besides, she added, there was Granny to think of. She didn't want to leave her alone.

Ernie didn't even bother trying to convince me not to move in with her, or to remind me, as he had in the past, that she lives just a half-hour away. He knew it was futile. Ernie has watched me get up from the table when we've had guests to go sit with Granny; he's seen the way I broke out in hives on the rare occasions my mother came to our house on Robin Hood Drive; he's seen how jumpy and nervous I get afterwards and can't eat or sleep for days; and he's listened to me scream in my sleep.

"All right, Meg," he said. "Do whatever you have to do. But I sure as hell hope you're not going to be there over Christmas."

"It'll just be for a few days," I said to him. "And I'll have Cameron with me. You know how my mother is when he's around—don't touch this, don't touch that, stay right there in front of the TV, don't make a mess. She doesn't want anything in her precious house disturbed. She'll ask us to leave in a few days, you watch."

At night, Cameron slept with me in my old bedroom, in the single bed beneath the window. Or rather, Cameron slept. The slightest sound—Cameron moving his hand across the pillow, a creak when the wind blew—made me bolt upright. In the middle of the night, I had to talk myself down: *He's dead, Meg. He's not here, he can't do a damn thing to you anymore, he's not coming for you anymore.*

Still, in the mornings, Donald was waiting for me. His face stared out from silver frames on the mantle above the fireplace, on the kitchen counter, on the shelf above the dining room table. There was Donald on his yacht, Donald beside his red Lincoln, Donald standing under the Arc de Triomphe. There were two pictures of Nick, taken a few years before the drug rehab hospital, but none of me. And none of Cameron.

My mother was polite to me, but her face had an enduring expression, the kind people have when a distant cousin unexpectedly comes to stay from out of state. Sometimes I think that's how she preferred to see me, too: as a distant relative, someone whose features in no way resemble her own, someone whose skin color is different, someone who comes from a world she'd rather not think about, rather not remember. For twenty years she listened mutely to Donald's remarks about me—hey little nigger girl, hey little pickaninny, I've got nothin' against niggers, everyone should own one; and now, sometimes, I think she feels the same way about me. All my life she reminded me she never wanted me in the first place, that I ruined her music career, that she tried to leave me behind in Barbados. But now that Donald is dead it's as if she has forgotten I am her daughter at all, that the black blood in my veins came from a man she once loved.

To remember any of it, of course, would be an admission. It would mean acknowledging what she has done to me, and neither of us can do that. Maybe what both of us have done—me with my confession to Father Venard, and her treating me like her maid—are just separate ways of doing anything we can to avoid that truth, to keep the wolves of memory away from the door. To go onward, we both had to pretend: It was completely normal that we were living in the same house again; nothing, at all, had happened between us.

Every day I did my best to clean, even though Carmen, her cleaning woman from St. Patrick's, still came once or twice a week. Occasionally, Carmen and I chatted in the kitchen about meaningless things: How was your weekend, isn't it hot for December. I shopped for groceries, tended the orchids out back, cooked "healthful" chicken and fish meals the way my mother liked them. Ernie usually came over each evening around dinnertime, and sometimes he offered to take us all out to a restaurant. Even though I knew what she thought of him, my mother put on her best face for him. She turned her cheek to let him kiss it, something he'd been doing ever since Donald died. Privately, Ernie told me he did it because he didn't want any more friction with her.

Not once did I see my mother cry over her dead husband. Not once did she appear even remotely sad. When people from St. Patrick's came over and told her how well she was holding up, she told them it was because Donald was sick for so long and she had time to prepare herself. And then she added with a sniff, "But of course you never can really prepare yourself for something like that, not with a man like Donald."

After the people would leave she'd play with her big white dog, Napoleon. While Granny stared with her usual blankness at the television, my mother walked through the sliding-glass door to the pool area and began dancing in place next to the dog like a marionette being made to walk over hot coals. "Na-po-leon!" she crooned, her knees jerking up and down as if pulled by invisible strings. "Oh, Na-po-leon!" The dog looked up at her expectantly, wagging his bushy tail. And then, after a few minutes, she'd come back inside and lock the dog out. He always stood there bewildered, as if he couldn't figure out what he did wrong. I knew exactly how he felt.

As the days blended into each other, I tried not to think about what I said to Father Venard or what my mother would do if she ever found out. As one week turned into two, I told myself *it's over now,* that nothing would ever come of it. But one day my mother came home from doing an errand. She'd been gone several hours, and she had a strange expression on her face. All her words were the same—how's Granny, has the dog been fed—but there was something cold in her face. Something scary. And a little flashing yellow light of warning went off inside me.

That night at the dinner table, my mother lifted a forkful of vegetables to her mouth. She said, "I think it's time for you to go home now, Margaret." And then she took the bite and chewed slowly, purposefully, staring straight ahead of her.

"You do?"

"Yes, I do."

"All right. So, tomorrow?"

"No, tonight. After you clean up the dishes. And keep your child under control while you do them, Margaret. I don't want him getting into any more things."

I looked across the table at Cameron, who was silently chewing a piece of bread. Whenever he was over at Mom and Donald's house, he was always like a different child: quiet, still, inside himself. He had done nothing while we had been staying there—touched nothing, disturbed nothing, gotten into no mischief. Whenever I wasn't playing with him, he sat in front of the television on the rug, holding his favorite stuffed animal on his lap, just as my mother instructed him to do. *Your child,* she said. *Keep your child under control.*

What could prompt such anger in her toward him, unless it was the same thing that prompted it toward me? What other reason could she have for spitting it out that way, unless her coldness toward him was an extension of what she felt toward me? It hit me then: *I am not the only one with a secret. My mother has one, too.* I could feel it.

And for the first time since Donald died, a knot of fear returned. I could not wait to get back to Ernie's house, to get away from her.

Ernie's not big on Christmas music so he had James Brown blasting on the stereo singing about how good he feels, just like he knew that he would. It was Christmas Eve, and I was bouncing my head to the saxophones and wrapping presents in front of the huge tree, which was covered with so many ornaments and lights you could barely see a speck of green. I'd bought a sweater and perfume for my mother, some shirts and a silver cigarette lighter for Ernie, some body powder for Granny, and a stack of toys for Cameron.

Maybe it was the music, but I was feeling good, too. I couldn't believe it, but I was actually feeling happier. Ernie says the only way to get any contentment is to convince yourself you've earned it; otherwise, he says, you go around thinking it's just around the corner, that if only one more thing happened or if you finally bought the thing you wanted, then you'd be happy. That makes sense to me, because that's just how it was. I always thought if Donald were out of my life, if he'd just go away somewhere, then I could be happy. But right after he died, nothing was any better. Nothing really felt any different. So I started doing what Ernie suggested, telling myself each day that I'd already paid my dues, that I'd earned a bit of contentment. And by Christmas Eve, I was getting a glimmer of hope. If I just went on with my business and tried to forget about everything, I'd be all right.

The only thing that set me back was Father Venard's phone call. As soon as I heard his voice I felt the tightness in my chest, the thumping of my heart. "Hello, Margaret," he said. His voice sounded as if there was someone in the room with him. "I'm calling to wish you a merry Christmas," he said.

"Thank you, Father Venard. And merry Christmas to you, too."

"We haven't seen you at church lately, Margaret. Not since the service. Is everything all right?"

Why was he asking me that? Why did he even bother to pretend he wanted to see me? "Oh yes, everything's fine," I said. "Thank you. We've just been very busy with the holidays and, well, everything's just been very busy."

"I see. Well, please give my best to your mother when you see her."

Give her my best? My best what? And why didn't he give it to her himself? Except for when we were in Europe, my mother hadn't missed Mass at St. Patrick's since we moved to Tampa in 1974.

For two days after that call, I couldn't get rid of the feeling that something was wrong, that there was something I didn't know that might hurt me. It was the same feeling I had when we came home from Europe and I saw the strange look on Mike Cobaugh's face. But Ernie kept telling me to push it out of my thoughts, that I was just being paranoid. "Venard may be a son of a bitch," he said, "but he's still a priest. The man's not your enemy."

"You think so?"

"Yes, I do. You've got to stop thinking about him. It's over now."

I like living with Ernie, and I like his little house. He bought the land cheap and built on it a few years back, and it's still the only house on the cul-de-sac not far from the Tampa airport. There's a thick grove of vine-covered trees out back, a small screened-in pool, and at night you can sit on the patio and listen to the crickets and frogs, the cacophony of the jungle. Cameron loves living on Robin Hood Drive, a street named after someone who stole from the rich and gave to the poor, and he loves counting the planes that rise and descend over the house, too. Whenever I drop him off at Tom's, he tells his father how many planes have flown overhead since the last time he was there, almost as if it's his way of marking time between visits.

Tom's never said anything to me, but I can tell he thinks Ernie's house is a bad environment for Cameron. It never bothers me what Tom thinks, though, because the way I figure it, he lost his right to have a say in things that concern me. Sometimes, though, I've caught Tom looking at Ernie as if that's the biggest mystery of them all. Like: What does Ernie have that I didn't? I could if I wanted, spell it out for him. But you can't just hit someone over the head that way. You can't say to someone who's basically a happy person that they live their life like an ostrich, and that if they knew even half the truth the world wouldn't look so good.

Ernie, Cameron and I spent Christmas morning with my mother and Granny over at Occident Street. Nick had come, too, and it was the first time since the funeral I'd seen him. From what I could tell, Nick seemed fine to me. It was early in the day, so he probably hadn't had any drugs yet, and he and my mother stood next to the tree talking about when and where various ornaments were bought.

"Remember this one?" my mother asked. "We got that our first Christmas here in Tampa. Donald bought it, I think he got it at some crafts fair in Ybor City. And this one—I can't remember where that came from, but maybe we got it at Tarpon Springs, or else maybe it was that time we all went to, well, I guess it doesn't matter. . . ."

Nick nodded his head as if he was vastly interested. "Really?" he said. "It was really that long ago, Mom?" He gave no sign of what was going on inside of him—or what he was about to do that would blow all of our lives apart.

Five days later, Nick showed up at Ernie's house. He was dressed in his usual outfit, a pair of dirty jeans and T-shirt, and even though it wasn't dark yet, the smell of alcohol was strong on his breath. He plopped down on the living room sofa as if it was the most normal thing in the world and spread his arms out over the back. He started shaking his head.

"Well, Meg, I've really gone and done it this time," he said. "I've really gone and fucked things up. Oh man, oh man, I've really fucked things up bad."

"Gone and done what? What have you done?"

"I went over there today, Meg. To Mom's. And I told her everything."

"Everything? You told her—"

"Yeah. Everything Donald did to me. Starting in Guyana. I told her that's why I ran away to Pensacola, you know, to get away from him. Oh man, I shouldn't have told her. She's so mad, Meg, you wouldn't believe how mad she is. She looked like—"

"What did she say to you, Nick? What did she do when you told her?"

"Oh man, I shouldn't have ever gone over there. But I was drunk, you know?"

"You must have been. What made you do that?"

"I told you, I was drunk. Drunker than now. And it just made me mad, you know? I don't know what it was. See, she told me on the phone that Don Jr.'s going to be handling all her money from now on, and I don't think he should be doing that, you know? She should be handling her own finances, not just handing everything over to him."

"Why do you even care about that, Nick? What possible difference could that make to you?"

"Well, anyway. So I went over there, and I ended up saying everything like I told you. And she told me I was making it all up, that Donald would never do anything like that, that I was just a liar and to get out. She really told me to get out! So I said, 'Well, if you don't believe me, just ask Meg. He did it to her, too. Meg will tell you the same thing.'"

"Oh God, Nick. You told her about me?"

"I had to. So she's going to call you. I know she will. So you've got to back me up, Meg. You've got to, or she'll never speak to me again. I swear to God she was that mad. You should have seen her, Meg. She was like, crazy."

The next day, my mother did call me. All morning I'd been afraid to answer the phone, and the second I heard her voice I wanted to hang up, call Ernie at work and ask him what to say to her. She didn't even say hello. My mother said, "Your brother was over here yesterday, Margaret. And he said some things to me."

"Um-hmm."

"And I want you to come over right now. I want to talk with you. I want to ask you some things. So come over."

She waited for me to say something. I couldn't tell her I was too scared to go over alone, that there was no way in hell I was going to walk into that lion's den by myself, so I said, "I'll come over tomorrow, Mom. My car's being fixed and hopefully it'll be out of the shop by then. I'll try and come tomorrow."

The next day Ernie drove me over in his Bronco. My feet were pulled up beneath me on the front seat and my heart was racing. I told Ernie he had to do the talking for me, that he had to tell her what happened because I was certain I wouldn't be able to do it. I was too scared. The only time I've ever felt so scared was when Darley helped me pile my clothes in Tom's car, and I ran away from Occident Street.

Ernie said, "Okay, Meg, I'll be there to help you out if you need me. But you should be the one to talk to her. This is something you really have to do on your own."

I screamed at him. "Stop telling me that! You told me that with Father Venard and look how that turned out! Why are you always telling me I have to do things on my own?"

The rest of the way over to her house, Ernie held the

steering wheel with one hand and with the other he laced his fingers between mine. "It's going to be all right, Meg," he said. "You've waited your whole life to get this off your chest, and now you can. You know she's going to believe you. You know she will. Christ, she saw half of it herself."

My mother opened the door, and her face instantly registered what she thought about seeing Ernie beside me. Without any greeting she left the front door open, turned on her heel and walked into the kitchen. There was a pot of red sauce on the stove, and she picked up a wooden spoon and began stirring it. Ernie and I stood on the other side of the counter, facing her. She looked at Ernie as if she hoped her withering glance would send him into the next room, but he didn't flinch. Pretty soon I guess she realized she'd just have to say it in front of him.

"So, Nicholas was here yesterday," she said.

"Um-hmm."

"And he told me—well—he said Donald did some stuff to him. When he was little."

"Um-hmm."

"And he said Donald did stuff to you, too."

"Um-hmm."

"Well, did he?"

She was stirring the pot and staring at me as if she'd just asked me the most normal question in the world. As if she'd said, So I hear you're going back to school, is it true? But I didn't trust her detached look, her measured tone of voice.

Not one bit. I clutched Ernie's arm so hard it might have come out of its socket.

"Yes, he did," I said.

"He did?"

"Yes."

The wooden spoon went around and around and around. She looked at the sauce as if taking her eyes from it would cause disaster. "Well," she said, "so what did he do to you?"

"He—he abused me. The same as Nick. From the time we were in Guyana until—"

"I don't believe it," she said. The spoon suddenly stopped moving. She looked up and stared me straight in my eyes. "Donald was not that kind of man, Margaret, Donald would never do such a thing! He was a fine man, a good man, and you're just saying all of this because he didn't leave you any money."

"I don't want his money. I just—"

"Good! Because you're not getting any of it! You're just telling a bunch of lies!"

"It's not a lie. It's the truth. All my life he—"

"He did *nothing!* And I don't believe you! You're a *liar!* I don't believe a word you say! Donald would never do what you say, never! He was a good fine man, and you have no right to say these horrid things. No *right!* Do you hear me?"

I buried my head against Ernie's shoulder. That's when he took over for me. Ernie took a step forward and said, "You want to know what your precious husband did to Meg, Pat? I'll tell you what he did to her." And then Ernie described the horrible things Donald did to me on the boat, the horrible things in Bel Air, the horrible things when I was pregnant. His voice was shaking. He said, "*That's* the good fine man you were married to! And he *did* all those things to her. He did them to *Nick*, too. It's the *truth*."

She was so angry she couldn't speak. Suddenly she lifted the wooden spoon and hurled it. It hit the edge of the counter and red sauce splattered like blood. She screamed, "The minute you showed up here I should have thrown you out just like Dr. Arthur told me to do! He said to throw you out if you came over here and I should have done it!"

"But you asked me to come—"

"Get out of here!" she screamed. "Get out of my house and don't ever come back! I don't ever want to see your face again! Ever again! For as long as I live!"

She took a step toward me. I bolted to the front door and ran outside. Tears streamed so hard down my face that I couldn't see where to put my feet, I couldn't see a thing, and halfway down the walkway I stumbled and nearly fell. But Ernie was right behind me; he grabbed me just in time. He steadied me and helped me to the car.

My mother stood in the doorway and screamed after us. "You're both a bunch of damn liars! And you and your brother can rot in hell, you damn liars!"

From the deposition of Patricia Sahlman, conducted by Richard Gilbert

"When did Donald Sahlman pass away?"
"November 26, 1992."

"After that, did Meg ever come to you and advise you that she had been abused?"

"One month after. She and Ernie came to my house. . . . She said that she was sexually abused as a child, and she never told me anything about it before, but that she was going to tell it to me now. I told her I didn't believe it. And Ernie did the rest of the talking for her."

"What did Ernie tell you about the sexual abuse?"

"He said that she was always abused, that I didn't know the number of times she had that horrible thing in her mouth, and that I must know the type of man I was married to, that I had him on a pedestal and that he was no good."

"What did you respond?"

"I did not believe any of it."

"Did you call Meg a liar?"

"I didn't call anybody a liar. I said it was all a bunch of lies."

"Did you tell them to get out of the house?"

"No."

"Did you make a comment to Meg and Ernie that Dr. Arthur told you to throw them out of the house?"

"Yes. Because that's what he said. That same day."

"How did it come about that he told you that?"

"Because Nicholas came the night before. . . . I told him he was lying. I didn't believe it."

"So, after that, did you have a conversation with Dr. Arthur?"

"The next morning I did. He said he didn't believe it, [and] if any of them come back to me with such a thing, throw them out of the house."

"In your response to Interrogatory #11, which

asked you to identify all facts tending to disprove [Meg's] allegations, you indicate that her relationship with, and show of affection toward Donald Sahlman belie her claims that she was sexually abused. What do you mean by that?"

"They always had a wonderful father-daughter relationship. She was very affectionate toward him."

"In your answer to Interrogatory #12, you say that the evidence will show that she was flirtatious with him, seemed to enjoy being around him and in general did not exhibit any evidence prior to his death that she had been sexually abused by him. What do you mean by flirtatious?"

"She was always flirting with him. Flirt. She would flash herself in front of him. Try to rub up against him. She would in general be a general flirt. You know what a flirt is."

"Was there anything about this flirtatious activity between them that caused you some concern about their relationship?"

"No, it did not."

"You say that she did a complete about-face after his death, and after learning that she was not a beneficiary of his estate. What do you mean when you say she did a complete about-face?"

"She changed her attitude towards him and me. She went from this sweet, loving daughter to a mean, hateful person."

Twenty-Five

It has now been a month since my mother threw us out. I haven't seen or talked to her since that day. Neither has Nick. A few times I took out Ernie's gun while he was at work and held it to my head. I put the barrel in my mouth, and then I put it against my heart. I didn't want to screw it up, though; and I had to be sure it would work. But then I thought about Donald. Even if he's dead he still knows what I did, that I told his secret. And he'd be waiting for me if I killed myself. He'd be there on the other side, and he'd get me for it.

At night, when I'm able to sleep at all, I dream Donald isn't dead. He's on his boat, and he's standing on the deck. I try to run from him, to lift my feet off the weathered dock, but my shoes are nailed down. Donald watches me, amused. *Nice try, Margaret.* And then he opens his arms and grins. "Why don't you come and give your old dad a hug?" he says. "Because you don't want to make your old dad mad, do you?"

Three weeks ago—a week after my mother threw us out— the letter from her lawyer arrived at Ernie's house. It was the notice of administration I brought to Lynwood Arnold's office, the one that said Nick and I had thirty days to make a claim against Donald's estate. Nick and I read it together and were on the verge of throwing it away, of paying no attention to it, but Ernie was outraged. He told us my mother just fired off a "preemptive strike," and he warned us that if we didn't get a lawyer right away we'd never have the chance to change our minds. Ernie told me I couldn't just do nothing, not after everything I'd been through. He shook his head while I reminded him that Donald was dead, that it was too late now. "That's what she wants you to think," he said. "And you don't even know what your legal rights are, do you?"

I don't know anything about legal rights. Or any rights, really. But I should tell you this: Nick was only partially telling the truth when he told Lynwood why he thought my mother hired a lawyer about Donald's will. Nick told him it was because she thought we were a bunch of greedy liars, but that wasn't the real reason. At least, it wasn't the only one. The real reason is that my mother probably got worried after Nick and I both showed up at her door and told her everything. She told Ernie and me that Dr. Arthur, Granny's psychiatrist, advised her to throw us out. So maybe Dr. Arthur even warned her we might be about to do something. Something she thought might threaten everything she spent so many years trying to acquire.

Ernie's been wrong in the past, but he was right about one thing. Never in a million years would she think we'd do anything about that notice of administration. After all, why would she think we'd act differently now than we have our entire lives? We've always been silent, always done what she wanted, and that document was a warning. There is no doubt in my mind. She must have thought getting that piece of paper in the mail would scare us so bad, rattle us so much to think she'd gone and done something like that, that we'd both just disappear and forget we ever said a thing to her. And that's what she wants us to do, too, what she expects us to do: Sink into the ground, just like always.

Lynwood said we only have six more days to file an official response before the thirty-day deadline. I'm terrified, but I feel like I want to do it. I keep picturing her walking out to the curb to get her mail and opening an official-looking document from Nick and me, and she won't know what hit her. It'll be like a cannonball shot into her stomach, it's going to take her by such surprise. If Nick and I thought she hated us for what we told her, just wait until her lawyer explains what it means. She'll be like that cougar we once saw at the zoo, the one that bared its teeth and screeched any time anybody came near its cage.

But I could be wrong about that. Maybe it will be like

Lynwood said. Once she thinks it through, once she pictures how it would look to everyone if this ended up in the newspapers, maybe she'll calm down and talk to us. Even though Ernie would probably be mad and say I was chickening out, I honestly think that if she came to Nick and me and told us she was sorry for what happened to us, if she told us she loved us and believed us and was sorry, I'd drop the whole thing.

Actually, maybe all she would have to say is that she believes us. Maybe I could live without her saying she's sorry.

After what I went through right before Donald died, I learned you can't ever force another person to be sorry for anything. It's like demanding flowers. You can't make people feel something they don't, and if they apologize without meaning it, it's still no good. Still, maybe when she sees we haven't sunk into the ground quite so fast, maybe she'll start thinking about what happened to us. Maybe she'll start looking at things from our perspective, at what we went through.

At least, it's something to hope for.

—END OF CLIENT STATEMENT
February 1993

Part III

Dead Man on Trial

*A*nd behold, a certain lawyer stood up and tempted him, saying, Master, what shall I do to inherit eternal life? He said unto him, What is written in the law? How readest thou?

—Luke 10:25–26

*T*he Lord is known by the judgment which he executeth: the wicked is snared in the work of his own hands.

—Psalms 9:16

Twenty-Six

In early March 1993, less than a week after they agreed to
represent Nick and me, Richard Gilbert and Lynwood
Arnold filed a formal response to my mother's notice of
administration. There was no mention of sexual abuse,
which our lawyers said would have been immediately
snapped up by the newspapers, and the allegations were
intentionally vague: "assault, battery and other torts."
Lynwood, whose expertise was in estate law, told Nick and
me he planned to contact my mother's lawyer and spell out
the real nature of our allegations. After that, he said, my

mother would have thirty days to either accept or reject our claim.

My mother, though, didn't require that much time. Through her lawyer, Charlie Luckie, she said Donald couldn't possibly have abused me in Guyana because he'd been living in Florida. He couldn't have abused me in Florida, either, because she could prove he'd been in South America. According to her I was a chronic liar who'd made up stories my entire life, and already she could have scores of people who would testify to that. And Nick, she said, was a cocaine addict who'd say anything for money. Both of us had concocted a pack of lies just so we could get our hands on Donald's money.

Less than twenty-four hours after she received it, my mother rejected our claim. By law, Lynwood explained, Nick and I now had only thirty days to file a lawsuit. If we didn't, we forfeited any future right to do so.

"They're pushing us to the wall," Lynwood said. "And it sounds as if they're going for an alibi defense, too. Your mother's lawyer even said to me, 'If you try to place him in Guyana, we'll prove he was in Tampa.' He's clearly only hearing things from your mother's perspective, but I honestly don't think he understands how long a time we're talking about."

Rich Gilbert wasn't surprised my mother didn't immediately acknowledge what Nick and I had endured. He didn't expect her to promptly admit the role she'd played in it, either. In virtually every personal injury case he'd ever handled, he said, the initial response was one of denial.

"She's got a lot at stake right now," he told Nick and me one afternoon in his office, which like Lynwood's looked out over the harbor. "Several million dollars if your estimate of the estate is correct. That's enough money to make a lot of people hide the truth. And the only way she's apt to stop denying everything is if she's presented with enough credible evidence that she thinks she'd lose the case."

Even though my lawyers may have expected her denial, my mother's total rejection of Nick and me was more painful than anything I'd ever experienced. I simply couldn't believe what she was doing, how she'd completely thrown us away. Each day I tortured myself with images of things she'd seen— Donald grabbing me as I walked down a hallway, Donald yanking away my bath towel, Donald driving me away on another trip—and one thought went through my head: *How much had she really known, besides what she saw herself? Had she and Donald had some kind of understanding about everything?*

Rich and Lynwood told me I had to let things unfold, that they still thought a settlement offer might be made. Hearing that, though, sank me into an even deeper depression. It wasn't money I wanted; it was for her to say she believed me, that she'd help me, that she forgave me. But now the only belief and support I had was from Ernie and Nick, and two lawyers who barely knew me. My mother was forcing me to either admit that Nick and I had made everything up—or else file a lawsuit against her. If it hadn't been for my brother and his corroboration of what Donald did, I don't know what I would have done. Used Ernie's gun on myself, probably.

In April 1993, thirty days after our claim was rejected and no further word came, Nick and I gave our lawyers permission to file a lawsuit against my mother and the estate of Donald Sahlman. Our experiences were condensed into a slew of legal terms: assault and battery and intentional infliction of emotional distress and negligence, impersonal meaningless words that frightened me with their cold weight. Rich said no mention would be made of "child abuse" since, as far as he was concerned, the sexual abuse Nick and I had endured as children was only a small portion of my parents' "outrageous conduct." Equally important, he said, was what he saw as the mental cruelty I'd experienced my entire life, the sexual abuse throughout most of my adult life, as well as my mother's lifelong sanction of it. For that reason the lawsuit claimed the emotional and sexual abuse had been "continuing," a legal term that meant it had gone on without interruption. At the time I had no way of knowing how crucial that one word would turn out to be.

The day after the suit was filed, both the *Tampa Tribune* and *St. Petersburg Times* ran headlines that read, "Children Sue Stepfather's Estate, Mom," and "Stepchildren Allege Abuse in Legal Battle Over Estate." Rich and Lynwood had advised me not to read anything—it would be certain to just distress me—but I couldn't help myself.

"The stepchildren of a deceased seafood executive have sued his estate and their natural mother, claiming that she failed to protect them from severe sexual abuse that continued well into their adulthood," I read in the *St. Petersburg Times.* Nick and I, the article said, "charge that Donald

Sahlman, seventy-one, who died Nov. 26, coerced, threatened and intimidated them into long-term abusive relationships while their mother, Patricia Sahlman, fifty-six, permitted the abuse in return for Sahlman's financial support." My mother, it said, vehemently denied the allegations. "I am appalled by these allegations about my dead husband. They're absolutely untrue." Lynwood Arnold, the article went on to say, "would not let a reporter speak to his clients, nor would he detail their current occupations or conditions."

I crumpled the paper and threw it to the floor. *"Liar!"* I screamed. Ernie stood helplessly nearby. *"Liar!* How can she *lie* about us like that? How can she *say* that when she *knows?* When she was *there?"* I dissolved into tears. Ernie put his arms around me and comforted me as best he could. But I was inconsolable.

Looking back, maybe her lies and betrayal weren't as incomprehensible as they felt at that moment. Somewhere, in some innermost point inside me, I think I did glimpse the truth of what she was doing. It was a nameless understanding, wordless and hazy and deep inside a void; but something within me still must have alighted briefly enough upon the horror of it to at least sense it. And there's a reason I believe that, too. If that hadn't been true, there's no possible way I could have gone on after those first articles appeared. I'm not strong; I don't have that kind of courage to stand up for myself. Knowing that, what I have to think is this: If there hadn't been some deeper driving awareness at work, I would have stopped everything right there. If I hadn't known on some level what she was doing and why, the moment my mother publicly denounced Nick and me as liars I would have told Rich and Lynwood I couldn't go through with it. That I'd made a huge mistake by ever contacting them.

I'm not saying I had any understanding of that while everything was happening. I didn't. And I had even less understanding of any of the legal issues. Whether it was because they thought Nick and I were incapable of grasping their strategy or they feared we were too emotionally fragile to hear it, during the next several months Rich and Lynwood gave us information only when they deemed it necessary: to get a signature on a document, to have some sequence of events clarified. Usually they told us about threats only after they'd passed ("Your mother's lawyer filed a motion to have the case dismissed, but the judge denied it"), probably to save us unnecessary worry. Nick and I placed our faith in them, and they went forward.

In truth, I didn't really want to know what they were doing. And my lawyers, I think, sensed that. The moment I realized that Rich and Lynwood both believed me, that they knew I hadn't just come up with some strike-it-rich scheme, I became like a panicked cancer patient handing her fate to a doctor. Rich was compassionate but indignantly furious about what had happened to me, detached but also passionate, and I trusted him. He'd take over; he'd decide how to proceed. And if everything blew up in our faces I was certain he'd let me know.

There were only two legal obstacles that Rich did describe to Nick and me in any detail. I assume it's because he knew, even then, that they were the things most likely to stop us in our tracks. The first obstacle was the fact that Donald was dead. Beyond the obvious—removing the opportunity to question him—Rich said Donald also became shielded by something called the "dead man's statute." What that meant was that no statements made by Donald could be introduced at trial, if it ever came to that, since he wasn't around to defend himself. The minute I heard that, I pictured Donald smiling in his casket. *Round One goes to me, Margaret!* Not one word of any of the threats he'd made to me would ever be heard by a jury. So how could I convince anyone why I'd been silent for so long? How could I make anyone believe why I'd never told a soul?

Rich also said that Nick and I needed to understand the statute of limitations on sexual abuse cases. In Florida, he told us, child abuse victims typically have to make their case against their abusers before age twenty-five. That, he said, or else within four years after the victims no longer are dependent upon their abusers.

"Before age twenty-five?" I said, jerking upright on Rich's leather sofa. "You have to say everything before then or else forget it?"

"Let me finish," Rich said. "That's what the law has been until just last year. But let me explain." In 1992, he said, the Florida legislature passed an amendment to that law in an attempt to allow more victims to get justice. Under that amendment, Rich said, anyone can file a lawsuit claiming sexual abuse—regardless of how long ago the abuse occurred—but only up until four years from the passage of the law. "In other words," he explained, "it wouldn't matter how old a person was when the abuse stopped, but a lawsuit could only be filed up until 1996. And based on that amendment, both you and Nick would be well within that statute of limitations."

Even though it helped Nick and me, that amendment still didn't seem right. What about someone who got abused after 1996? Or someone who's too afraid to come forward right away and has to wait until the abuser is dead? "It's just the way the law is written," Rich said. "The law is always changing, but that's how things are right now. But it's at least encouraging for us."

Ever since March, when Nick and I were forced to decide whether to go forward with a lawsuit, we'd both been seeing therapists. Within a few months, though, it seemed as though I'd met with an army of them: the counselor recommended to me by Jeanne Becker at St. Patrick's, a psychologist and psychiatrist Rich wanted Nick and me to see, the psychologist hired by my mother's lawyer. Each time I was asked to tell my story again and then perform a battery of tests, often with hundreds of statements to be answered true or false. But how was I supposed to answer? I did, for example, think "people are out to get me"—my mother and her lawyer, for starters. But what if those therapists thought I was just paranoid? And what if they thought I was lying about everything? Dr. Blau, who'd been hired to evaluate me for Charlie Luckie, scared me the worst. The way he watched me immediately reminded me of Father Venard's face the day I left his rectory office.

Lynwood must have known how deeply the whole process was affecting me. Every day he called me, becoming, in many respects, the therapist I trusted most. While Rich focused on gathering a list of witnesses, Lynwood listened to me talk about how I was haunted by Donald and had nightmares about him every night; how I thought about killing myself every day; how I was certain Donald was going to win. He encouraged me, told me to have faith. He kept reminding me I hadn't lost this battle yet. "Try not to think about the case, Meg," he said. "That's what Rich and I are here for. We're fighting for you, but this could go on for a long time. I know it's hard, but the less you think about it, the better."

Lynwood was right: Not thinking about it was hard. That was especially true in May, when Rich was preparing to question his first witness: my mother. He wanted me to be there during the deposition, but he said he'd understand if I didn't feel that I could. Ernie convinced me I had to. "I'll wait right outside that room for you, Meg," Ernie said.

Dressed in a dark blue suit that now was too large for me, I sat beside Rich and the court reporter on one side of the long table. My mother sat on the other side next to Charlie Luckie and Don Jr., who had been named in the lawsuit as the estate's personal representative. My mother stared icily at me, and then coolly lied about everything: No, Donald had never examined me to see if I was a virgin. No, he had never been prejudiced against black people. No, she and Donald never threw my clothes on Tom Cassedy's porch. No, she never threw Ernie and me out of the house. Out of the nearly thirty depositions that eventually would be taken by Rich,

Lynwood or Charlie Luckie, hers was the only one I attended. After that, I couldn't face the idea of listening to any more lies.

Nick's deposition by Charlie Luckie was a few weeks later, and then came my own. Rich knew how terrified I was, and he counseled me outside the downtown conference room. "When you go in there, just tell the truth," he said. "You have the truth on your side, Meg. Listen carefully to the question, answer each one to the best of your ability, and if you can't remember just say that. And whatever you do, don't volunteer any information. Tell him only what he asks and nothing more."

That was what I tried to do. But instantly I could tell by Charlie Luckie's questions where he was going. "Do you usually walk around the house naked?" he asked. *No,* I said, *I did not.* "If your mother said that, she'd be wrong?" *She would be.* "Did you ever accuse Father Fausto of making advances toward you?" *No, I did not.* "Did you ever leave your son Cameron for two or three days with Mr. Sahlman and your mother?" *Yes, sir.* "Do you have a close friend named Darley?" *Yes, sir.* "And you never told her about the abuse before Donald Sahlman died?" *No, sir.* The more questions like that he asked, the more upset I got. If my mother stuck to everything she was saying and kept lying about me, what hope did I have?

Then he asked, "When was the last time that you claim Mr. Sahlman abused you?" At the time I had no idea how critical this one answer would be—how, years later, it would come back to haunt me. To me, Donald's abuse of *me* was when he put his mouth on me, probed me, when he shined a light on me. After he got mouth cancer, that stopped. From then on he only made me do things to *him*—and mentally I went to far-off places. I wasn't present when my hand moved; I thought about the pictures Cameron had drawn for me or whether I needed to go to the dry cleaners or whether tonight I'd try cooking that new recipe. I had learned that: to go away.

I thought back to the last time Donald had put his hands between my legs, the day Cameron had gotten locked in the upstairs bedroom. It was not long before he was diagnosed with mouth cancer. I said to Charlie Luckie, "When I was twenty-seven." "So you say that he assaulted you while you were still married to Thomas Cassedy?" "Yes, sir." "Before that incident, when was the last incident that you say he assaulted you?" I told him about the time we'd been renovating our kitchen, when Donald came by and took me to his boat. Before that, I said, Donald took me upstairs while Tom was still at work. "What year was that?" he asked. I was twenty-six, I said. So, four years ago.

After it was over, Rich walked across the street with me to his office. "I think it went well," he said. "And now the best thing you can do is put everything out of your mind, Meg. I'm contacting people you told me about. Don't think about it anymore."

I was only able to do that, though, when something more pressing happened at home. One night Ernie came into my bedroom. He'd given up sleeping with me because I screamed too much in my sleep. "Have you seen my gun?" he asked. "I always keep it above the bed and it's gone." Ernie didn't have to tell me where he kept it. And I knew the last time I'd seen it, too: a few days earlier when I'd put it in my mouth and thought about pulling the trigger. Ernie walked back into his bedroom and then a few moments later came back. He was livid. "All my jewelry from the pawnshop's gone, and someone broke the lock on the sliding glass door. I'm calling the police, Meg. Some son of a bitch broke in here."

There were plenty of things the thief could have taken but didn't—the television and stereo, for starters. It was almost as if the person knew exactly where to look for the jewelry Ernie brought home each night, where to find his gun. But who would have done it? And how could they have known when Ernie and I both would be gone? From that day on, I was terrified to be alone in the house. I kept all the doors and windows locked, and the slightest sound, even the phone ringing, made me jump nearly out of my skin.

And then came the thing that shattered what little security I'd been clinging to.

A month after the robbery and six months since filing the lawsuit, Nick vanished. He didn't show up for his appointments with therapists, he didn't show up for meetings with Rich and Lynwood. At first I thought he was probably on another drug binge, but after I hadn't heard from him in weeks I got truly worried. Something was wrong.

Nick had been unemployed for a long time. For the past several months he'd been living with a woman named Frances in a run-down apartment without a phone. Frances, who wanted to help Nick after Kim Hourigan gave up, was in her late forties, gaunt and unemployed, too. I had no idea how they scraped by. Several times I'd driven Frances various places after Nick drove off in her beat-up car and disappeared for days, and in the past she'd always been friendly to me. But this time, when I went to her apartment to find Nick, she wouldn't even look at me. That's when I knew.

"He's changing his mind, isn't he?" I asked her. "He's not going to go through with it, is he?" Frances became very nervous and told me I should leave.

A few days later, Nick called Rich and told him he'd made a decision. He was dropping out of the lawsuit. He'd thought it over, he said, and realized it would be just too painful for my mother. He just couldn't put her through a trial, and all of this had been terribly hard on her. Rich asked him to sign a document that spelled out those reasons, and not long afterward he did that.

But then came the bombshell. Rich told it to me as gently as he could.

A few days after signing the document for Rich, Nick went to Charlie Luckie and gave him a formal statement. In it, Nick said Donald had never abused him. Ever. He'd made up the entire story, he said, fabricated everything. He lied in his deposition in May, he said, because Ernie and I had offered him five thousand dollars so we could win the case.

We had pushed him into it, Nick said. Ernie and I had told him everything to say, put the words in his mouth. And now his conscience was bothering him so much that he needed to set the record straight, to come clean.

He said he was very sorry for the pain he'd caused my mother.

Twenty-Seven

Mom had gotten her claws into him. I didn't know how, but I was certain she was behind it. And if Nick got up there on the witness stand and said Ernie and I had offered him money to lie, I was just as certain what a jury would think of me. It was over. I couldn't go on anymore. Not now. I couldn't do it without Nick.

"Yes, you can, Meg, you're stronger than that," Ernie said to me in Rich's office. The two of us were sitting on the leather sofa, and Rich was leaning forward, his elbows on his knees, in a wingback chair. "You're stronger than you know, stronger than you have any idea of," Ernie said. "And Nick would have just hurt you anyway."

"I'm sorry, but I can't do this anymore." I was fighting tears. "How could he do this to me? How *could* he? And I'm *not* strong. I'm *not.*"

"Yes, you are," Rich said. "And we *don't* need him, Meg. We can keep going and do whatever we have to do. This isn't over. And Ernie's right—Nick probably would have just hurt you in the long run."

It didn't take long for me to realize what Nick was doing and why. He must have decided we were fighting a losing battle, that my mother was going to win. And when she did, Nick knew he'd be frozen out of her life—and her bank account—forever. Nick must have figured he was on the losing team with me, and this was his chance to jump to the other side. If he helped her win the case, even if it meant lying on a witness stand under oath, then she'd have to be grateful to him. She'd *have* to.

Rich and Ernie both sat quietly, waiting for me to say something. The thought of going on now, alone, was the most frightening thing I'd ever imagined. At the same time, though, I knew that if I quit I might as well wear a sign saying I was a liar, that everything Nick and I had said was pure fabrication. And the idea of that was worse. If what Rich said was true—that we didn't need Nick, that it wasn't over yet—then it could only mean one thing: Not only would Rich have to prove that my mother was a liar, but that Nick was one, too.

I looked at Rich, at his piercing blue eyes beneath bangs that had fallen onto his forehead as he hunched forward. I didn't want to think about what might happen to Nick if I kept going all alone. Maybe he'd change his mind again, realize what he was doing. But if Rich truly believed there was still a chance, I'd just have to keep trusting him. "All right," I said finally. "Do whatever you have to do, Rich."

For the next few months I spent every day reading the Bible, praying to God to help me, to watch over me. I held the blue rosary Father Morrison had given me in Guyana and said, *I'm not asking you to do anything except protect me, God. As long as you don't leave me, too, I'll be all right. Please don't leave me now. Please help me through this.*

And it was then that my prayers began to be answered, one by one.

One day Ernie got a phone call from the detective assigned to our home robbery several months earlier. None of Ernie's jewelry had turned up, the detective said, but someone had taken his .357 Magnum and tried to pawn it. Did Ernie by chance have any idea who Nicholas Clairmonte was?

"Oh, that's excellent," Rich said when I told him. "Excellent. Now if we could just get some help with some of these other witnesses."

Rich had been having a hard time getting statements from several people. In particular, he wanted to talk to Hans Meixner, the German tour guide, and Jeanne Becker from St. Patrick's. But there were problems. After so many years I didn't have the slightest idea where to find Hans, and so far every attempt to locate him had failed. And Jeanne Becker was sick. Terribly sick. Rich told me she was terminally ill with cancer, unable to get out of bed. Jeanne had been so kind to me, had helped me so many nights over the phone, and immediately I prayed for her.

But maybe Jeanne prayed for me, too.

A few months later, Jeanne said she'd be willing to have her deposition taken—but only if Rich wrote out his questions and allowed her to write down her answers. Charlie Luckie didn't fight it, and so Rich confined his questions to three things: Had I ever told her Donald had abused me? Had she offered me any counseling or advice? And had my mother ever indicated she had any concerns about my relationship with Donald?

About a week later, Rich asked me to come down to his office. Immediately I knew he had something difficult to say and wasn't sure how to break the news. "Meg, do you remember what you told me about your conversation with Father Venard the day after the funeral?" Of course I remembered. "And you told me Father Venard said the conversation would be under the seal, that he wouldn't and couldn't ever reveal it to anyone?" I felt what was coming, but I didn't want to believe it. "Meg, did you ever give him permission to talk to anyone else about what you told him? Did you ever release him from the seal?"

I couldn't do more than numbly shake my head. It was as if I'd been stabbed through the heart. "He told someone, Rich?" Everything was collapsing, everything was falling apart. "Father Venard told someone what I said to him?"

He nodded slowly. "I'm very sorry, Meg. He did."

"He told someone." Rich nodded again. "How did you find out?"

"Do you want me to tell you," he asked, holding up Jeanne Becker's responses, "or do you want to read this yourself?" Rich had never shown me any of the depositions before, and I'd never asked to read any of them. But this time I needed to know what was in it; I needed to understand what Father Venard had done to me. He handed me Jeanne Becker's six-page response and pointed to the third page:

"Then I asked Meg how she was doing when I received the most rapid speech back. 'All I ever wanted him to say was that he was sorry he ever did this to me.' How she was glad it was finally over. And she began to tell me of the sexual abuse that began as a little child in Guyana, how she felt dirty, how she wanted to receive Holy Communion. All of this in this extremely rapid speech. I told her all she needed to do was go to confession. At this she asked, 'How could God let this happen to a little child? I cannot go to the wake or funeral.' I told her, 'God got you this far, and He will get you through the next few days.'"

I turned the page. *"Her next phone call came to my home late at night. Meg kept saying, 'Bad Meg! Bad Meg! She caused this to happen!' I told her, 'Meg, no child causes abuse. Start to journal in a notebook all you can, good or bad, until we can find a professional abuse counselor.'*

"The next day I went to the pastor, my boss. I told him I needed a professional abuse therapist, as I was trying to help a young woman who threatened to kill herself last night. Father Venard Moffitt asked, 'Who?' I told him I could not break a confidence. He asked me three times. He said he also was handling a sexual abuse case. Out of obedience to my boss, I told

him! I told Father Venard when she first told me—before the wake service—and the ensuing memories: the 'little pink thing in her mouth,' the checking after she began to date. Father said he could not believe any of it about Don Sahlman."

I looked up at Rich. "One more," he said. I turned to the final page. *"Within the next week or two, Father Venard said that he got permission to speak to Pat and Donald Sahlman Jr. Father said that Pat admitted that she and Donald did check Meg's vagina, as it was a custom in the islands to be sure that the father of the bride would be selling a virgin."*

For a long time I just sat there. Rich didn't say anything. "He told my mother," I said. "The son of a bitch went and told my mother what I said to him. And Don Jr., too!"

Rich reached out his hand.

"That son of a bitch, that—" I was having a hard time believing what he'd done to me, when it could have happened. But then I remembered how Cameron and I had moved in with my mother right after Donald died. That last day I was there she was gone several hours, and when she came home she'd had that cold expression right before she asked me to leave. *And keep your child under control, Margaret.* A few days later Father Venard called me at Ernie's to wish me a merry Christmas. I'd *known* something was wrong, I could hear it in his voice. But Ernie convinced me I was just being paranoid.

Rich squeezed my hand as I stared numbly at the floor, shaking my head. "I'm very sorry for you, Meg. I really am."

I looked up at him. "But what, Rich? I can hear it in your voice. You're sorry for me, but what?"

"Well, okay, you're right," he said slowly. "But I'm not sorry for us. But I'm not sorry for the case." He leaned forward in his chair, and I could tell he was excited. "Do you see? Father Venard broke the seal, Meg. So it's too late for him to claim that whatever conversation he had with Pat and Don Jr. is confidential. If you never gave him permission to reveal it, we can *ask* him about that conversation he had with Pat and Don Jr. According to Jeanne Becker, your mother *admitted* to Father Venard that she and Don checked you! All along she's been denying that—it's been your word against hers—and here she goes and admits it to her priest! I'm going to nail him, Meg. I know it's a blow he did that to you, I know how it must hurt you, but it might be the best thing that ever happened to you."

It took several moments for his words to sink in. "But Rich," I said. "What if Father Venard lies?"

I had lost most of my friends—and people from my past I hoped would treat me as friends—since the lawsuit was filed. Some had called me after reading the newspaper stories to ask what was going on; others I had contacted myself. There was a time I would have been devastated by the doubt I heard in their voices, by their obvious disbelief, but too much had happened for it to register as more than a brief stab of pain and anger. Maybe I was simply becoming numb, impervious to stings. When my friends Kathleen Murphy and Sue Sparks skeptically asked why I'd never told anyone before—and added that they couldn't or wouldn't help me—I simply put down the phone. They didn't believe me; so be it. They thought I was doing it for money; I would not argue with them. I had no room in my life now for anyone who didn't support me.

Only one person did cut me to the quick. It was Kathy Mann Beville, Donald's now-married niece. Even though we'd never been close, I'd seen her at enough family functions over the years to have been friendly with her and to hope she might be willing to corroborate the breast exams Donald performed in her presence. But I didn't have a chance to say anything to her. As soon as she heard my name, her voice became a low growl. "I can't even *believe* you'd call me, Margaret. It's *despicable* what you're doing. *Despicable!* Even if it did happen, you should have gone to the *grave* with it." She slammed down the receiver.

Of everyone, only Darley, Carol Llosa and Kim Hourigan, Nick's ex-girlfriend, stood by me. When I told Darley about Jeanne Becker's deposition, she punched her fist into the air and let out a whoop. And when I said that my mother's lawyer had finally come up with a settlement offer—fifty thousand dollars—she told me she didn't think I should take it. It was the same thing Ernie told me. "You've come too far, Meg," Ernie had said. "You're not going to let those bastards buy you off after everything they've done, are you?"

Ernie was right. Six months earlier, I would have dropped everything for an apology. But that was before my mother roped Nick into lying for her, before Father Venard's betrayal. The lawsuit had never been about money, but now I needed more than ever to be believed, to prove I wasn't the greedy liar my mother was making me out to be.

Still, Darley could tell I was worried. Without Jeanne's testimony at the trial—and if something happened to prevent her deposition from being introduced (I was getting smarter about the way lawyers did things)—there was a good chance I'd lose. My mother had a long line of people who were prepared to say what a great relationship Donald and I always had right up until he died, and that would be hard for a jury to ignore.

"Well," Darley said, "then maybe I could help you."

"You help me so much, Darley. Really you do."

"That's not what I mean," she said. "I meant, help you with everything you told me on the airplane going to England. You know. I guess I could testify about what you told me."

I gasped. "Oh my God," I whispered. How could I have forgotten that?

"And there was something else, Meg," she said slowly. "Something I couldn't—there's something I've never told you before."

It was the day I ran away from Occident Street to live with Tom. After Darley helped me load everything into Tom's car, she went home. Later that day, my mother and Donald showed up at her front door.

"It was totally bizarre, Meg. At least it was to me then. Because when you moved out—and I hate to say this—but until then I thought you'd had this princess kind of life there, and I didn't understand why you were in such a big fat rush to move out. I mean, you'd waited all those years, right? But you were so crazed that day. I'd never seen you like that. And then afterwards—well, you told me yourself what a mess you were. So I guess I didn't want to make things worse for you.

"Anyway," she went on, "they came over. I don't remember the whole conversation, but they kept asking me whether I thought you were still a virgin. They were totally frantic about it, like it was the most important thing on Earth. Don did most of the talking. He kept asking, 'Do you think she's still a virgin? Do you know? Do you think she still could be?' And I was thinking the whole conversation was ridiculous. Bizarre, but ridiculous. Because by then, I guess I'd just assumed you weren't a virgin. You were twenty-five or something, weren't you? But that was the only thing they asked me about. When they figured out I wasn't going to tell them anything, they left."

It wasn't until our trip to England two years later that she understood what my parents' conversation that day had been all about. "I'll never forget what you said to me on that plane," she said. "You started out by confessing that you were half black—as if I gave a damn. And then you told me about all the icky comments Don had always made about your black relatives. Do you remember?"

Some of it, I said. But it was strange: I remembered so many things in my life, but not everything I told her on that flight. Why was that? How could that have happened?

"I don't know, Meg, maybe some psychological thing," she said. She told me I'd described meeting Anthony in Colorado, how he'd been the love of my life, and then "how Don blasted him about making sure you were a virgin. And do you remember what I asked you then? About how Don would know if you were a virgin? That's when you told me about all the checking, how it started way back in Guyana, how he took naked pictures of you. And you made me promise never to tell anyone, Meg. I remember asking you if it was still going on, and that's when you clammed up. It was obvious you weren't going to say one more word about it. And then you made me promise. Do you remember? You said, 'Promise me you'll forget what I told you, Darley. Promise me you'll never let them know what I said, that you'll always treat them exactly the same as you always have.'"

I've got this philosophy: The moment you think you're on top of things, God reminds you who's in charge. I was feeling confident after Darley said she'd testify for me—and that's when I got reminded of who was in control.

"We don't want you to give up," Rich said to me one afternoon in mid-1994, nearly nine months since Nick had withdrawn from the lawsuit. We were in Rich's office, and Lynwood was sitting next to Rich in a leather executive chair looking stern-faced. I knew it was going to be bad. "And we don't want you to think everything's over, either," Rich went on. "This is just a setback, an obstacle to be overcome, and there's a very good chance we can do that. Lynwood and I just need you to keep on being strong."

"What is it, Rich? Just tell me quick, because if you don't I'll go—"

"Meg."

"It's very bad, isn't it?"

Lynwood and Rich looked at each other. "Meg," Rich

asked, "do you remember how I explained to you, after we first filed the lawsuit, about that new amendment to the statute of limitations? How the legislature passed it in 1992 so more people could come forward if they'd been abused?"

"Sure I do. You called it our four-year window of opportunity."

"Well, there was a case that challenged the legality of that amendment, challenged the length of time a person could take to come forward. A lot of the claims made in the case were similar to yours, although your abuse went on a lot longer."

"And?"

"And it went to the state Supreme Court, Meg."

He didn't have to say anything more. "And the court struck it down, didn't they? They said you can't file a claim no matter how old you are, didn't they? That thing about being able to file until 1996—that's gone, isn't it? And it's back to the way things were before. Right?"

Rich and Lynwood both nodded.

"Meg," Rich said gently, "based on that ruling, your mother's lawyer filed a motion claiming that all of your allegations are legally barred by the statute of limitations. Since the Supreme Court basically said that any claim that had expired prior to the 1992 amendment couldn't be revived, Charlie Luckie filed a motion to throw out our case. And right now we honestly don't know what will happen."

I was so angry I was shaking. "You know what? Those guys on the Supreme Court, those guys giving out the rules? They wouldn't *do* that if they'd gone through what I did! If they were getting abused like me, if they knew how it felt, they wouldn't make that decision! They'd never say you can tell the truth until you're a certain age and then after that, forget it!" I felt totally, completely defeated. Already it felt as though I'd been dealing with the idea of a trial for years and years, and now it was all for nothing. Everything I'd gone through—and now it was over just like that. "You know what's new?" I said, furious. *"Nothing's* new! All my life I got beaten down, got squashed into being silent, and now they're doing it to me again! They're *still* protecting Donald. Here the man is dead, and he's still winning!"

"Meg," Lynwood said. "Please don't give up. You can't give up now. It's not over. Donald hasn't won yet." I couldn't tell if he was saying it to be kind or because he thought I'd go home and kill myself or if he really believed it. But it didn't even matter anymore. Either I was going to get a trial or I wasn't.

"You want to know what I think?" I said.

"What?" Rich and Lynwood answered in unison.

"Those guys on the Supreme Court?" Rich and Lynwood nodded. "They're all probably just a bunch of dirty old men."

Maybe it was the tension, but Rich and Lynwood both burst out laughing.

The way I understood it, my entire case, and the possibility of getting a trial, now hinged on two statements: "Twenty-seven," and "continuing."

In my deposition, I had told my mother's lawyer that Donald's last act of abuse had been when I was twenty-seven. Charlie Luckie hadn't asked me if Donald ever made me do anything to *him* after his ritual had ended—when he got mouth cancer—and Rich had told me not to volunteer anything. If the judge hearing all our pretrial evidence now believed those had been the last times anything happened to me, it was over. The statute of limitations would mean we couldn't go to trial.

Rich and Lynwood told me I had to write out an affidavit explaining, in detail, why I answered the way I did. After that I'd also have to give a second deposition and let Charlie Luckie try to rip me to shreds. They didn't have to tell me that's what he'd do; it was already obvious. And so, in my second deposition, I rattled off everything Donald made me do up until his death at a mile a minute, barely stopping for breath, leaving nothing out. I was so angry I didn't once look at my mother staring at me with hatred from the other side of the table.

After it was over, because of one word Rich had used in our initial lawsuit—"continuing"—we still had a chance. Rich argued to the judge that all of my psychological injuries were the cumulative result of years of uninterrupted abuse. He said that under something called the "continuing tort doctrine," the statute of limitations shouldn't even apply to my case. Donald Sahlman and my mother physically and emotionally abused me right up until the end, and while Donald was alive I'd been too fearful to say anything.

The judge gave us only a partial victory. It was one that gave us hope and kept the case alive—but at the same time made the task facing Rich even more difficult. The judge agreed with Rich's argument about the continuing tort doctrine. But he also said that Charlie Luckie was right about throwing out some of the earlier charges like battery, for which the statute of limitations already had expired. We could go to trial, the judge ruled, but the jury would only be allowed to consider two allegations. And if the jury didn't believe that Donald's abuse had been continuous—that he'd abused me until he died—the only acts of abuse they'd be allowed to consider would be the last three instances I'd recounted to Charlie Luckie. Three instances, out of all those years and years!

The first allegation the jury would be allowed to consider was "intentional infliction of emotional distress." Had Donald and my mother *knowingly* hurt me? Rich said it wouldn't be enough to prove that my mother had been "negligent"—that she simply allowed things to happen because she wasn't attentive enough. Lots of mothers deny they ever knew their children were being abused, Rich said, and sometimes they're telling the truth. For me, the jury would have to be convinced that she'd *known* what was happening—and had allowed it to go on anyway.

The second count the jury could consider was conspiracy. Did my mother conspire with Donald to hurt me? Did she have a motive to let him do everything to me, a reason to turn her back on me all those years?

The judge set a trial date for August 1995. Even though Rich was relieved the case hadn't been thrown out, he also was clearly disappointed that the number of charges was now reduced to two. To me, though, there was something strangely fitting about those questions a jury would have to answer.

They were the same ones I'd been asking myself since the day Donald died.

Ever since my lawsuit had been filed, Rich and Lynwood had watched the legal process alternatingly buoy me up or cast me into despair. They'd seen my hope replaced by anguish in the course of a single day, my anxiety and sense of impending doom deepen whenever Charlie Luckie filed still another motion that delayed my trial. To me, it seemed my mother's lawyer was doing everything in his power to make sure I never got one.

In mid-1995, a few months before my trial was scheduled to begin, Charlie Luckie filed another motion—this time to have Rich and Lynwood dismissed as my attorneys because they'd previously represented Nick. I simply couldn't have started all over again with a new lawyer or gone on without them, something he must have known, and for weeks, while the judge considered it, I barely slept or ate at the prospect.

When that motion failed, and the August trial date approached, the reality of what I was facing began to hit me. I pictured having to walk into the courtroom and get up on the witness stand—something Rich said would be a vital part of my case—and at times I became so nauseated with fear that I thought I'd faint. All through July, I was a nervous wreck, snapping at Ernie and Cameron over nothing, dragging myself through each day and lying awake every night. I was a mess. For the first time in my life, on the advice of Dr. Deminico, my psychiatrist, I began taking medication for my anxiety. I could tell by the way Rich and Lynwood looked at me that they didn't know whether I'd be able to hold up much longer, and I wasn't sure I could either.

The trial was now one week away. Lynwood called me as often as two or three times a day to reassure me, to soothe and encourage me, but nothing he said helped. Every minute seemed like an eternity, every hour as if time had ground to a halt.

On the Friday preceding the trial's Monday starting date, Charlie Luckie used a different tactic. This time he filed a motion to dismiss Judge Menendez, who'd heard all the pre-trial arguments over the previous two years. Charlie Luckie's motion was based on some obscure technicality, one the judge said gave him a "heavy heart" to see employed for such an obvious reason. Still, the motion was legally sound enough that Judge Menendez reluctantly was forced to remove himself from the case—and my trial was delayed once again. A new date, with a new judge, was set for the following June 1996.

Only many years later did I learn that Rich and Lynwood, at that point, didn't believe I'd be able to withstand the stress of an actual trial. At the time, they told me only that in light of certain events, the conditions might be right for a settlement offer. I was exhausted and depressed, and I truly believed we were fighting a losing battle. Donald had always won, and he clearly was going to win again. And so finally, reluctantly, I agreed.

Charlie Luckie, however, had no interest in a settlement. My mother, he reported to Rich and Lynwood, didn't even plan to entertain the idea. I was a liar, and she had nothing to say to me. Once again my mother was forcing me to quit—and essentially admit I'd lied—or else press onward into what seemed like an endless, horrible unknown.

"They're trying to wear you down, Meg, they're trying to crush you," Rich said. "And you can't let them. You've got to keep hanging in there. You're going to get your trial. You have to just keep having faith in that."

I was so exhausted, so beaten down, that I fell into a kind of gallows humor. "Gee, Rich, you're starting to sound like Lynwood," I said. "The pep talks are usually his job. He hasn't quit on me, has he? You know, jumping off a sinking ship? I wouldn't blame him, you know. I'd probably do the same thing."

Rich smiled gently. "No one's quitting on you, Meg. We're in this for the long haul. We've got a case to win." He put his hand on my shoulder. "We're still fighting for you, Meg. And don't *you* go giving up on *us*. Promise me?"

After I left Rich's office, I went home and sat on the sofa with Ernie. Cameron was playing with a puzzle on the floor, and I sank back into the cushions. I was just so damn tired. They were trying to wear me down all right—and they'd succeeded. Everything my mother had done to me was as if she'd taken a chisel to soapstone, as if hammer by hammer she'd whittled me down to nothingness. I didn't have my mother's diamond hardness, her steely resolution. I wasn't strong like her. And she was going to win, Donald was going to win, I could feel it. Rich and Lynwood could do all the legal gymnastics they wanted to, jump through all her hoops, but my mother always got what she wanted in the end. And what she wanted was to destroy me, whatever the cost.

That was my frame of mind when, a few weeks later in September 1995, I walked into the downtown courthouse and married Ernie.

"You—you got married?" Rich stuttered after I told him. It took a moment for it to register. "Yesterday? Did I miss something?"

"It was—" What? A lifeboat? At least something to hold on to? "It was kind of a spur-of-the-moment thing."

"Okay. Well, great, Meg. Congratulations," Rich said. But one look at his face told me he thought I'd just made a terrible, stupid mistake. After a moment, he smiled awkwardly and said, "Well, it looks as if Lynwood and I need to change your name on a few documents."

Twenty-Eight

eep down, I hadn't believed I'd ever get a trial. But Rich and Lynwood had. And finally that day approached. There were no last-minute motions filed by Charlie Luckie, no sudden unforeseen delays. And suddenly everything I'd been going through for more than three years was becoming real. The entire night before the trial was set to begin, I stared at the ceiling with a knot inside me. *Please God,* I prayed. *Please help me through this.*

On June 11, 1996, the civil trial of *Margaret Haefele, formerly known as Margaret Cassedy vs. Donald Sahlman Jr., as personal representative of the estate of Donald Sahlman, and Patricia Sahlman, defendants,* finally began in a third-floor courtroom in downtown Tampa.

While the jurors waited to come into the jury box, Rich and Lynwood took their places at the plaintiff's table. My mother, Charlie Luckie and his assistant sat at the defense table on the other side of the aisle. Judge James Arnold was in his black robe at the front of the packed courtroom, and against the back wall reporters and photographers were lined up to observe the proceedings. There was only one notable person missing.

Me.

Since May 1993, Rich and Lynwood had taken depositions from scores of people who'd come in and out of my life— some peripherally, some very importantly. But, for the most part, I'd been shielded from what anyone had said about me. My lawyers had reduced each person's hours-long question-ing session into the simplest terms: "It went well, Meg." Or, "He confirmed what you told us." Or, "There was a conflict about the dates. Are you certain this happened in 1975?" But the bulk of whatever had been disclosed remained unknown to me.

But now that the trial was about to begin, my lawyers told me they still thought it best if I didn't hear everything— which was another way of telling me they didn't want me to be there. I was strong, Rich said, but he saw no reason to put me through it. I didn't have to sit in that courtroom and listen to people lie about me, because it would just hurt me. Just upset me. And the jury—well, he said, he'd already told them in the selection process, during voir dire, that some things would be too painful for me to hear. He'd already told them I wouldn't be in the courtroom, he said, and he honestly didn't think they'd hold my absence against me.

And so, except for two times, I never entered the courtroom. I allowed myself to be kept in the dark during the two-week trial; I sat or paced in a small room with one window while the battle was waged across the hall. Most of the time I was alone. Ernie had offered to testify, but Rich said it wasn't necessary. And then, for some reason, Rich told me it probably was best if Ernie didn't come to court at all. I've always done what I'm told; I didn't question it. Ernie shrugged when I told him. "They've got you this far," he said, "so they must know what they're doing."

At the lunch break or end of the day, Rich or Lynwood reported to me in a general way what had happened, what witnesses had said—but they never let on when disaster neared, they never once hinted when our fight was about to be lost. The same was true for my few friends who sometimes sat in the courtroom. When they came to me they hugged and reassured me, and told me things like, "Don't worry, Meg, Rich will get them in the end." And all through it, I tried to tell myself the same thing. I prayed they were right, prayed the jury wouldn't view my absence like an accused person who refuses to testify on his own behalf.

For several years after the trial, I didn't want to know what really happened inside that courtroom. Rich and Lynwood never went into the details of how I was betrayed, and I never asked. There are many reasons, I'm sure, for my prolonged denial, but what it comes down to is this: It's taken me nearly four years to be able to go back and face everything, to hear every word that was spoken, to talk to people who saw it, to finally confront the truth. I wasn't ready for it then and couldn't have stood knowing.

But I know the truth now.

I've recreated those scenes in my head, played them over and over.

I know every word.

Twenty-Nine

The judge threatened to send the sheriff after Father Venard.

The priest was supposed to be Rich's first witness. But by 9:30 A.M., when the jury was getting impatient to come into the courtroom, there still was no sign of him. Father Venard had been served with a subpoena, and a lawyer representing him had assured Rich he'd be there. But now Rich realized he was a no-show—and that opening statements couldn't begin until it was resolved.

"Father Venard is a very reluctant witness, Your Honor,"

Rich said to Judge Arnold, a lean blond-haired man who appeared to be in his late forties. In fact, Rich added, he might even have to treat him as a hostile witness. What he didn't say was that he had a strong feeling Father Venard was going to lie.

Charlie Luckie, who stood next to Rich in front of the judge, argued that the priest shouldn't have to come into court at all since he'd already given a deposition months earlier. But Judge Arnold didn't buy it. "You tell him the subpoena is not an invitation," the judge said. "I don't care whether the witness is a lay witness, a priest, a doctor or whoever. A witness is a witness, and a subpoena is not an invitation you can RSVP on." The judge looked at Rich. "Do you have another witness you can put on?"

"Yes, sir."

"Okay," Judge Arnold said. "Bring in the jury."

Rich rose from the table. "May it please the Court," he said, and then walked over and stood in front of the jury. He was dressed in a dark blue suit and had nothing in his hands. By now he knew my entire story backward and forward and required no notes.

"An eighteen-year-old girl comes home from a date," he began. "She's called into her parents' room and told to remove her clothing. She's laid on the bed. A flashlight is focused on her genitals. She's told to spread her legs, and she's examined by her stepfather to determine whether she's had sex. The mother is present and condones the activity.

"This case is about that girl. This case is not about broken bones or open wounds that you can see or feel. It's about a broken spirit that you must feel. This case is about Don Sahlman, that stepfather, who conducted that examination. This case is about Pat Sahlman, the mother who participated in and condoned much of the abuse." He paused to let his words sink in. "Good morning. My name is Richard Gilbert, and along with Lynwood Arnold I'm representing Margaret Haefele."

The purpose of an opening statement, Rich told the jury, is to describe what the evidence will be and how all the testimony will fit together. "The evidence in this case is about a girl, a child, who has grown to be a woman, but in many respects remains a small child," he said. "She's trapped in a prison of sexual and psychological abuse. The evidence in this case is about a mother who abandons her parental responsibility, turns her child over to her boyfriend and eventual stepfather in order to secure financial safety and security. The evidence will be about a man, a boyfriend who becomes a stepfather, who assumes the role of parent and violates that trust, seduces a child and trains that child to be sexually compliant at his request. Sexual abuse does not occur in the open—but in this case, much of the evidence about sexual abuse will come from persons other than Margaret."

Rich told the jury who some of those witnesses would be and what he expected them to say. He outlined how I was the product of an interracial marriage, how my mother left me behind in Barbados and moved to Guyana where she got a job at one of Donald's companies. She and Donald started a long-term affair while Donald "was living in Tampa, married, and had a son, Don Jr., who sits behind me.

"During the early years they were together, the evidence will show that Pat relinquished her maternal obligations of caring for the child, caring for the child's hygiene, teaching the child about her body's development," he said. "She turned over those obligations to her boyfriend, and he performed those responsibilities: He taught Meg how to clean herself; he taught her how to use a feminine hygiene pad; he taught her how to take a douche. But while he was doing all these things, he was also training her to be sexually compliant to his demands."

Rich told the jury all of the horrible things Donald did to me beginning when I was four years old until we moved to Tampa when I was twelve. "During her teenage years, from twelve to eighteen, the evidence will show Meg was isolated. She was restricted. She couldn't do the things other children do. And during this period of time she's also a servant in the household: She does the laundry, the cooking, the cleaning. She runs errands. She's at their beck and call. And I apologize—but Don calls her his little nigger girl. His little pickaninny. And the evidence will also show that during this time his threats began to increase in intensity."

By now, the jury must have been following Rich's every move as he paused, moved in front of them, gestured with his hands. He led them quickly through the course of my life: Donald's ritual on the boat, the nude photographs, how my mother provided the opportunities for him to abuse me, the inspections after I began to go on dates. He told them about my marriage to Tom, what Donald did to me during and after my pregnancy.

Rich said, "One of the issues you'll need to consider in this case is: Why did Meg allow the abuse to continue? Why didn't she report it? The evidence will be that she couldn't. Studies will show that few victims report abuse, and they are powerless to stop the abuse until the abuser's control ends." And that control ended, he said, when Donald was near death. It was then I was able to tell certain people about what had been happening to me, although there had been others. Before Donald died, Rich emphasized, there had been others.

"All through this case, you'll see the many faces of Margaret," he said. "But one constant will always come through, and that constant is Don Sahlman's control—and Meg's perception of Don as being all-powerful. At the end of this case, I'm going to ask you to find that Donald Sahlman sexually and emotionally abused Margaret Cassedy, and that much of the abuse was with the knowledge and consent of her mother, Pat Sahlman."

He thanked the jury and sat down. Judge Arnold told Charlie Luckie he could proceed. My mother's lawyer walked in front of the jury box.

"Members of the jury," Charlie Luckie began. "This is a case, rather than being about sexual abuse and emotional damage, that is about greed. You will find from the evidence that Donald Sahlman Sr. made a will in 1991 before he died in 1992. In that will, he left his property and money to his natural son and only child, Don Sahlman Jr., and to his wife, Pat Sahlman, both of whom are named as defendants in this lawsuit. While Don Sahlman was ill with cancer—he had mouth cancer, and then he got lung cancer, and his death was imminent—Margaret Cassedy was told during his last illness that she was not a beneficiary under the will."

It must have been impossible for the jury not to have hung on his words. With his silver hair, flaccid face and expensive dark suit, my mother's lawyer was undeniably distinguished looking. His conviction that I was nothing but a greedy liar must have seemed genuine. "Up until that time, the relationship between Margaret Cassedy and Don Sahlman had been a good one," he went on. "It had been a relationship where he had taken care of her, had taken care of her mother, her brother, had sent her to private schools, had provided her with beautiful clothes, gifts, automobiles. And this was a family that took many photographs. We have boxes of photographs and albums.

"As the Chinese might say, pictures are worth ten thousand words," he said. "Those photographs depict a happy person as far as the plaintiff in this case is concerned. They depict a person in various places and doing various things where she was happy, where she was smiling. She was afforded love and affection by Don Sahlman, as well as her mother. And those pictures depict her happiness and her affection toward Don Sahlman and her mother."

But then, after Donald died and I found out I wasn't named in his will, what did I do? I hatched a plan. "By this time she had gotten to know a person by the name of Ernie Haefele, who is a pawnbroker." He might as well have said *criminal.* "The evidence will show that Ernie Haefele urged Margaret

Cassedy to make a claim against the estate. He went with her to talk to Pat Sahlman, making accusations and threatening to bring suit." The jury would hear testimony that "not only did Ernie Haefele participate and urge the bringing of an action for money, but he also talked and assisted in getting Nicholas Clairmonte, who is her brother, to join in that action. And in fact, Nicholas Clairmonte and Margaret Cassedy filed this suit together with these attorneys."

Rich was on his feet in a flash. "Objection!" Out of earshot of the jury Rich told the judge that a motion had already been granted by Judge Menendez—who'd been dismissed after hearing all the pretrial motions—not to permit any mention of the fact that Nick had once joined me in the lawsuit. But Charlie Luckie argued that Nick was going to testify against me, and the jury had to have a context for his testimony.

Judge Arnold sustained Rich's objection. He told the jury to disregard the last statement. But the bell had already been rung; the jury had to be wondering why my brother had withdrawn from the suit. Charlie Luckie stepped back in front of the jury. "The fact remains, ladies and gentlemen, that Nicholas Clairmonte did, in fact, bring a lawsuit along with Margaret Cassedy."

"Counsel!" Judge Arnold snapped. "I sustained the objection. I told the jury to disregard it, and I don't want to hear it again!" But it was too late; now they'd heard it twice.

"But Nicholas Clairmonte will testify in this case, and he'll tell you what happened," Charlie Luckie went on, unfazed by the judge's rebuke. "He'll tell you that Ernie Haefele and his sister talked him into doing certain things—and that he did them—and that the deposition given by him was not true. He gave that deposition with a promise on the part of Ernie Haefele and Margaret Cassedy that he'd be given five thousand dollars. It's true Nicholas has been a drug abuser—and that he had some debts that were related to that. But Nicholas will testify that what he did was induced by Ernie Haefele and Margaret Cassedy."

Charlie Luckie didn't mention what Rich thought was an important fact: that a few days earlier Nick had landed in jail. It was because of a drug charge, but Charlie Luckie made it sound as though Ernie and I were responsible for Nick's troubles. "The testimony will be that after Nick gave the deposition and he asked for his money, they would not give it to him. So he burglarized their house, got some stuff and sold it."

Then he told the jury about everything good Donald had done for our family, beginning when he helped us move from Guyana. He said I'd had numerous opportunities in my life to confide in someone but never had. There'd been Father Morrison, for starters, a priest in Guyana. "We expect Father Morrison to be here to testify in this case," he said. And what about Tom Cassedy? He'd never known a thing. In fact, he said, Tom is a prominent stockbroker and his father is an attorney. Certainly I could have told one of them if the abuse really was going on.

He told the jury about my first deposition, in which I claimed that Donald's last acts of abuse had been on three occasions after I moved away from Occident Street. "Now, by saying this, I'm not admitting that the abuse took place," he said. But after that deposition, he said, I amended my earlier statements in an affidavit and explained "that the things that occurred later were not really abuse of *her*—but things she had done to *Don Sahlman*." There would be psychiatrists and psychologists brought in to testify, he added, but none could be sure what happened to me. In fact, no one could really know anything except for what I'd told them—and I was a liar.

"The evidence in this case will show that Margaret Cassedy is not a truthful person. She changed her testimony to suit a circumstance." There were two sides to this story, he reminded the jury. "And one side points to greed."

"Call your first witness."

"Thank you, Your Honor. At this time, the plaintiff would call Patricia Sahlman to the stand as a hostile witness."

My mother, dressed in a tasteful dark suit with no jewelry, held up her hand and swore to tell the whole truth so help her God, and then took her seat. Rich started off with simple things: when she was born, when she married my father, and then whether Ronald Clairmonte had been a black man.

"No," she said. "He wasn't."

Rich retrieved a photograph from the table, introduced it as exhibit number 4 and handed out copies to the jury. She couldn't have known that photo still existed; it was the one picture of my father I'd rescued when she destroyed her Barbados album. "Mrs. Sahlman," Rich asked, "is that a photograph of Ronald Clairmonte's family?"

"Friends and family," she answered.

"And could you point out for me—I'd like to show this to the jury—can you point out Ronald Clairmonte?" It must have killed her to do that—pointing to his black face, plain as day. "This one," she said. Rich told the jury which face was my father's. Denying my father's blackness had been a lie she'd told since I was four years old—to me, to Donald, to everyone in Guyana and at St. Patrick's—and I truly think Rich's next question was mostly for me. "Ma'am, would you identify yourself in this photograph?" There was no need, really; hers was the only white face there. Reluctantly she put the tip of her finger on the image of herself thirty-four years earlier. She said nothing.

Rich then asked when she moved to Guyana, whom she'd taken with her, where she worked when she got there. She said her job was at Georgetown Seafoods. "You weren't working for Don Sahlman's company, then?" he asked. She shook her head. She said she never worked for Don Sahlman.

"When did you meet Don Sahlman?"

"In 1974," she said. "No, that's wrong. About 1973." *When I was eleven years old.* She explained they weren't intimate back then, just friends, and he came to Guyana two or three times a year. She said he gave her no financial support during that time.

Rich asked permission to approach the witness. "Let me hand you what's been marked as exhibits 9A, 9B and 9C, which have been identified by your counsel as your employment records. Did Don Sahlman assist you in finding employment in Tampa after you moved?" She said he hadn't. Rich directed her to look at the employment applications in her hand. Hadn't she, in fact, listed Donald as a reference on her application to the Chamber of Commerce?

"I never worked for Don Sahlman," she repeated.

Well, what about her application to the University of Tampa? Whom had she listed as her next-to-last employer? "Sahlman Seafoods," she read. She explained that was the parent company of Georgetown Seafoods. "But I never worked for them."

"Where it says, 'name and title of your immediate supervisor,' who did you put?"

"Donald Sahlman. Because I could not put an out-of-town person."

"So is it your testimony you lied on this application?"

"No, I did not," she responded. "I never worked for Donald Sahlman."

Rich changed subjects. He asked whether Donald provided financial support for her move to Tampa, and whether he'd paid the deposit on our Aegean Towers apartment. He had, she said, but she denied she'd engaged in an "open affair" with him while he was still married to bedridden Bette Louise. He never spent the night at our apartment either, she said, "because we didn't want to do that in front of the kids."

Rich backed off one subject as quickly and easily as he went on to another. "And in 1977, he helped you purchase a house? He put down an eighteen-thousand-dollar cash deposit on it?"

"Yes."

"And for the next two years, he loaned you approximately

twenty-four thousand dollars? And provided you with cash gifts of approximately two hundred dollars every two weeks?"

"Yes."

Rich walked over to the desk and handed three new documents to Charlie Luckie that itemized all the loans Donald had made to her. "Isn't it true, ma'am, that those loans were forgiven by Don Sahlman?"

"The majority of them were."

"Ma'am," he went on, "what role did you play in Don and Bette Louise Sahlman's divorce?"

My mother lifted her shoulders, as if he'd asked her the impossible. "I don't know what role I played," she said, "because I was not called into the divorce."

"You were not called?" When she denied it again, Rich walked over to the table, picked up another document and introduced it into evidence: the 1979 deposition my mother had been called to give in Donald's divorce proceedings. Months earlier Lynwood had told me that Bette Louise ended up walking away with millions; he said it had been the biggest divorce settlement in Hillsborough County history. "During that deposition, ma'am, isn't it true you were asked how much money you'd been provided by Don Sahlman? And didn't you *deny* you had received any money from him, other than the twenty-four-thousand-dollar loan?"

"I do not remember."

"And didn't you *deny* that Don Sahlman provided any financial support for your move to Tampa?"

"I do not remember."

Rich refreshed her memory. He read from the divorce deposition: "Question: And when you left Guyana, did you receive any financial aid in moving, or anything in the way of a loan? Answer: *No*. Question: No money? Answer: *No*. Question: He did not support you in any way? Answer: *No*." Rich looked up at her. "You don't recall those questions and answers?"

"I really don't recall it," she said. "No, sir."

Rich wanted to make certain the jury understood that she was the primary beneficiary under Donald's will, and that any money paid to me as a result of the lawsuit would come out of her pocket. Once she conceded that, he asked her about when I was a child. "You didn't teach her how to take care of her private parts, did you? You were too shy and embarrassed?"

"Yeah," she said. It was Donald who had done that, she said, but in her presence. He showed Nick and me how to bathe when we were around nine or ten. "And during the day," Rich asked, "outside of those baths, did Don periodically inspect her genitals to see if she was clean?"

"Not that I know of," she replied. "No."

Rich was making a lot of trips back and forth to the plaintiff's table. He picked up a copy of the deposition she'd given in May 1993, one month after my lawsuit was filed. "Do you recall this testimony? Question: Did he periodically check them to see if they were cleaning themselves? Answer. *Yes*. Question: How would he check Meg? Answer: *She would tell him to come and see if she bathed clean*. Question: She would ask him to come in and look at her? Answer: *Yes*. Question: How old was she when she did this? Answer:

Twelve, thirteen. Question: Up to what age? Answer: *Around eighteen.*" He paused to let her previous answers sink in for the jury. "Is that what you said, ma'am?"

My mother shrugged. "We always stressed the fact that you have to have proper hygiene, and she wanted to be sure she was clean. She would ask him to do it, and I would be present so as to avoid misunderstandings."

My mother did concede that during my puberty she'd never had any conversations with me about my body, that Donald had taken that job. But as if to prove how involved she'd really been, she claimed I'd had a persistent infection that lasted four years, starting when I was twelve. After nagging me, she told Rich, she finally got me to go to a gynecologist. But I had refused to be examined.

"She was scared?"

"Yeah."

"Did you ask her why?"

"The gynecologist told me that all young girls are scared, and he didn't want to force her. I'm still scared of gynecologists. So it's a natural thing to be afraid of them."

"My question to you, ma'am, is: Did you ever ask Meg why she was scared?" She said she hadn't. "You never went in and talked to your daughter privately without Don?"

"Not privately, no."

"Objection, Your Honor," Charlie Luckie said. "Counsel's arguing with the witness. It's been asked and answered."

"Overruled," Judge Arnold said.

"And when Meg reaches puberty," Rich went on, "Don examines her breasts for lumps, correct?"

The lumps, she said, didn't develop until I was about eighteen; after that she showed me how to examine myself. Rich went over and grabbed her deposition from three years earlier. "Do you recall this question: Did you talk to her about doing breast examinations? Answer: *No.* Do you recall that question and answer?" She said she really couldn't recall. "Isn't it a fact, ma'am, that instead of talking to her or showing her how to do them, you let Don Sahlman do the breast examinations? Isn't that correct, ma'am?"

With Rich talking to her that way, maybe she was reminded of the way Donald had leaned over her when he found out Father Morrison had come to Tampa years earlier, how he'd glowered at her and said, "Tell me you won't see the priest again. Say it so I hear you." Finally she said yes. It had been Donald who conducted those examinations, and not her.

Rich asked her about my jaw and back problems. She told him she'd taken me to doctors, that she'd been very concerned. "So, when Meg had back problems you took her to a back doctor," Rich said. "When she had TMJ in her jaw you took her to another specialist. But when Meg had a genital infection for *four years,* you took her to a gynecologist *one time?*"

"Right," she answered.

He asked her about the trips. She'd never known what the sleeping arrangements were when we went to Key West or Fernandina Beach or Colorado, she said, and she'd never asked, either. But she'd had no cause for suspicion. She'd seen pictures of our hotel rooms—but they always had two beds. Never once had she had an ounce of concern.

"Ma'am," Rich asked, "do you recall talking to Jeanne Becker at your church about whether or not it was normal for Don to take Meg on these trips alone?"

"I don't recall any such conversation," she said, shaking her head.

Jeanne Becker, by that time, had died. Obviously there was no way Jeanne could come into the courtroom and accuse my mother of lying—and even Jeanne's six-page deposition probably wouldn't get introduced. Earlier, Charlie Luckie had argued in the judge's chambers that her statements shouldn't be allowed to be read to the jury, and the judge hadn't ruled on it yet. So maybe my mother was simply gambling. Gambling that no one was going to contradict her.

"Ma'am, do you recall a trip you took to Europe and a tour bus driver by the name of Hans? And he took Meg out on a date? She was twenty-one or twenty-two at the time?" Yes, she remembered that. "And do you recall that after that date, Don confronted Hans in front of everybody else on the tour and angrily accused him of having sex with his daughter?"

"No, he did not," she retorted. "That never happened."

"None of it ever happened? He never mentioned anything to Hans?"

"No. Never. Donald was angry and he wanted to cut short the trip, but I talked him out of it. We were angry," she said, "because we were embarrassed."

Rich nodded slowly, as if to say, *Well, gee, maybe I misunderstood that part.* "You indicated you were embarrassed. Why was that?"

"Well, first of all, because one does not go flirting with strange men who don't speak English—and she doesn't speak German. Besides, she was flirting with him so outrageously that it became the talk of the group. You could actually hear their tongues wagging about her outrageous flirting with Hans."

"You say that Hans does not speak English? But he's a tour bus operator for Americans?"

"He still doesn't speak much English."

Rich nodded again, as if there was only one thing still bothering him. "Why are you so concerned about these things, ma'am?"

"Because I was strictly brought up by my mother," she replied. "And in turn, I'm afraid I was an overly strict mother."

"You were strictly brought up by your mother," he said slowly. "And yet you engaged in a sixteen-year relationship with a married man?"

"Yes," she said, "but that is me."

Rich asked whether she recalled Donald taking "nude and provocative" pictures of me after I'd reached puberty. Of course she didn't, she said; she had nude pictures of me as a baby, but that was it. "Do you recall a confrontation with Michael Cobaugh where he found nude and provocative photographs, and confronted you and Don about that?" No she said, she didn't. That never happened.

"You don't recall calling Michael Cobaugh a swine?"

"No, sir."

He moved on. He asked her about when I moved out to live

with Tom. Had she and Donald taken my clothes and thrown them on Tom's front porch? Of course they hadn't, she said. They packed my things neatly in boxes. "I was hurt and angry she'd run off to live with a man outside of marriage," she said. "I didn't bring her up that way."

"So your testimony is that everything was neatly packed in boxes?"

"Yes." She nodded. "I didn't throw clothes on the front porch."

"Do you recall a phone conversation shortly after Meg moved out when you called her a slut and a whore?"

"That's not the way it was," she insisted. "I said, 'This is not the way I brought you up.'"

"So you did not viciously attack her in that phone call? You didn't call her any names?"

"No," she said. She did not ever do that.

Rich went back to the day I moved out. Did she and Donald go over to Darley Davies's house to find out whether I was still a virgin?

They'd gone, yes, but that hadn't been the purpose of the visit at all. They needed to get Tom's address from Darley so they could take me my things.

"So when you went to see Darley Davies that day and had a conversation with her," Rich asked, "the point of your inquiry was not the status of Meg's virginity? Is that what you're telling us?"

She shook her head.

"You have to answer, ma'am."

"Yes, that's right."

"Ma'am," Rich asked, "when Meg began dating, when she was about eighteen years old, do you recall that when she came home from dates Don would manually check her genitals to see if she'd had sex?"

"I don't . . . no . . . I never said that."

"Did that happen, ma'am?"

"No," she said, regaining her composure. "No, it did not." Rich asked her the same question a second time—and got the same answer—just so the jury would be sure to remember it.

"Mrs. Sahlman," he said, "did you have a conversation with Father Venard Moffitt in which you *admitted* to him that Don used to check Meg when she came home from dates to see if she was still a virgin?"

"No, sir," she answered flatly. "I never told Father Venard that."

Rich nodded thoughtfully. "Was it a custom in Barbados for fathers to check their daughters to make certain they were still virgins?"

"No, it was not."

"And Mrs. Sahlman, if you had become aware of Don Sahlman checking Meg to determine the status of her virginity, would you have become concerned about possible abuse?"

My mother's lawyer objected—calls for speculation—but the judge overruled him. My mother, Judge Arnold said, could answer the question. "I don't know," she said after a pause. "You'd have to have a reason for doing that. Maybe if he suspected."

"So if Don suspected Meg of having sex," Rich asked, "that would be justification?" No, she said, it wouldn't. "Isn't that what you just said?"

Charlie Luckie objected, and again was overruled. "Let me ask you again, Mrs. Sahlman." Rich spoke slowly, forcefully, enunciating each word. *"If you had become aware* that Don was checking Meg to determine the status of her virginity, *would you have been concerned* about child sexual abuse?"

She stared back at him. "Yes, I would have," she said finally. "But that never happened."

"Would you have felt it was appropriate for him to do such a thing?"

She shook her head. "No," she said. "No, it wouldn't be."

Rich turned, and then put one finger to his forehead as if he'd just remembered one last thing. My mother and Nicholas were still on very friendly terms, he asked, were they not? Yes, she said, they were. And wasn't it true that she had been paying his rent? She had, she said. But she paid the rent directly to his landlord and not to him.

"And there's a reason why you don't pay it directly to Nick?" Rich asked. "Because he's a drug abuser?"

"That's right," she said.

Rich walked back to the plaintiff's table. He didn't look at her again. "Your Honor," he said, "that's all I have."

Maybe Charlie Luckie wasn't worried about his case, even then. During his brief cross-examination of my mother, he displayed all the confidence of a man who's discovered his opponent's fatal weakness but doesn't mind still playing the game a bit longer. He asked her primarily about the trips Donald had taken me on and whose idea they'd been. According to her, I was the one who instigated every one of them, begged Donald to take me, including one trip to Australia.

We went to Sydney, she explained, to meet a man who wanted to marry me. But I had recognized I was too young and so we came home. But Donald was always doing generous things like that for me; in fact, she said, Donald's relationship with me had always been loving, right from the start. It wasn't until just a month after his death that I changed so dramatically. That was when Ernie and I showed up saying all kinds of horrible things about Donald, telling all of our lies. She told us to get out of her house because she hadn't believed a word of it.

Charlie Luckie had no further questions.

Judge Arnold told my mother the witness could step down. My mother, excused, rose primly out of the witness box and took her seat.

Thirty

At this time, Your Honor," Rich said, "the plaintiff calls Tom Cassedy."

Tom was dressed in a suit and tie, and I heard later he looked uncomfortable being on the witness stand. I had told Tom about the lawsuit a few months after filing it, in the parking lot of Nevada Bob's restaurant where he met me each week to pick up Cameron. Oddly, he hadn't been shocked. He opened his car door for Cameron and said, "Well, it explains a lot." Cameron got into the front seat. "A lot of things make sense now." He never asked me why I'd never told him before, and I didn't volunteer to tell him.

Tom gave a rundown of his educational and employment background, and then described how we met at the Halloween party. We dated for six months before I moved in with him. Rich asked him if I'd been a sexually aggressive person. "No, not at all," he said. "It was funny because, outwardly she wore a lot of makeup, that sort of thing, but as a person she was extremely shy. At the Halloween party, for example, she was trying to get back into a corner to get away from everybody." I was so timid, he added, that I wouldn't even go to the mall by myself. "She always had to go with her mom and dad or her friend."

My relationship with my parents was harder for him to describe. "Volatile" and "extreme" seemed most accurate. "Either it was very loving"—that was when he said that Donald called me "darling"—or else "he was very, very upset with her." He said I was dramatically affected by their moods. "If she did something that wasn't in her father's favor, something he didn't like, she was terrified by him. She was like a child. A three- or four-year-old child. He had very strong control over her." And that control, he added, lasted even after we were married. It caused problems between us, especially because I was always going over to their house to cook or clean or run errands.

Tom told the jury about how "absolutely terrified" I'd been the day I moved in with him. He couldn't, though, remember if we'd slept together for the first time the night before. After he picked me up from his friend's house, he recalled, I seemed to have calmed down a bit—but then we pulled up to his house. "Stuff was thrown all over, scattered all over," he said. "Clothes, stuffed animals, everything she'd left at her parents' house that we didn't get into the car."

"It wasn't in boxes?" Rich asked.

"No, absolutely not," Tom said. "It took me five or ten minutes to pick it all up."

"Before Meg moved out of Don's house to live with you," Rich asked, "did Don know where you lived?" Sure, Tom said. Don and Pat had been over to his house for dinner. He wasn't sure when they'd come, but they had. "So Don didn't have to ask anybody where you lived?" No, Tom said, "They knew exactly where I lived."

Tom recounted that, after the day I moved out, I broke out in hives and was so upset I couldn't eat or sleep. For two or three weeks, he said, "she wouldn't go out of the house." And then came the phone call. Tom said he'd been on the downstairs phone when my parents talked to me, that he'd heard everything. But he preferred not to say what names my mother called me.

"I understand," Rich said, "and I apologize for asking you again."

"Well," Tom said reluctantly, "she called her a whore and a cunt."

Rich asked him about the events leading up to our wedding and our honeymoon in Barbados. Tom said it was there that he learned some things he hadn't known about me. "I didn't know that her father was from Barbados and that he was black," he said. "That was a big thing. We went to his grave."

"Meg had not told you that before?"

"She told me it was something her parents had told her never to tell me."

Charlie Luckie objected—hearsay—and asked the judge to strike Tom's last statement. The jury was told to disregard it. But when Tom was asked about another incident, he described a conversation he once had with my mother. "I don't know how it came up," he said, "but Pat flat-out denied that Meg's father was black. I said to her, 'But, Pat, I met his *brother.*'"

Tom told the jury I'd been too terrified to tell my parents I was pregnant and that he had gotten "the lucky job." Afterwards, they didn't talk to us for two months.

"And did there come a time," Rich asked, "when you attended an intervention on behalf of Nick at Suncoast Hospital?" Tom described the trip in the car with Nick. After a few minutes in the therapist's office, he said, "Don got real upset and said, 'I don't need this anymore' and walked out." He couldn't remember anything about Kim Hourigan handing a letter to the therapist.

Rich apologized for once again having to ask a sensitive question. But would he be willing to describe any problems in our sex life? That must have been difficult for Tom to do, in front of all those people. "Well, at the beginning, everything seemed somewhat normal," he said. "But not long after that, she came right out and said one time, 'I don't like it.'"

Charlie Luckie objected again—hearsay.

"But she did say that to me," Tom protested, before the judge admonished him.

Rich moved on. Did there come a time when we got divorced? And could he talk about the reasons?

Tom didn't answer straight off. "I really don't know what the reason was. She told me that I was never home. But to be honest with you," he said slowly, "to this day, I'm not really sure."

Charlie Luckie didn't take long in his cross-examination of Tom. Clearly he didn't consider him a critical witness. After a few questions about our wedding and whether Donald had, in fact, walked me down the aisle—yes, Tom said, he had—my mother's lawyer focused on one incident: the time Cameron got locked in an upstairs bedroom. Had Tom left his work to go over and help get Cameron out?

Tom explained that he hadn't been able to leave work right away, and suggested I call Donald. By the time he got home, less than two hours later, Cameron was already safe and Donald was there with me. Cameron wasn't yet two, so it would have been sometime in 1989.

"And what were Donald and Margaret doing when you got there?"

"Nothing," Tom said. "Just kind of walking around."

Charlie Luckie handed Tom a document and asked him if it accurately described the date he'd bought our Davis Island house—1989—and then how long afterward the incident with Cameron had occurred. He seemed satisfied with Tom's answers. He walked back to the defense table.

Charlie Luckie, obviously, was a different kind of lawyer than Rich—and he was building an altogether different kind of case. But it would have been a mistake to underestimate what he was doing, how carefully he was laying one brick on top of the other. Because even though they were invisible bricks, they'd turn out to have considerable weight. Probably only two other people in that courtroom—Rich and Judge Arnold—fully understood how devastating his strategy might be.

Tom was excused as a witness.

"At this time," Rich said, "the plaintiff calls Father Venard Moffitt."

Father Venard clearly wasn't happy about being summoned to court—and certainly not under threat of arrest by the sheriff. He'd been in a church meeting earlier in the morning, his lawyer had explained to Judge Arnold, and he'd been under the mistaken impression his testimony wouldn't be required. Still, as he walked down the aisle, Father Venard didn't look like someone who willingly was taking the witness stand. As he held up his right hand and was sworn in, I was told he looked stiff, awkward, his jaw clenched.

He'd been a priest for forty-two years, he said in response to Rich's questions, a priest at St. Patrick's for eight. He met Donald in 1986, and over time they "became good friends." The same, he said, was true for my mother. Donald and Pat had both been extremely active in the church, he said, and Donald had been a regular financial contributor. Father Venard had interacted with me over the years and had seen me every Sunday. "She was very well-groomed, a beautiful young woman, very excellent," he said. "The best of taste, really."

Rich asked him about the meeting I had with him the day

after Donald's funeral. How had I seemed to him? "She was crying," he said. "She didn't think I would believe her. And I said, 'I don't know what it is unless you tell me. We can have a confidential talk and I can't divulge it.'"

"Was it under the seal?" Rich asked.

"Not really under the confessional seal," he said, "but just not divulge it."

Rich asked him if, shortly thereafter, he had a conference with my mother. Father Venard said he had—but that he'd first called me to get my permission. "She said that anything she told me, I was free to discuss with her mother."

The meeting took place at his residence at St. Patrick's. My mother showed up with Don Sahlman Jr., along with Don Jr.'s wife, Peggy. Father Venard recounted how he told them about the accusations I'd made, and that it was his desire to help me reconcile with my mother.

"What did Pat, the mother, tell you about checking Margaret to determine the status of her virginity?" Rich asked.

"She said because of the promiscuity, there were times when Margaret came home when she was checked by her— by Donald Sahlman. Patricia was present."

Rich took a moment to let that statement sink in—perhaps as much for himself as for the jury. So Father Venard had told the truth after all. Lynwood had won the bet. "So Pat told you that when Meg would come home from dates, Donald would check her to determine whether she still was a virgin?"

"Not every date," he said. "But at times, yes."

"And Pat was present during these checkings?"

"Yes."

"And Pat told you this, in that meeting in the rectory with Don Jr. present?"

"Yes."

"What did Patricia Sahlman tell you about where the custom of this checking came about?"

"I think she said it was a way that they had used in the islands," he answered. "To make sure that there was no pregnancy. She said it was the only way they had to make sure that she was behaving and conducting herself properly."

"And how did you respond when she told you this?"

"I—I was amazed," he answered. "I couldn't condone it. Donald was deceased, and so it was post factum, but I couldn't agree to it, I couldn't condone it." And had he conveyed any of those feelings to my mother? "I said it wouldn't be the right way," he answered. "And she said, 'We had no other way because of what she was doing. Because of the promiscuity.'"

"The promiscuity? So did they ever discover during those inspections that Meg wasn't still a virgin?" They hadn't, Father Venard said.

"They never found that she'd ever engaged in sex?"

He nodded. "Right."

Father Venard did recall having a conversation with Jeanne Becker, but he didn't remember telling her that my mother's explanation for the checking had been to determine whether "they'd be selling a virgin." He also didn't remember my mother ever telling him that she'd thrown me out of her house. "But she did say the accusations Margaret brought simply weren't true," Father Venard said. "She said they were absolutely false."

Rich started walking back to the table. But then he turned around. Just one more thing. "Father Venard," he asked slowly, "did you ever call Margaret and offer to help her?" Father Venard shook his head. He said he'd heard I was considering a lawsuit, and from that point forward I'd never asked for his advice. Rich nodded. "My question is: After you heard what Patricia Sahlman admitted to you, did you ever offer to counsel Meg?"

Father Venard took a moment to answer. "Not in that particular frame," he said. "No, I didn't."

Charlie Luckie again made short shrift of his cross-examination. He seemed completely unconcerned about my mother's meeting with the priest or what she'd admitted to him. He asked Father Venard how we'd seemed as a family— "always very amiable, always friendly, appeared very loving"—and then what he'd thought of my relationship with Donald. "She always seemed very loving, very gracious to him," Father Venard said. "She always seemed like a very loving daughter, really." In fact, he told the jury, there had never been *anything* about my demeanor to suggest I was ever emotionally distressed—and I'd had ample opportunity to confide in him over the years.

"Was there a change in her, as you observed, after Donald Sahlman died?" Charlie Luckie asked.

"Dramatic," Father Venard answered.

Charlie Luckie had no further questions.

But Rich did. I can picture him getting up to walk in front

of that priest, how mad Rich must have been on redirect. His voice dropped down low. "Father Venard," he said, "you were asked a moment ago whether you saw any emotional distress in Meg, and you said you didn't. Is that correct?" Yes, he said. "But *you weren't there*, were you?" He took a step closer. "You didn't see her face when she would come home from a date and they'd put a flashlight to her genitals and observe her, did you? You didn't *see her face* on *those occasions*, did you?"

Father Venard shook his head. I was told he looked stunned, shamed. "No, I didn't," he said softly. "I had no knowledge of it."

"And Father, let me ask you this: What did Meg tell you was the *reason* why she didn't report the abuse earlier?"

"She—she told me her stepfather—she said Donald had threatened to send her and her mother and Nicholas back to the islands. That they would go back to the islands."

"Thank you," Rich said coolly. "That's all I have."

But Rich did, of course, have more. His last witness for the day was someone I'd been trying to find for more than a year—someone who, miraculously, had received a letter I'd written only a few days earlier. After talking with Lynwood on the phone, he said he'd be more than happy to fly halfway around the world to help me.

"Your Honor," Rich said, "we now call Hans Meixner to the stand."

Oh, how I would have given anything to be in that courtroom when my mother turned and first spotted him, when she saw him walk past her and step into the witness box! Later Hans told me that her jaw dropped, that "her face, it went all white." Hans Meixner, a man who supposedly spoke no English, a man I hadn't seen or talked to for more than eleven years!

Hans told the jury he and Rich had never spoken to each other before, that he'd just arrived from Augsburg, a small town near Munich, the night before. "We'll just wing it then," Rich said to him. For many years Hans said his job had been as a bus driver and tour operator, arranging and booking tours all over Europe. The last conversation he'd had with me, he said, was in May 1985. That was when he met me on a two-week European tour with Donald and my mother.

"It was a little bit strange, because the whole group talked about this family," Hans said. "Because always the stepfather was very close to her, and sometimes he keep her away." Sometimes, he added, only my mother came down for dinner. "She told us then she wanted to excuse her daughter because she don't feel well, and also the stepfather to care for her."

"Do you know how many rooms they had?" Rich asked.

"That was another problem," Hans said, "because the Sahlmans have only one room. And some of the hotels have very small rooms. Donald was told he could have a second room free of charge because it's impossible to take a third person inside, and he actually was fighting: 'If you don't get a third bed in this room, then I will stay in another hotel.' He say, 'All three stay in the same room or we're moving to another place.'"

The tour went to Venice, where Hans said he had a date with me. "We just had a gondola ride, and it was a little bit late when we went back to the hotel. And then she was in trouble with her stepfather. It was because I can't understand when she says she has to go back. She was at this time twenty-two or twenty-three," he said, "so five or ten minutes late?"

Hans said he had a clear memory of the conversation he had with Donald two days later. "We went to Monte Carlo, and I'm walking the street, and somebody walk behind me and I don't realize it. And then he came up to me and told me, 'I don't want you talking to my daughter again. I don't want that you see her again.' I said, 'Sorry, but if she talks to me, I can't refuse. I can't say don't talk to me because your stepfather don't allow it. She's old enough.' And that was all. He was very angry."

"Did you have another conversation with him?" Rich asked.

"Yeah, a very bad one, actually," Hans said, nodding. "We went to Paris, and two days before the tour finished we had a beautiful dinner on a boat cruise on the Seine River. Very expensive. And we sitting at a long table, about fifteen or twenty people together. And then he got up and talk to two men, that he don't want that I sit with them. I asked if there some problem, and—excuse me, but I have to talk like this— he say, 'I know you fuck my daughter!' At this moment, I was struck."

Hans said he told Donald he didn't understand. Donald yelled louder. "He repeat again, 'I know you fuck my daughter!'

And everybody was shocked. It was all the people that hear this. Then he went back and take Meg and his wife, and they be going. Nobody saw them anymore, and they disappear."

"Was Pat present?" Rich asked.

"She was sitting at the table also," Hans said. "Right in front. And after this—on the tour was a lady, she was a social worker, and this social worker says—"

Charlie Luckie cut him off with a sustained objection of hearsay. I didn't learn until later what that social worker told the group after we left: "I have seen cases like this," Hans told me the woman whispered as we walked off the boat, nodding knowingly to the group. "He marries the mother," she said, "to get to the daughter."

"And did you ever see them again?" Rich asked.

Hans shook his head. "Even when the departure and the group fly back," he said, "they didn't show up. We don't have any more contact, ever."

"Thank you," Rich said. I know now how much he truly meant that.

Charlie Luckie had no questions of the witness. Hans stepped down.

Thirty-One

Father Venard's testimony made headlines in the next day's newspapers: "Priest Testifies in Battle Between Mother, Daughter," and "Priest 'Amazed' at Parents' Account."

"Patricia Sahlman took the stand Tuesday and denied she and her husband abused her daughter," the *Tampa Tribune* reported. "But the pastor of St. Patrick's Church in Tampa testified the mother told him about actions she had allowed that he could not condone." Accompanying the story was a picture of Father Venard on the witness stand, his fingers pointing toward his heart. Beneath it the caption read:

"Father Venard Moffitt said it was difficult for him to testify about what he was told, 'But the truth is the truth.'"

The truth is the truth. How strange those words were to see—and coming from him! Did he remember at all, I wondered, the words he'd said to me, his tone of voice, just moments before I left his office? *"You know what they say, Margaret. The truth shall set you free."* But maybe, though, Father Venard was right after all—just not in the way he imagined.

The truth, I've learned, isn't like some jailer dangling the keys to your freedom who one day shows up to spring open a door that's been locked all your life. It doesn't just *voila!* set you free that way. The way I see it, it's more like a person with a sword slashing through a dense thicket, slowly and laboriously cutting a narrow path to walk through. Because to me, at least, that's what Rich was doing for me.

That morning, out of sight from the jury or media, Rich was fighting for survival inside the judge's chamber. And if he lost this one fight, if he couldn't cut the path, my trial would end on the spot.

My mother's lawyer didn't view the previous day's testimony as damaging. To the contrary, everything seemed to support the case he'd been building all along. Charlie Luckie asked the judge for a directed verdict. Based on the testimony of my very own witnesses, he said, the statute of limitations had "clearly run" for any claims against my mother. If Judge Arnold granted his request, the trial would halt then and there. Victory would be declared for Donald and my mother.

Charlie Luckie had based his motion on two issues: the "hygienic cleansing in Guyana" and "the checking." "The mother also participated in it," he said to Judge Arnold, "but as a matter of law, I don't believe the court could say that the conduct was atrocious and was of such a conduct that no reasonable person would have been involved in it." Furthermore, he argued, the "checking" stopped when I moved away from Occident Street in April 1987. And since I didn't file my lawsuit until 1993, he said, my claim of intentional infliction of emotional distress was therefore barred by the statute of limitations. Even if there *was* a judgment that my mother engaged in a conspiracy, he said, "it was a conspiracy as to the checking." Once that conspiracy stopped, "then the statute of limitations commences."

Judge Arnold turned to Rich. To keep the case alive, Rich had to provide a compelling argument that my mother's wrongful acts also occurred *after* the statute of limitations cut-off date, which already had been determined to be April 1989. The cutoff date for Donald's acts was November 26, 1988—exactly four years prior to his death. That was probably why, in his cross-examinations, Charlie Luckie had placed less attention on earlier events in my life, and more on those that occurred in the four years before Donald died.

"What I want you to do," Judge Arnold said to Rich, "is address the issue of *acts* committed by Patricia Sahlman after April 12, 1989. Not the conspiracy, but the *acts*." Rich, of course, knew what the judge was really saying: Here's your last chance to convince me.

I can picture Rich now, taking a deep breath and squaring

his shoulders. "An element of conspiracy is silence," he began. "Perpetrating these events in silence and keeping them covered, keeping them in the closet, keeping them in the shadows—that's how you can accomplish sexual abuse. One of the most dramatic things Patricia Sahlman did that has caused severe emotional damage to the plaintiff in this case was when she threw the plaintiff out. When, after Don's death, in furtherance of her own desires to keep this thing quiet, when Meg came to her and explained what had happened, she called her a liar. Now, that is coming from a person who *knows* what happened," he said. "And I would *dispute* that cleaning a child to the age of eighteen years old, whether that constitutes abuse. The law on conspiracy is that if you can prove the conspiracy by circumstantial evidence—and in this case, with the opportunities Patricia Sahlman presented, with Don's apparent interest in Meg's genitals and the status of her virginity—it can be concluded from circumstantial evidence that she was *aware* of the sexual activity going on."

Judge Arnold shook his head. He still wasn't convinced. "Other than the silence and throwing her daughter out after this came to light," he asked Rich, "what did Patricia Sahlman *individually* do after the April 12, 1989, date?"

If Rich failed now, it was over. "Your Honor," he said. "I think there is evidence in the record of her continual humiliation and intimidation. It doesn't *end.* They threw her clothes on the porch. Called her names. The events at the wedding. 'You're worthless.' That attitude—the servant attitude. Meg's having to come over and perform for these people, even after she left home and was married. This is a picture that has been presented to the jury, of a half-black child who is literally treated as a piece of property owned by her parents, utilized by her parents for deviant sexual practices. The mother was a *part* of this process. And it was to obtain the financial security she could get from Don, by allowing him to dominate, control, belittle, intimidate and utilize her daughter."

Judge Arnold didn't answer right away. After a long moment he said, "I'm going to deny the defense motion for a directed verdict," he said, "to all counts except the one, to individual acts of Mrs. Sahlman. And I'm going to reserve on that."

Rich and Charlie Luckie walked out of the judge's chambers toward the courtroom. They both knew what it meant. Rich still hadn't proved his case to satisfy the statute of limitations issue. And if he didn't do it soon—before the issue went to the jury and Charlie Luckie asked for another directed verdict—my case was lost.

Over the next several days, Rich brought on witness after witness who not only contradicted everything my mother swore to on the stand, but also supported everything I'd told Rich and Lynwood all along.

There was my high school friend, Valerie Eyring, who recalled our boat trip to Key West. "Terry and myself slept in the living area," she said, "and Meg and Don slept back in the bedroom." During high school, Valerie said, "she never was allowed to go out with us, especially if we had something at nighttime." She also remembered the strange comment I'd once made offhandedly that I'd be "checked" if I ever went on a date.

There was Norma Llosa, Carol's mother, who had a clear memory of pictures I showed her from Aspen and Vail. There was one picture in particular: the one hotel room with one bed where Donald and I had stayed at the St. Moritz Lodge. The picture stuck in her mind, she said, because immediately she noticed that Donald's clothes and mine hung in the same small closet. "I thought it was strange," she said.

There was Mike Cobaugh, who said he got some of Donald's pictures developed at a drugstore photo lab and actually "feared for my own safety from the police" if he ever got asked about them. "Some of them were in what you could tell was an expensive motel," he said. "The dressers had gold handles, there was plush carpeting and magnificent pictures on the walls—and they seemed to be casual pictures of their total nudity, of the mother and the daughter." In one, he said, a large mirror showed Donald's reflection holding the camera: "It was definitely him." He also recalled a time I made a comment about being checked—even though I'd forgotten it. "It was repeatedly brought up by her: 'Be careful, be careful, be careful.'" My mother's use of the word "swine" after he confronted Donald over the phone was also lodged in his memory because he wondered later if it was a term used in Barbados instead of "pig." After that conversation, he said, "My relationship with Margaret ended. Instantly I was a persona non grata." Mike said he kept the pictures for several years "in case the whole thing ever blew up." He kept them, he said, until he became involved in another serious relationship and worried how he'd explain them if his girl-friend ever came across them.

Darley also took the stand. She described in detail the frantic conversation Donald and my mother had at her house after I ran away from Occident Street. "They weren't concerned if Tom was a nice guy and would he treat her good," she said. "They were concerned about her virginity and her virginity only." She broke down in tears while she recounted my conversation on the airplane going to England. It had pained her to see me so ashamed "to admit she was half black," she said; then she'd been "horrified" when I told her everything else. That was why, after my divorce, she always stayed with me at my apartment whenever Donald visited me. I was "a nervous wreck," she said, until he left.

Father Fausto, too, came to help me. He told the jury about the phone call I made to him right before my thirtieth birthday when I first informed him of Donald's cancer. "I said, 'I'm truly sorry. I know you must feel truly down,'" he recalled. "And she said, 'No, it's not that. I'm just mad.' And I said, 'Are you mad at God for sending the illness, or because he hasn't heard your prayers?' She said, 'I'm mad at Don. I want him to do something for me before he dies.' And then she just burst out, a torrent of words. She said, 'I've been abused by him. I want him to apologize to me.'" Father Fausto also told the jury what I said to him at lunch the following day about Donald and the bedpan, and another comment months later at Donald's wake. "She took me aside and said, 'The son of a bitch died without telling me that he loved me truly.'" Father Fausto shrugged. "And well," he said to the jury, "what could I say?"

Rich also introduced into evidence a travel agent's itinerary, which was passed around for the jury to see. It was the reservation Donald had made for one room, with one bed, at the Hyatt Regency in Australia. He'd made it right before Anthony convinced my mother to go along too and ruined all his plans. I had saved it all those years in my "Anthony" bag, which I've kept to this day.

Thirty-Two

I have no memory of faces, no memory of how I got through
the courtroom doors, down the aisle to the witness stand.
I do remember being led by someone, a hand under my
elbow, but not whose it was. As soon as Rich stepped in front
of me, I focused on a spot above the jury's heads; I let the
bodies sitting all around me darken until I couldn't see them
anymore, and instantly the lights in the room seemed to dim.
I was present, and not present. I was enduring it, answering
his questions in front of all these strangers, but I also had
gone to another place. I'd learned how to do that in my life: to

go away. My eyes didn't move from that one spot on the wall.

Rich led me through the course of my life, beginning when I was a child in Guyana at Bel Air to our move to America. To each of his questions I let the words come on their own, the memories floating out, almost as if they were happening to me once again. I remembered the yellow sheets at the boat, Tom's green sheets, the sound of Donald's red Lincoln backing up from Tom's house to take me to the boat. I heard myself saying things I never imagined I could: Donald running the bath water to make me urinate, his dipping his fingers under my stream. Rich's voice was gentle, hypnotic, and I went wherever he led me. "Thank you, Meg," he said finally, before returning to his seat.

It was now Charlie Luckie's turn to interrogate me.

Lynwood told me once that Charlie Luckie had won a lot of his cases, that he had a great reputation as a "bulldog lawyer." And that's just how he was with me, too, gnawing at me over three isolated incidents like I was a bone. They were the incidents I'd told him about in my deposition, and all of them were after the statute of limitations cut-off date.

In the beginning I simply answered everything he asked me, repeating what I already had said about the time Cameron got locked in the upstairs bedroom. How long afterward, Charlie Luckie asked again, had Donald arrived to get him out? How long after that did Tom come home? What happened then? But then he kept going back to that: Was it ten or fifteen or twenty minutes later that Tom arrived? Well, hadn't I said before that maybe it was forty-five minutes? Wasn't it a fact—

Maybe that was what pulled me back into a fully wakeful state. I looked him straight in the eye. "I don't *know* the time, sir. All I know is what I can tell you happened after I got my son out of the room." With no forethought, I pounded my fist down on the witness stand. *"It happened!"* The jury jumped.

Charlie Luckie read for the jury the answers I'd given in my first deposition. He focused on the last time I'd claimed Donald had taken me to his boat. "Question: What year was that? Answer: *This was at least four years ago, five years ago.* Question: Why did you go to the boat with him? Answer: *Because he asked me to.* Question: You didn't tell him you didn't want to go? Answer: *No sir, I did not.* Question: Why did you not tell him you did not want to go? Answer: *I do not know.* Question: And before that occasion on Angeles, when was the last time he—* Answer: *When I lived at Occident.*

"You remember that testimony?" he asked.

He handed me the affidavit I'd written that explained those answers. He noted that my testimony had changed in it: In addition to what I'd said earlier, "there were other acts of abuse that took place" after moving away.

"You said, did you not: *'When I was asked in my deposition when was the last time that I was abused by Donald Sahlman, I only thought back to the period of time when the ritual still existed'*?" Yes, I said, I had. "So you didn't consider it abuse when you did something to him, is that right?"

"No," I said. "Because—no, I didn't."

"Thank you," he answered. A flash of smugness crossed his face, as if he'd just proved something important.

It went on like that for an entire afternoon of one day and

the entire morning of the next. He showed me pictures of Bel Air, pictures of me standing on a bed with mosquito netting and smiling, a picture of me in diapers when I was a year old in Barbados. He asked me to identify each one, to tell the jury what I was doing when the picture was taken. "Do you know why you were crying in Barbados?" he asked, pointing to the picture of me in diapers. "I was crying?" I responded. "Weren't you?" he asked. Then came a slew of other pictures taken through the years: Nick and me standing beside Mom and Donald at their wedding, me skiing with Anthony in Vail, Valerie and Terry and me on a dinghy. In all of them I looked happy, as if I were having a great time. Charlie Luckie didn't produce a single example of the horrid kind of pictures Mike Cobaugh had seen—and which Rich assumed my mother had either destroyed or conveniently lost.

"You say that you were abused by Don Sahlman." The doubt and sarcasm in his voice were obvious. "How old were you when you knew?"

"I guess when I got into my teens," I answered.

He nodded. And had I made a recent phone call to someone and used the word "closure"? Yes, I said, I had. "And where did you get that term? What does it mean to you?" My mother had always called me stupid. Did Charlie Luckie believe I couldn't understand that word without the prompting of some oversuggestive psychologist?

Right then I stopped being afraid of him. I don't know how or why, but something came over me, almost as if a friend had come to sit down beside me. "I think I've always known that term," I said. "To me it means when something has been done and you need to go on. You need to get closure on that part, in order to go on with the rest of your life."

Charlie Luckie nodded, satisfied. He looked at the judge. "That's all I have, Your Honor."

Finally, I was allowed to return to the little room across the hall.

I'm glad now that I wasn't in the courtroom for the last part of Rich's case. He was probably right; I couldn't have stood it back then to hear everything that was said about me. All of the psychiatrists and psychologists and therapists I'd seen over the last few years—with the exception of Dr. Blau, the psychologist for the defense—got up and testified about their professional opinions of me. All the tests I'd performed were analyzed and described in detail, along with reams of studies about symptoms that victims of sexual abuse often exhibit.

According to my test results, I was "a lost little child in the body of a woman who lived a robotic existence." I suffered from a host of psychological injuries: chronic post-traumatic stress disorder, depression, obsessive-compulsive disorder, panic disorder with agoraphobia, borderline personality disorder, low self-image, impaired sexual functioning, dissociative disorders, paranoia, recurring nightmares, bulimia and a high propensity for suicide.

Dr. Karen Moorhead, a psychologist I'd seen many times, told the jury some of what I'd revealed to her. "She said she was directly told by her mother that she was an accident, that she wasn't wanted, that her heritage was not to be respected—and this was a source of shame, a source of great distress," she said. "She said repeatedly, 'I just don't know why she never loved me.' This was as big an issue to her as why she would have been abused."

Dr. Moorhead said that because of the deep shame that comes with sexual abuse, it's not uncommon for people to recant, to later claim the abuse never happened. And while that wasn't true in my own case, she said she couldn't offer a prognosis for my future. "I truly question her longevity, or whether or not she will effect suicide one of these days," she said. "She believes she is ugly, stupid, bad; that she will be punished, that she is not loved, that she is not worthy to be on the Earth. She believes this," she went on, "and the depth of her shame—helping a person recover from such deep shame is very difficult."

Rich had one final witness from my past—someone who testified on my behalf from the grave.

Rich and Charlie Luckie had argued vehemently in the judge's chambers about what portions, if any, of Jeanne Becker's deposition should be admitted into evidence. Finally the judge had ruled that all but one statement could be read for the jury. My mother had claimed on the witness stand that she never once "had an ounce of concern" about any trips Donald took me on, and Rich wanted to show that, too, had been a lie.

Standing in front of the jury, Sondra Fryrear, Rich's legal assistant, spoke Jeanne's words. Jeanne described going to Father Venard to get the name of a counselor for me, Father Venard's insistence that she reveal my name to him, and then what I had told her the day of Donald's wake. The jury heard what I tearfully had told her in late-night phone calls, how she finally located a counselor and gave me the woman's name, and then Father Venard's comment a few weeks later about what my mother admitted to him about checking my virginity.

Unfortunately, Rich hadn't been permitted to let the jury hear Jeanne's final statement, which was considered hearsay: "Pat and I were on our way to a concert on her tickets. And from nowhere, Pat asked if I thought it was normal for a father or stepfather to go on trips."

Jeanne's entire deposition had been typed at her bedside by a court reporter shortly before she died. Strangely, though, those last few words were the only ones she had written—almost as an afterthought, on the last page—in her own unsteady hand. Jeanne had been in severe pain and on heavy medication at the time she gave her deposition—something the jury had been advised of. But her intent, even if the jury never heard it, even if I'm the only one who knows it, was clear.

Jeanne was trying to help me, even then. *The truth is the truth.*

In my prayers, I have always thanked her for that final act of kindness.

Rich turned to Judge Arnold. "Your Honor," he said, "the plaintiff rests."

Thirty-Three

It's gone well, Meg."

"So you're confident? You feel confident about it?"

"I never feel confident, Meg. Not until it's over."

Rich had done the best that he could. I knew that, even if I didn't know the details. But now it was Charlie Luckie's turn to present my mother's case in front of the jury, and the defense was far from resting. Charlie Luckie still had a legal ace in the hole—and it was a simple one that could blow our whole case apart.

He began by calling Father Andrew Morrison to the stand.

I never saw the priest the entire time he was in Tampa helping my mother, nor would I have wanted to. Of all the betray-
als, his had stabbed me among the deepest.

Father Morrison, my "Uncle Andy," held up a picture for the
jury. It was one of me smiling broadly and holding a Hula-hoop.
"This is the Margaret I knew," he said. "M. M. was a very cheerful, friendly girl." Even in front of those strangers he lapsed into
the nickname he'd called me ever since that long ago day in his
car. Never once, he testified, had he ever seen anything that
would lead him to believe I'd been abused in any way. My relationship with my mother was "loving" and "very close."

Father Morrison said he came to Tampa in 1975 for "knee
surgery," a trip he'd told us at the time had been for church
business. And even though my mother had met him secretly
in a variety store parking lot—and Donald had practically hit
her when he found out about it and made her promise never
to see him again—Father Morrison made it sound as if he'd
been welcomed by Donald with open arms. "Donald invited
me to go for a boat ride," he told the jury. "Margaret came
along. We went in his launch on the Tampa Bay." He said
there wasn't even a hint that I was afraid of Donald. "Just the
opposite," Father Morrison said. "It seemed to be a very
good relationship."

And then he told the jury about the phone call I'd made to
him just a week before the trial began, when I first had
learned Father Morrison was coming from Guyana to testify
against me. "She said she wanted to give her side of the
story," he said. "And then she spoke in a very excitable
manner. She just poured herself out. And I said, 'Margaret, I

can't believe this.' Well, she kept on telling me of the abuse that had taken place, describing in very graphic terms what had happened to her. And I said to her, *'It is unbelievable.'*" He said he'd asked me if I was doing it for money. Was that what I wanted? "She said no. She said, 'I have to have a closure of this matter.' She repeated that word. She wanted to have 'closure' to this awful experience she had suffered."

Rich didn't take long on cross-examination. He had, essentially, one question. "Father Morrison, did Pat Sahlman ever tell you in Guyana that she was allowing Don to examine Meg's genitals?"

"No, never."

"And would that shock you?"

"It would shock me, yes," he said after a moment. "But never, never—such a thing never came up."

Charlie Luckie's next witness was Sam Fazio, Donald's one-time business associate in Guyana. He testified he lived at the Bel Air house off and on for more than a year. Never once did he see me for more than half an hour, he said; I was zooming in and out of the kitchen, eating cookies and drinking Pepsi and talking to Lucille, the cook. Lucille, I'd learned, had died many years earlier.

"This house that the Sahlmans owned, it was a big house?" Rich asked on cross-examination. "So if somebody chose to go in and out to take a nap they could shut the door and the maid and cook would not see what was going on?"

"Yes," Sam Fazio said. Rich had no more questions of him.

Donald's former business friend left the courtroom as I entered it.

Rich had told me earlier in the morning that I could be in the courtroom for this next witness—especially since he thought my presence would send a strong message to the jury. But I also think he knew that no matter how bad it was, this was something I needed to hear for myself. I walked quickly, nervously, to the plaintiff's table and sat beside Lynwood, while Rich flipped quickly through pages of a yellow legal pad. My hands were shaking, and I was too afraid to look at the jury.

"Your Honor," Charlie Luckie said, "at this time the defense calls Nicholas Clairmonte to the stand."

My brother, dressed in slacks and a long-sleeved shirt, walked stiffly to the stand. He swore to tell the truth, the whole truth and nothing but the truth, and sat down, bolt upright, staring straight ahead of him. *Don't do this, Nick.* But I knew he would; I just didn't know the extent. Finally he looked over at me. To this day I have no idea what Nick was thinking, what possibly could have been going through him. He looked away.

Nick described how he'd become involved in my lawsuit. "I was approached by my sister," he said, in answer to Charlie Luckie's question. "She asked me if I'd ever been abused by my dad, my stepdad, and I told her that—I asked her what she was talking about? She told me she'd been abused, and I said, 'Well, I've never been abused.'" He talked about the offer of money, how I'd urged him to go to my mother "and see what her reaction would be, if she accepted it or not," how he later lied in his deposition after Ernie and I coached him what to say.

Charlie Luckie turned to Rich with a satisfied expression. "You may inquire."

Rich walked in front of Nick. He was controlled, his voice was even, but I knew how outraged he was. "Mr. Clairmonte, I notice you have a bracelet on," he began almost conversationally. The jury hadn't been informed where Nick had been for the last few weeks. "What is that bracelet?"

"It's the booking number for the jail," Nick said. There wasn't a hint of embarrassment in his voice, and instantly I was reminded of something he said before he placed his bet on my mother. "Don't worry about the trial, Meg," he'd said. "I can have that jury crying one minute and laughing the next. I'll have them eating out of my hand."

"So you're in jail now?" Rich asked. "When you walk out of here you go back to jail?"

"Yes, sir."

"And those clothes you're wearing—they're not the ones you had on this morning?"

"No, sir."

"Let me just make sure I understand the sequence of events," Rich said. "You gave a sworn deposition on May 20, 1993, and you raised your hand and swore to God to tell the truth? And now you're testifying to this jury that you did not do that, that you intentionally committed perjury? You gave that testimony in exchange for five thousand dollars?"

"Yes, sir." *Oh God, Nick. What are you doing? Why are you doing this to yourself?*

He admitted he broke into our house and stole Ernie's "stuff" because he needed money to pay off a drug dealer. "And you were arrested," Rich said, "because the fence to whom you sold the items stolen from your sister turned you into the police?"

"Yes, sir."

"This was your friend who turned you in?"

"Yes, sir."

Nick said he'd been placed on three years probation, during which time he "had a relapse" of drug use. His most recent arrest was because he violated the terms of the probation. Prior to his most recent arrest, he conceded, my mother helped him with the rent and drove him back and forth to a new job. "And she provides you with painkillers that are not prescribed for you?" Rich asked. *How did he know that?* Nick said she didn't. "Sir, wasn't she giving you Darvocet, which is a painkiller? Didn't she give you Darvocet when you gave your sworn statement changing your testimony on August 9, 1995?"

"Yes, sir," he answered. Maybe that reminded him of when Father Morrison came to Tampa years earlier, when Donald knew he'd met my mother in a parking lot. All of us knew Donald had found out; we just didn't know how.

"Now, let me ask you about what you're testifying to here today," Rich said, taking a step closer. "You're not saying that Meg is making up the nude photographs? Or the breast examinations? Or the checkings or cleanings? Or whether or not Meg was abused by Don? You're not testifying that anything she says is not true?"

"No, sir."

Rich reminded him about the testimony in his first deposition, that Donald had subjected him "to various types of anal and oral sex," and that my mother had been present "on several occasions when he tried stuff." Rich asked, "And you're saying now that was a lie?" It was, yes. But Nick didn't remember "three-quarters" of what he'd said in the deposition because it had been under "duress and stress."

Until then I had tried to control myself, but right then my jaw dropped and my head jerked. *She must have offered him a lot more than painkillers to make him do this. How could he do this to me? Did he think he'd never have to look me in my face ever again? Or didn't he even care?*

For the next hour, Rich punched away at him. He read statements from his first deposition; Nick said they were all lies. Rich asked about statements Nick made to numerous therapists and psychologists; those had been lies, too.

"And you're lying now?" Rich asked. "You would lie to make sure she provided you the material comforts she always provided you?"

"No, sir," Nick answered. "I provide my own material comforts."

I was almost relieved for Nick when, after another half-hour of being battered like that, he finally was allowed to step down. Nick looked at me briefly, blankly, as he was led out of the courtroom, back to jail. A moment later I got up and left, too, back to the little room across the hall.

For the next week, Charlie Luckie produced scores of other witnesses from my past who either attempted to disprove that I ever could have been abused, or else show that things simply couldn't have occurred the way I said they did.

Olivia Brooks, the former maid for Donald and bedridden Bette Louise, told the jury how she was sent as an "investigator" to spy on Donald's comings and goings. She reiterated what she'd said in her deposition: that Donald's boat, up until his divorce in 1979, had been right behind his house on Culbreath Isles. Rich, at that point, introduced into evidence a document Lynwood had tracked down. It was a boat slip rental receipt from the Imperial Yacht Basin—and dated four years earlier, in 1975.

My former friends, Kathleen Macado Murphy and Sue Sparks, were on the stand only a short time. To this day I don't know why they betrayed me the way they did, but they both recalled how I phoned them to talk about the lawsuit— and then how they severed their relationships with me afterward. Never had they seen anything to indicate any abuse, they said; in fact, to them my relationship with Donald had always seemed extremely loving and close. What's more, they said, I had a "bad reputation" for telling the truth.

On cross-examination, Rich asked them both if they'd ever contacted me again after my initial disclosure. They hadn't, they said; I'd never called them again and so, well, that was that. "So your friend calls you up and admits she was abused all her life," Rich said, "and then you never call her again to talk about it?" He sat down, disgusted. "No further questions," he said.

Kathy Mann Beville, Donald's now-married niece, also testified to what a loving, close relationship her uncle always had with me. I was the daughter he never had, and Donald's devotion to me was eclipsed only by his devotion to my mother. Kathy described for Charlie Luckie how she and I had driven together to the hospital on Thanksgiving Day four years earlier, and how she stood next to me in the hospital room when Donald died. "Margaret was devastated, heartbroken, what you'd expect to see from someone who lost a father," Kathy said. "She was physically crying, shaking."

On cross-examination by Rich, Kathy did admit to seeing Donald perform breast exams. "And when Meg first told you of the abuse," Rich asked, "you told her she should have kept her mouth shut and gone to the grave with it. Correct?"

"I asked her why, if it had been going on for twenty-odd years, why she had never brought it forward before, why she waited until the man was dead," Kathy answered. "I asked her how she could hurt her mother like this. If she had problems I hoped she got help, but I thought she should have kept her mouth shut. Yes, sir, I did."

Rich's face flushed red as he took a step toward her. "So here's a woman who just told you about twenty-five years of sexual abuse," he said angrily, "and your concern about her was *nothing*? You were only concerned about the *family* and how she was hurting her *mother*?"

"Absolutely," Kathy answered.

Rich asked her if she'd ever known about the cleanings or checkings or nude photographs. She hadn't. "And if that were proven to be true," Rich asked, "would that be inconsistent with the Don Sahlman that you knew?" She said it would be inconsistent. She'd be totally surprised. "But it hasn't been proved," Kathy said.

Carmen Clift, my mother's cleaning woman from St. Patrick's, testified to how attentive I'd been to Donald during his last illness, what a loving daughter I'd been. Even though we'd barely talked about anything more than the weather, Carmen claimed I'd had numerous intimate discussions with her about my sexual conquests, and how "hot" various men were in bed.

And then came Dr. Blau. That psychologist had always terrified me, had always looked at me like Father Venard. During one test, Dr. Blau told the jury, I slipped off my shoes under the table—a clear indication I wasn't as distressed during the test taking as I wanted him to believe. He also reiterated what he'd said in his deposition: My test results indicated a propensity toward malingering, toward deceit. In the world of psychology, he said, it was known by a simple term: "faking bad." I did have psychological problems, he conceded, a "borderline personality disorder." But there was no way to tell whether it had been the result of abuse. He described Donald's breast exams and nude photographs as "bad parenting," and refused to characterize them as necessarily abusive.

Rich went at him like a pit bull. Wasn't it true he had virtually no experience treating victims of child sexual abuse? Hadn't he asked me open-ended questions ("describe your symptoms") rather than specific ones, as authoritative experts recommend? Wasn't it true he compiled his report prior to seeing Father Venard's deposition and then, after reviewing it, made only one notation? Rich read from Dr. Blau's report: "Father Venard notes that she lied" about whether I'd ever told my story to anyone else. "*That's* what you considered significant?" he asked incredulously. "It wasn't that the *mother* had lied about the abuse? And you didn't write down that the abuse had, in fact, occurred? And after a priest testified under oath that the checking did occur, you *still* could not say whether the abuse occurred? That was the conclusion in your report?"

"That was my conclusion," Dr. Blau said.

As a rebuttal to previous defense testimony, Rich was permitted to call another witness to the stand. Kim Hourigan, Nick's ex-girlfriend, was sworn in. She recalled for the jury Nick's intervention several years before Donald's death, how all of us drove together to Suncoast Hospital. Kim said she took a letter she'd written with her, and at the hospital handed it to the therapist. "I didn't want to say it in front of Donald or Pat," Kim said, "so I chose to put it down in black and white." And what was in that letter, Rich asked. "I told in the letter what Nicholas told me," Kim answered. "That he had been raped by Donald Sahlman."

Rich said he had no further questions. Neither did Charlie Luckie.

The trial had gone on for two weeks. Finally, on June 20, it came to an end. "Your Honor," Charlie Luckie said, "the defense rests."

Thirty-Four

The little room across the hallway from Courtroom Number One seemed suddenly smaller. I paced back and forth, sat down, and then got up and paced again, picturing what was going on just a few feet away. I had told Rich I thought I could bear to hear the closing arguments, that I was strong enough to listen, but Rich didn't think I should. "I'll come to you the minute it's over, Meg," he'd said, taking both my hands. "I promise you I will. You've been so strong, and for so very long—can you be strong just a little longer?" I pressed my lips tightly together so I wouldn't cry, and nodded. Rich rested one hand gently on my shoulder, smiled encouragingly at me, and then disappeared across the hall.

Rich's closing argument lasted nearly two hours. He reminded the jury what witnesses had said, what the evidence had proved, the litany of lies my mother most surely had told them. He talked about Nick's testimony, how previous experts had testified that recanting sexual abuse isn't at all uncommon, and that if my brother would admittedly lie about his mother for five thousand dollars, how much would it take for him to lie about his sister? And don't forget Kim Hourigan, he told them. Kim wrote that letter years before Donald got cancer, years before Nick claimed I approached him and asked him to lie about being abused.

Rich talked about the cleanings and the checkings and all the emotional abuse I'd endured over the years, and why. And that, he said, was a very complex issue—but at the same time distressingly simple.

"This is a case of child sexual abuse," he said. "It was the family environment created by the mother that allowed the abuse to begin and progress to greater levels of deviant behavior. The man, Don Sahlman, has violated the sacred trust of being a father in the worst possible way. The evidence shows that there was a progression of events, a progression of abandonment, a progression of abuse, a progression of threats and rewards. As Meg got older, the threats became more personal, more forceful: 'You will go back. Your mother, your brother and your grandmother will go back to South America and live in poverty.' How powerful was that?

"Meg had the world on her shoulders," Rich said. "She was protecting her mother. She was protecting her family. What else could she do? There were progressive perverse acts until a final resistance—when the power was lessened, the power was reduced, the power died."

He reminded them of the trips, of my mother telling me I had to go to the boat because Donald had been so good to us, all while Donald was examining me in front of her. "You heard Meg tell that compelling story about having to eat lunch, and she would sometimes vomit to avoid having to go back to take naps with Don. Children will jump through hoops for parental attention and affection. They'll endure pain. They'll do anything they have to do to get the love and attention of their parents. And when you take a child like that and you abuse it, you have a condition called learned helplessness. They learn it's futile to resist."

He reminded them of Donald's boat, how the evidence had shown that he moved it from behind his house shortly after we moved to Tampa. "Suddenly, Donald needs a boat slip." He reminded them how terrified I was when I ran away from Occident Street to live with Tom, how terrified I was to tell them I was pregnant. "She's twenty-five years old, pregnant, and what's the normal healthy family response? Joy? Happiness? They're going to be grandparents. They ought to be ecstatic." But he reminded them what Tom said. "They didn't talk to them for two months."

Rich talked about Donald's ritual on the boat, how I was subjected to it even while married, even after my child was born. "And one day her child gets locked in a room. She's frantic. She calls him to help her. And what does he do? He comes over and *abuses* her. He's her *stepfather,* for God's sake. And the abuse continues until shortly before Don's death, when she's able for the first time in her life to refuse.

"You repeatedly heard from defense witnesses," he went on. "When asked to describe the family relationship, it was, 'Oh, these are normal folks. They were a happy, loving family.' And I'd ask these folks, 'Well, what if you knew when you saw them and they were looking like a normal healthy family that the cleaning was going on and the checking was going on?' All of them: 'I would be surprised. It would be totally inconsistent with the people I knew.'"

The defense, he said, claimed I made everything up when I realized I was cut out of Donald's will. What about all the people I had told over the years? There'd been Valerie Eyring and Mike Cobaugh and Darley Davies, and a few months before Donald's death, Father Fausto. "And don't forget Jeanne Becker," he said. "She was here, talking to you, too."

I heard later that Rich looked searchingly at the jury. "There's nothing in the law that requires Don to have sex every day to find that this was a continuing and repetitious wrong, where the injuries are the cumulative effect of the conduct of Don and Pat," he said. "And we're not only talking about sexual abuse—we're talking about emotional abuse. About intimidation. About humiliation. Belittlement. We're talking about treating Meg like a thing, like a servant, like she was a toy that could be taken down off a shelf like one of his cars, one of his boats. She was *never* treated with dignity or respect."

And what happened after Donald died, he asked, when finally I went to my mother and told her what I'd gone through? "She throws her out," he said. "How abusive was that? Now, if she knew nothing, if she were the perfect housewife, the perfect mother, then maybe I would say she just rejected it. *But this woman knew.* We *know* that she knew. That almost caused Meg to commit suicide. The mother comes into this trial this very week and denies it again, and she blames her daughter for the abuse. And I submit to you that it's continuing and cumulative. It is a conspiracy of silence. Donald Sahlman was speaking to you through the mouth of Kathy Beville, his niece, when she told Meg, '*You should have kept your mouth shut and taken it to the grave.*'"

Rich let his eyes sweep over the jury once more, looking into each of their faces. "Patricia Sahlman sold her child into sexual and emotional slavery for *financial security*," he said. "She intentionally condones abusive activity, and she gave Don Sahlman every opportunity he needed to use Meg as his personal toy. You've heard the expert testimony that human life is ruined by abuse. And then to blame that child for how she's turned out is just not fair. Meg feels the guilt and shame, but she is *not responsible* for the abuse—and you should *tell* her that by your verdict."

He paused, and seemed swept by emotion. "Last Sunday was Father's Day," he said, his voice thick. "Father's Day is a day to honor all men who choose to be fathers, who hold a little hand, who give a child a safe place in the world. Let this week now end with a declaration: That fathers, while they should be respected, have a duty to their children to earn that respect. That in this community in 1996, we *will not tolerate* the breach of a child's trust. That children are a gift from God, and we will *punish* those who abuse that gift. And that while we honor fathers, we will hold abusive fathers responsible for the damage they cause. That justice be done."

He looked at them once more. "Thank you."

After Rich took his seat, Charlie Luckie rose and walked in front of the jury. "Ladies and gentlemen, we've now found out what this case is all about," he began. "The case is about money. The case is about greed, as I told you you'd find out when this case got started. This case is about a presentation made in this courtroom by the attorneys, the psychologists, the psychiatrists, which is acted out by Margaret Haefele."

Charlie Luckie's voice was heavy with disgust and contempt. "You've probably seen her coming in and out of the courtroom with people holding onto her arms as if she is an invalid," he went on. "She hasn't been in the courtroom, and this is part of the *show*—that she simply can't sit here and listen to the music."

He reminded them of the two depositions I gave, where "the last thing that happened to her as far as abuse was concerned was when she was twenty-seven years of age. And she testified further in those depositions that there were *three* things that occurred from the time she left home in April 1987," he said. "*Three* events. And those events amounted to him taking her to the boat one time, and his having taken her upstairs on a date, when there was a very brief occurrence between them."

The final event I had claimed, he said, was when Cameron got locked in a room. "So who did she call then to help her get her son out? Don Sahlman, the man who she *says* has abused her since she was four years old."

He turned the jury's attention to the affidavit I wrote after my second deposition. Rich had told me to list every symptom, every problem, every fear I now had. "Now, what does she delineate in this affidavit that she never testified to in her depositions? She says, *'I'm often depressed. I do not trust, and I'm afraid of people. I usually sleep only two or three hours a night. I have frequent nightmares. I have nervous habits, such as picking hairs from my eyebrows. When I'm nervous I itch and scratch myself, occasionally to the point where I bleed. The only reason I haven't killed myself is I can see Donald Sahlman waiting for me, and I believe he is angry with me for telling about the abuse. I often see a red Lincoln, which was Donald Sahlman's car, and this frightens me. I feel dirty and bad, that God is punishing me for doing bad things.'*

"That brings up something you need to think about very carefully in this case," he said. "Why in the world didn't this woman do something about this from the time she was grown? She said she was eighteen years old by the time she knew what was happening to her—and then for twelve, thirteen years she does nothing."

Nothing, that is, until I discovered I wasn't going to be in Donald's will. "And then the build-up for this case begins," he said, taking a few steps closer to the jury. "And where does it begin? She goes to the Italian priest, Father Fausto Stampaglia, on her birthday. And she tells him a story of

long-standing abuse." According to Father Fausto's testimony, he reminded them, the only thing I wanted was an
apology. "Then Don Sahlman dies. Two or three days after
that she goes to Father Venard Moffitt—and this is the second part of the build-up. She tells her story again, but now
she goes beyond the time she left the home. She's embel-
lished it. She also tells Father Moffitt, 'I'm going to bring a
lawsuit.'"

Charlie Luckie was like Father Venard and Dr. Blau and
Father Morrison all rolled into one, their voices all utilizing
Charlie Luckie's mouth to say the same thing.

"Father Moffitt says to her, 'Do you want me to help you?
Can I counsel you? Can I get the family back together?'" he
went on. But I had no interest in the priest's help, he said; I
turned it down. "No. She didn't go back to Father Moffitt. She
was going ahead with her lawsuit."

Charlie Luckie told the jury to remember all "the holes" in
my story, beginning with everything that happened in
Guyana. Sam Fazio, he reminded them, was there at Bel Air
and never saw a thing. And Father Morrison never saw a hint
of anything either. "He said, 'M. M. was a happy, bubbly girl.'
He showed you the picture of her with her Hula-hoop." My
mother's lawyer held up that picture for the jury to see again.
"Now, can you believe that child depicted in that photograph
was abused?" He moved the picture so they each could see it.
"Can you reasonably believe that a child who was abused to
the extent that Margaret Haefele has testified to in Guyana
would not have shown severe signs of depression, being
afraid, just in a state that you could hardly even imagine?"

He recalled Olivia Brook's testimony about Donald's boat being kept behind his Culbreath Isles house up until his divorce in 1979, five years after our arrival in America. He recalled, too, my claim that Donald had abused me on Juno Street, even though "there is no evidence Donald Sahlman ever lived there." And finally, he reminded them of all the psychiatric testimony in the case.

"They say she is so messed up now that she is virtually a *basket* case," he said. He pointed a finger. "Margaret Cassedy Haefele's trauma—if she suffered it—was when *Don Sahlman* died." He looked at their faces. "She was traumatized because she knew that Easy Street might be over for her. She could not cozy up to Uncle Don or Daddy Don and get what she wanted—automobiles, college, whatever."

Did I show any trauma in any of the pictures he'd shown the jury? Did they see any sign of it when I was on the slopes of Vail? "Witnesses say that she adored him." And if that weren't true, then what about Cameron? No mother, he said, would allow her son to be alone with a man who had sexually abused her from the time she was four years old. "Further, if she is as bad off as has been depicted in this case, I would suggest to you that she has no *business* having and taking care of a child."

Oh God, how those words hurt me now, even after all these years. I can stand to think he called me a liar and con- niver and a gold-digger—but telling that jury I didn't deserve to have a child because of what Donald did to *me* as a child, that is still unbearable. I can't think about that for long or it feels as though it'll eat me alive.

Finally, he moved to the heart of his case. It was the one issue the jury wouldn't be allowed to ignore—no matter what they thought had happened in the distant past.

There is a statute of limitations in the state of Florida, he told the jury. The judge would give them instructions about it. But basically, he explained, what it all boiled down to was this: "One aspect of this case they hound and harp on is the checking," he said. "The checking stopped in April 1987 when she moved out of the house. Even if you find that it happened, there was no continuity. Four years from April 1987 would be April 1991. So, this claim was dead as far as the statute of limitations is concerned. This claim died long before four years from the date of Don Sahlman's death. And if you find that to be so, then her claim is barred. She does not have a right to recover anything."

The jury, he said, should consider carefully the last three incidents of abuse I'd claimed in my deposition. By my own admission I hadn't considered later acts to be abuse against *me*. So how, he asked, could I then claim to have been distressed by them?

"The conclusion you come to is that Dr. Blau was right when he said Margaret is deceitful and fakes bad," he said. Everything else I'd said, well, no one could ever know the truth. "There's one thing that *is* certain, though," he said. "And that is that Margaret Haefele has caused emotional distress to her mother and Don Sahlman Jr.'s family. Margaret Haefele has been successful in causing extreme emotional distress to her *mother*. Her mother was good to her. She was a good mother as she was growing up. And now Margaret

Haefele comes in here wanting money."

Charlie Luckie reached into his pocket and pulled out a stack of dollar bills. He waved them in front of the jury. "She wants a lot of these," he said, fanning the money up and down. "And that's what this case is all about."

Thirty-Five

Rich and Lynwood sat at the plaintiff's table, and across the aisle from them sat my mother with Charlie Luckie. All the testimony had been heard, all the lawyers' arguments made.

"Members of the jury," Judge Arnold said. "I shall now instruct you on the law that you must follow in reaching your verdicts. It is your duty as jurors to decide the issues—and only those issues—that I submit for determination by your verdict."

The jurors were to consider two distinct claims. The first,

against Donald, was for intentional infliction of emotional distress; and the second, also for intentional infliction, was against my mother. "Although these claims have been tried together," he explained, "each is separate from the other."

In order to make a determination of intentional infliction, he said, the jury should consider four separate issues: Whether Donald and/or my mother "engaged in extreme and outrageous conduct by sexually and emotionally" abusing me; whether Donald and/or my mother acted with the intent to cause severe emotional distress, or had reckless disregard for the "high probability" of causing it; whether, in fact, I *had* suffered emotional distress; and if so, whether the conduct of Donald and my mother was "a legal cause of Margaret Haefele's severe emotional distress."

Judge Arnold told the jury that "outrageous conduct," according to the law, is "behavior which under the circumstances goes beyond all possible bounds of decency." Further, the law recognizes that "an intent to injure is inherent in an act of sexual abuse."

But then came the caveat, Charlie Luckie's ace in the hole.

Because of the state's statute of limitations, the judge explained, the only way I could be *legally entitled to damages* was if the evidence showed that the emotional distress caused by Donald "was continuing after November 26, 1988." For my mother, the date was April 12, 1989.

The next issue for the jury's determination, he said, "is whether Patricia Sahlman was a joint-venture partner, aider and abettor and conspirator" with Donald to engage in intentional infliction of emotional distress. By legal definition, he said, a conspiracy is a combination of two or more people who by their "concerted action attempt to accomplish an unlawful purpose," and that they commit some "overt act" in the furtherance of the conspiracy.

"A conspirator," he said, "need not participate in the planning, inception or conclusion of the conspiracy to be liable for *all the acts* that took place during the conspiracy. The conspirator need only know of some of the other conspirator's plan, behavior or actions—and assist in it in some way to be held responsible for *all* of the acts of the co-conspirator."

Judge Arnold instructed the jury about the final issue before them. Had the intentional infliction of emotional distress by my mother and Donald been continuous? In order to reach that conclusion, he said, they had to determine that my parents' conduct was "a continuing and repetitious wrong," and that my psychological injuries were the "cumulative effect" of that conduct "rather than the result of each individual act."

If the jury found in favor of Donald and my mother, there obviously would be no need to consider the issue of damages. But if they found for me, he said, "you should award Margaret Haefele an amount of money that the greater weight of the evidence shows will fairly and adequately compensate her for such injury or damage."

If the jury found for me, they also could consider punitive damages "as a punishment and as a deterrent to others" and base their decision "on the enormity of the wrong."

Finally, he said, they should be aware that Florida law only permits punitive damages against a person, and not an estate. "You may consider an award for punitive damages against Patricia Sahlman only," he said. "You may, in your discretion, also decline to award punitive damages."

Before sending the jury to deliberate, Judge Arnold reminded them that their decision had to be unanimous— and that they could not be swayed from their duty by "prejudice, sympathy or any other sentiment" for or against any party. "Please disregard anything I may have said or done during the course of this trial," Judge Arnold added, "which makes you think that I prefer one verdict over another."

With that, the jury left the room.

My fate was now in their hands.

Rich came to me, just as he promised he would. Lynwood was beside him.

"It's over?"

They both nodded. None of us said anything. What could we say? It had gone on nearly three and a half years, and now it was done. Everything was out, every piece of it. All the horrible secrets that had been buried for thirty years, and now those secrets were gone. They had belonged to all of us— Mom, Donald, Nick—and not just me. There was nothing to do now but wait.

Lynwood thought it might be a while before the jury reached a verdict, and very possibly it wouldn't even happen that day. There were lots of legal issues for them to consider. He patted my shoulder and smiled at me, and said he was going back to his office. "No matter what happens, Meg," he said, "you told the truth. You got to tell *your* truth."

Rich stayed with me in the little room. Occasionally I stood up and walked around, but I wasn't pacing anymore; it was out of my hands. Donald had won all his life, and he probably would now, too. Even in death he was more powerful than I. And I had to be ready for *that* truth; when I heard it spoken out loud I had to be prepared.

Rich sat on a metal chair with a vinyl seat, his elbows on his knees and hands laced together under his chin. It was the same way he'd looked at me the first day I came to his office, when he'd listened so carefully to me, when his mind already seemed to be galloping ahead to what he must do to prove it, to how he could possibly help me.

"You okay, Meg?"

I nodded. I was so grateful to that man. No matter what happened now, no matter how things turned out, he had fought for me like no one else in my entire life. "Yeah, Rich," I said. "I'm okay."

I walked to the window and looked out. The cluster of office buildings blocked any view of the harbor and stood in stark relief against the sky. It was an early summer sky, when the cloudless blue often turns a strange bright white. I knew what it meant: It was the pale color of the coming heat, of the coming humidity that would pull heavy into our lungs and bead on our skin for the next three months.

There was a knock on the door. Sondra Fryrear, Rich's legal assistant, poked her head in. Rich jerked up; we both stared at her.

Sondra gave a tight smile. "The jury's back."

"Now?" Rich asked.

"They're waiting to come in."

My heart began pounding. It had been less than an hour. Rich asked Sondra to call Lynwood and tell him to hurry back. He looked at me. "What does it mean, Rich? So fast like that? It's a bad sign, isn't it?"

"I don't know, Meg."

"Donald won, didn't he?"

Rich put his hands on my shoulders and hunched down so he could look straight into my eyes. It was the same way that, years before, Anthony had stopped in the middle of that snow-covered road in Colorado, under all those stars, and peered at me to make sure I was all right after Donald's horrible comment.

"Do you want to be there, Meg?" Rich asked. "Whichever way you prefer it, whatever you decide."

I know what he was trying to do, to prepare me for the worst. He couldn't come right out and ask, *Are you going to go to pieces in that courtroom if this goes against you? Are you going to fall apart completely?* And in honesty, I don't know whether I could have answered that.

I only knew one thing.

"I have to be there, Rich," I said. "I need to hear it myself."

Thirty-Six

Rich and Lynwood sat on either side of me at the plaintiff's table. My mother sat ramrod straight on the other side of Charlie Luckie, although I couldn't see her face. My fingers were dug into my palms until Rich reached over and took one of my hands. He gripped it firmly, and I felt my shoulders drop. I took a deep breath and blew out slowly. *Here it comes.*

Judge Arnold turned to the jury. "Has the jury in this case reached a verdict?"

The foreman, a white man in his forties, was standing. "We have, Your Honor."

"Would you hand that paperwork to the bailiff?" A single piece of paper was taken by the bailiff and given to the clerk. "Madam Clerk," Judge Arnold said, "publish the verdict."

My heart was thudding in my ears. Rich grasped my hand tighter, and I could feel the same tension in him, too.

"We, the jury, return the following verdict," the clerk read. "Question Number One: Did Donald Sahlman Sr. engage in the intentional infliction of emotional distress against Margaret Haefele, which was a legal cause of injury or damage to her?

"Yes."

I jerked my head. Had I heard that wrong?

"Question Number Two: Did an act of intentional infliction of emotional distress by Donald Sahlman Sr. take place after November 26, 1988?

"Yes."

"Question Number Three: Did Patricia Sahlman engage in the intentional infliction of emotional distress against Margaret Haefele, which was a legal cause of injury or damage to her?

"Yes."

"Question Number Four: Did an act of intentional infliction of emotional distress by Patricia Sahlman take place after April 12, 1989?

"Yes."

"Question Number Five: Did Patricia Sahlman engage in a

conspiracy with Donald Sahlman Sr. to sexually and/or emo- tionally abuse Margaret Haefele?

"Yes."

I could barely see their faces anymore; tears were stream- ing down my face.

"Were the wrongful acts of Donald Sahlman Sr. and/or Patricia Sahlman continuing?

"Yes."

"What is the total amount of any damages sustained by Margaret Haefele and caused by the abuse in question?

"Three million dollars."

Rich squeezed my hand, but neither of us moved.

"Question Number Eight: Is Margaret Haefele entitled to punitive damages from Patricia Sahlman?

"Yes. So say we all, dated this twentieth day of June, 1996, at Tampa, Hillsborough County."

Judge Arnold thanked the jury for their sacrifices over the long trial, for the disruption to their work and private lives. He told them they were free to talk to reporters, but they also could choose not to comment if they wished.

The bailiff stood up. "This court stands adjourned."

Only then did I turn to Rich. I threw my arms around him, buried my head against his shoulder and sobbed. Lynwood, on the other side, was patting my back. "We won, Rich? We really won? Donald lost?"

I could feel Rich's shoulders move as he nodded. "*You* won," he said softly. "Meg, *you* won."

We didn't leave right away. I called Ernie to tell him, and then everyone from Rich's office, all the people I'd seen for the last three years, came to congratulate me. Part of me still couldn't believe what happened. I hadn't seen my mother leave the courtroom, and I didn't see her face after the verdict was read, either. But as people hugged me, I heard Donald's voice whispering to me, saying the same words he had since I was a stick-thin girl looking out an apartment window. *Who do you think they're goin' to believe, Margaret? A rich white man like me, or a little nigger girl like you?* And for the first time, I mentally said something back to him. *Me, Donald. They believed ME.*

Rich and Lynwood walked with me down to the lobby of the courthouse. Outside the glass and metal doors a throng of reporters had gathered. Lynwood put his hand on my arm. "We don't have to go out the front," he said. "If you want, we can go out a back way. Not see them."

I looked up at them both, these two men who had cared so much about me, who had carried me for so long. If it hadn't been for them, I would have given up long ago. For some reason I'd trusted them from the very start—and for God knows what reason they'd done the same about me.

I looked outside at the news van parked by the curb and the cluster of men and women standing near it. "No, it's all right," I said after a moment. "I don't want to talk to them, but I think I can face them. But you'll go with me, won't you?"

With my lawyers on either side of me, I walked out the doors into the pale bright light of June, and down the courthouse steps.

✝   ✝   ✝

Epilogue

By Aurora Mackey

Although a mother's active promotion of incest is shocking and, for many people, difficult to conceive of, Patricia Sahlman's actions by no means represent an isolated case. In their groundbreaking book, *Betrayal of Innocence: Incest and Its Devastation,* first published in 1978, coauthors Dr. Susan Forward and Craig Buck described this type of mother and her motives. Unlike the "silent partner," a mother who may be so preoccupied with her own emotional difficulties that she's unavailable to her children, the actively involved mother is "a more disturbed, perhaps psychotic personality."

"The actively participating mother tends to be a dependent woman," the authors wrote. "At first she leans on her husband, but as her daughter assumes more and more responsibility for household duties the mother shifts this dependence to her. The mother begins to resent her daughter, as if her daughter were stealing the maternal role instead of having it thrust upon her. As this resentment grows, the mother becomes hostile toward her daughter, driving the girl closer to her father, and causing the mother to want to see her daughter punished, demeaned."

On the more innocent end of the scale, the authors said, is the mother who convinces herself there is nothing incestuous about what she's doing. "On the darker end of the scale is the mother whose hostility toward her daughter and lack of normal maternal instincts are so great that she actually participates in her daughter's sexual abuse." In the vast majority of such cases, the authors added, this mother's classic response is one of denial. Further, such a mother usually refuses to enter therapy—a vital part of the healing process for her daughter—since to do so would require an acceptance of blame. "Only through treatment will the mother escape her own corner of the incest hell," Forward and Buck wrote, "and, in the process, release her daughter."

In 1996 Patricia Sahlman appealed the lower court's decision, claiming that her daughter's allegations were barred by the statute of limitations and that trial error had occurred by allowing the jury to hear certain statements protected under the state's "dead man's statute." In December 1997, Florida's Second District Court of Appeal upheld the lower court's three-million-dollar verdict. Lawyers representing Patricia Sahlman then asked the district court to certify the case to the state's Supreme Court.

Their request was denied.

Meg's victory had a resounding impact on similar childhood sexual abuse cases pending in Florida. In early 1998, the *Wall Street Journal* wrote: "The Sahlman case is significant in

Florida because plaintiffs here have long struggled to prove old claims of abuse. Unlike other states, Florida had few exceptions in its statute of limitations that abuse victims could use." As a result of Richard Gilbert's innovative use of the continuing tort doctrine in Meg's case, the article continued, "other lawyers say a number of older cases could benefit if the ruling gains acceptance among state judges."

As part of the punitive damages against Patricia Sahlman, Meg was given full ownership of the Occident Street house and all its contents, including her mother's jewelry collection. She also was given half ownership, with Donald Sahlman's brother Jack, of the Bel Air house in Guyana. Meg wanted nothing to do with either one. Although not required to do so, Meg asked her lawyers to draw up an agreement in which her mother would be permitted to live at the Occident house rent-free until Mrs. Sahlman's death.

Stripped of Donald Sahlman's remaining estate, Patricia Sahlman today is virtually penniless. She lives alone and works for a low-paying hourly wage as a secretary in Tampa. Occasionally she plays violin in a small community orchestra. Mrs. Sahlman rarely sees her daughter. According to Meg she has never once mentioned the trial, and says only that she still finds her daughter's allegations "difficult to believe."

After the trial, Meg was informed she could press perjury charges against her brother. She declined to do so. Although Nick and his mother still see each other regularly, Meg has seen her brother only once since his testimony. He came to her house asking for money, and Meg gave it to him. Nick never contacted her again.

Meg and Ernie Haefele were divorced a year after the trial, in 1997.

Meg is continuing with therapy and attempting to heal. She prays every day.

About the Authors

Meg Clairmonte was born in Barbados, the West Indies, and grew up in British Guyana before moving to Tampa, Florida, at age twelve. She attended Hillsborough Community College and currently lives in Tampa with her two sons.

Aurora Mackey is a former staff writer and columnist with the *Los Angeles Times* and medical reporter for the *Los Angeles Daily News*. Her articles have appeared in publications nationwide, including the *San Francisco Chronicle, San Jose Mercury News, Chicago Tribune, Miami Herald* and *Shape* magazine. Since 1993 she has focused on legal and health issues, most notably for *California Lawyer* magazine as a feature writer and columnist. A native of the San Francisco Bay Area, she has a master's degree in writing from the University of San Francisco.

True Inspiration

Angel Watch

Bestselling author Catherine Lanigan brings you this provoking and uplifting collection of real-life miracles and reveals how unexplained synchronicity brings positive changes into our lives.

Code #8199 • Quality Paperback • $12.95

Defending Andy

A powerful memoir of one mother's painful journey to fight against the health care system and try to save her son from cancer.

Code #9063 • Quality Paperback • $12.95